The Urban Millennium

THE CITY-BUILDING PROCESS FROM THE EARLY MIDDLE AGES TO THE PRESENT &

Josef W. Konvitz

SOUTHERN ILLINOIS UNIVERSITY PRESS

Carbondale and Edwardsville

Copyright © 1985 by the Board of Trustees, Southern Illinois University
All rights reserved
Printed in the United States of America
Edited and designed by The Bookworks, Inc.
Production supervised by Kathleen Giencke
88 87 86 85   4 3 2 1
Library of Congress Cataloging in Publication Data
Konvitz, Josef W.
The urban millennium.
Bibliography: p.
Includes index.
1. Cities and towns—History. 2. Urbanization—History. 3. Cities and towns—
Growth—History. 4. City planning—History. I. Title.
HT111.K58 1985   307.7′6′09   84–13908
ISBN 0–8093–1201–8

COVER ILLUSTRATION: From Paul Lacroix, *The Eighteenth Century*
(London: Chapman and Hall, 1876).
Courtesy Historical Pictures Service, Chicago.

For my mother and father,
who taught me the value of values

Contents

Illustrations

Preface

THIS BOOK DERIVES FROM A SERIES OF LECTURES on European urban history which I presented in 1975 to a faculty seminar at Michigan State University. I structured the seminar around several dynamic, long-term trends in European urban development. What factors, I wanted to know, made possible an increase both in the number of cities and in the size of the largest cities in Europe in nearly every century since the early Middle Ages? Why did efforts to limit city size in both the preindustrial and industrial eras fail, and how have cities coped with the problems of growth and decline in the past? What impact did preindustrial urban developments have on industrialization and modern urbanization? And, finally, what relevance has urban history to the study of contemporary urban conditions?

As I prepared my lectures, the role of the city-building process began to stand out from other variables and factors as a topic for further study. This topic appeared all the more important to me given contemporary concern about such man-environment issues as how people perceive a city and structure it mentally, what needs people try to satisfy through the environment, how environmental choices are made, and who pays for the costs of environmental change. Had I been less aware of modern trends related to design, I might have chosen a different set of historical issues to study. In response to questions and comments from the seminar participants, I committed myself to undertake a more profound analysis of the ways Europeans and Americans built, perceived, exploited, and modified city space.

This study touches upon many topics which are rarely considered in relation to each other. My intention has been to compose an essay in general terms about an aspect of urban history that has received little attention either from historians or from specialists in current urban problems. Had I tried to write a longer book with detailed case studies and extensive documentation, I would still be at work. Given the variety of conditions affecting and present in cities over time, the historian who attempts a general interpretation of urban development must necessarily omit or abbreviate discussions of many examples and variables. By focusing on the city-building process I have not meant to imply that other factors are irrelevant. The city-building process is a lens which brings certain patterns into focus; others looking through this lens might see different patterns than I have.

I am grateful to the Office of the Provost of Michigan State University for inviting me to offer a faculty seminar, to the participants who came to learn and taught me much, and in particular to Lawrence Sommers, John F. A. Taylor, and John Mullin for invaluable criticism and support. My wife, Isa, and Kevin and Grace Gottlieb, dear friends, encouraged me to transform my seminar notes into a book. Some of my ideas began as observations gathered in the course of trips to many European and American cities and several extended stays in Paris. On many occasions I saw more because Steven Kramer and Christopher Friedrichs were there; they also read parts of the manuscript and offered many useful comments. For any factual errors in the book I am of course responsible.

Introduction

CITIES HAVE SURVIVED IN THE WESTERN WORLD by adapting to the changes which their very presence has precipitated and diffused. The city-building process describes how architecture, vernacular construction, and planning together shape the urban environment, relate to each other, and affect the modification of cities. What is known about adaptability in city building is in inverse proportion to its importance. No one has treated this topic systematically. A few contemporary critics have called for greater flexibility and renewability, implying that modern cities are less easily modified than cities in the past, but they do not provide evidence against which this assertion can be tested. James E. Vance, Jr. refers to adaptability in the introduction to his historical study of urban morphology.[1] His richly detailed text describes how city forms in one period differ from those of another as a function of social, political, and economic trends. Vance also differentiates between periods characterized by the maintenance of existing patterns and periods when new forms or functions are created. But as he carries his story from the Middle Ages to the present, the role of adaptation, the characteristics of cities in different periods which affected adaptability, and the causes of transitions receive progressively less attention. If adaptability is desirable, one would like to know more about its spatial, social, and institutional variables, about the degree to which it has been present in different periods, and about its effectiveness in facilitating change.

These and other related matters interested Kevin Lynch for many years. Admitting that much of his thinking on the subject is sheer speculation, Lynch composed a list of questions which could keep

scholars busy for years. "How are cities adapted during abrupt transformations, such as disasters or social revolutions? What were the
typical sequences of adaptation in an urban district, and to what
extent were they blocked or diverted by physical rigidities? Can
people be taught how to adapt their settings more effectively? What
has been the actual experience with buildings and areas that were
designed to be flexible? What new devices for adaptability might be
used, both physical and administrative? How can adaptability be
measured?"[2] Lynch has not engaged in historical analysis, but his
concept of adaptability suggests that comparative historical research
is inseparable from the study of contemporary issues.

Although Lynch's discussion of adaptation is not based on exhaus-
tive investigation, it deserves to be taken seriously as the fruit of
considerable experience and reflection. Perceiving that adaptability is
usually a by-product of normative practices rather than something
deliberately provided, Lynch considers the processes "of control and
decision by which the environment is constantly being replanned" to
be as important as specific physical elements and structures of access
and communication.[3] Whether the opportunity for adaptive change
is seized depends on the attitudes and knowledge of people, "their
image of change and the future, their motives, confidence, and ability to accept and organize new information."[4] Adaptation of an existing environment is more likely to occur smoothly, almost impercep-
tibly, if that environment does not strictly prescribe use and
meaning. Often, aspects of city building to which planners and architects pay little attention matter significantly. Changes that are
easy to accept are "those we plan, or if caused by others, those which
are rapid, legible or come in modest, deferrable increments;" changes
"imposed without choice," or which are "overwhelming, . . . illegi-
ble, their pattern confused or seemingly random," are hard to accept.[5]

The ideas of latency and resiliency are intrinsic to adaptability.
Adaptability is a latent environmental charateristic which becomes
important when unforeseen circumstances or normal deterioration
and wastage render change desirable. The ease with which change
can be effected describes the environment's resiliency. To retain adaptability, contemporary changes should not diminish the degree to
which other changes can be made in the future.[6]

Besides adaptability, some other terms are relevant to the argument that follows. Architecture involves the design of buildings and spaces according to formalized rules and methods that take both structural principles and aesthetic values into account. By combining function with the symbolic expression of significant, enduring social, political, and intellectual principles, architecture makes a permanent claim on city space. It would seem that at no time has architecture directly shaped more than 10 to 15 percent of all built structures.

The overwhelming majority of all structures fall into the category of vernacular construction. Its objective is to satisfy the need for shelter in a direct and simple manner, unaffected by intellectual considerations about truth and beauty. Many vernacular buildings may nonetheless be beautiful. The skills needed to build in the vernacular are informal, widely accessible, and evolve slowly, in contrast to architectural knowledge. The vernacular builder works with common knowledge, when "common means not rude or vulgar" but belonging to everybody.[7]

Planning regulates construction and land use directly through such instruments as building codes, zoning, and control of streets; and indirectly as with fiscal, social, and public health policies. Planning can emphasize utilitarian and practical considerations or idealistic and aesthetic principles, or can attempt to combine both. Formal, abstract design and ad hoc, improvisational approaches are seldom combined in planning; instead, as George and Christiane Collins have observed, these two tendencies in planning "seem to see-saw cyclically over time."[8] Of course, architecture, vernacular construction, and planning are sensitive to other factors as varied as finance, religion, ethnicity, the organization of production, energy sources, education, and legal traditions. The city-building process, however, is more than the sum total of its parts.

Although city building affects the totality of the urban environment, it is a highly selective process, especially attentive to certain features and treating others as of marginal importance.[9] Implicit in city building are judgments about what can be done and what should or should not be done. By and large, these judgments are a matter of routine, of accepting conventional wisdom and of applying proven techniques. City building at any given time functions as a series of norms, perceptions, procedures, and techniques that have prima facie validity, that city builders try to improve but not to overturn, and that people internalize in their behavior and expectations. City building has a paradigmatic, self-perpetuating quality. The city-building process is an information system which selects and simplifies a vast quantity of facts into a manageable set of criteria and selection options. It is a metalanguage which directs the energies and resources of societies toward certain activities, transmits skills from one generation to another, and promotes attitudes and values about urban living.

For the purpose of advancing an investigation into city building, the past millennium can be divided into three periods, each characterized by a different mode or set of operative criteria. From the revival of cities in the early Middle Ages until the late seventeenth century, *cultural factors* heightened the intelligibility of city space and rendered it easier to manipulate. City building produced environments that everybody could understand and use, diffused construction skills widely, and focused public attention on urban affairs. During the eighteenth and nineteenth centuries, *economic considerations* dominated, the better to enhance the city as a place of production and exchange. Speculation made city building more complex and riskier, transforming relationships among lenders, owners, builders, and occupants. The skills and resources for city building, however, were still within the reach of most groups. Late in the nineteenth century, city building became subordinate to *political and social institutions*. As the scale and costs of development increased beyond the ability of individuals to control them, incentives arose to transfer the function of space allocation onto bureaucracies. Who controls city space, how tightly or loosely it is controlled, and how decisions about space are reached have become volatile political and social issues. In the cultural mode, emphasis is on the user; in the economic mode, on the investor; and in the political, on the regulator.

All three city-building modes have been present since the early Middle Ages; only the relative emphasis given to one or the other has changed. Periods of modal dominance are not stages of development on a linear progression. Earlier periods are no more a model of all that is good in city building than the contemporary is of all that is bad. No one mode is inherently superior, since in each some of the greatest architectural masterpieces and some of the worst slums have been built. Transitions between phases of modal dominance have occurred when an unprecedented set of problems overwhelmed builders, invalidating conventional methods and creating pressures for innovation. There have been only three periods of modal dominance in the past millennium because normative city-building techniques have proven satisfactory in a wide variety of circumstances over a long period.

This book focuses upon the responsiveness of city building to two kinds of problems. One kind is a function of forces outside the control of city builders such as sudden, unpredictable, and frequent changes in population size, economic conditions, political circumstances, and cultural trends. Until late in the nineteenth century, the modification of city space and buildings to change posed few problems, cost little, and did not inhibit the modification of cities in the future.

The latent adaptability of urban environments was compromised about a century ago. The worst aspects of industrialization, the prospect of further massive urban growth, rising social expectations, and the availability of several new technologies encouraged a major change in city building. Cities then acquired a relatively inflexible, energy-intensive, and costly capital infrastructure of zoned land uses, planning, building codes, utilities, and communications systems for entire urban regions as reforms essential to the public welfare.

This well-intentioned movement to improve city-building practices created an unprecedented set of problems: In twentieth-century Europe and America, cities have been built as if sudden, unpredictable, and frequent changes in the conditions affecting them are unlikely; yet in every decade such changes have occurred, burdening cities with prematurely obsolete buildings and districts that conform to outdated conditions and are costly to renovate, modify, or maintain. City building in the cultural and economic modes facilitated the modification of city space to changes in circumstances affecting cities; city building in the regulatory mode appears to retard and inhibit such adaptation.

Adaptability in city building involves not only factors and circumstances outside the control of city builders, but also the modification of city-building methods and the urban environment in response to latent contradictions and inherent limitations in a particular mode of city building. City building serves some higher goal for society than the provision of shelter and organization of space. The pursuit of such goals as economic growth, social betterment, or the preservation of certain values through city building, however, has also exposed cities to certain risks and problems. When city building in the cultural mode was dominant, political revolt and civil disorder constituted the primary danger. Later, the economic mode increased sensitivity to fire and epidemics. More recently, under regulatory city building, the threat of war has become the focus of attention. War, fire, epidemics, and revolts are not exclusively urban disasters and have been present at all times, but they have special consequences when they affect cities, and each city-building mode has been conditioned around one kind of disaster more than another.

City building in the cultural mode matured at a time when the interdependence of the various districts of a city and the distinctiveness of each city as an economic and political unit within a largely agrarian world heightened awareness of the city's potential to actualize some of society's higher values. City building in the cultural mode emphasized the perceptual and associational meanings of the environment. The urban environment often aroused strong feelings, contained multiple and overlapping channels of access and communication, blurred the boundary between public and private behavior and space, and intensified experiences—all factors which contributed to its politicization.

These characteristics enhanced civic rituals, fairs, and public processions as manifestations of social, economic, and political order. They also helped different groups to express their separate interests and identities. Parties to struggles used city space rhetorically, thereby dramatizing conflict at a time when the city was the sole focus of political activity for most people. Whether provoked by economic issues, internal power struggles, religious differences, or conflict with other political entities, urban riots and revolts were sharp reminders of the problems impeding attainment of civic virtue and communitarian unity. Charged with connotations having political and cultural significance and accessible to all groups, city space sometimes became a field on which contests for influence and control were held, a stage on which ideas and grievances were declared, or a prize which a victorious faction was proud to display. Reacting against disorder and conflict, upper-order elite groups and absolutist rulers eventually adopted some new city-building techniques in the cultural mode which, they believed, would inform, modify, and control popular behavior effectively. Their attempts to correlate spatial order with good government and social stability widened the difference between vernacular construction on the one hand and planning and architecture on the other.

By the eighteenth century, revolts and disorders which had been so common and threatening in the past diminished in frequency and shifted in nature for reasons which had little to do with city building. During the two centuries when the economic mode was dominant, fires and epidemics were the principal threats to the cities. Fires, epidemics, and regulations to prevent their outbreak had been familiar since the Middle Ages, but such disasters did not directly threaten the purposes of city building in the cultural mode. Economic city building promoted urban development as a source of profit and to facilitate production and distribution.

Economic criteria limited health and safety improvements to those groups with the ability to pay, but if a fire or epidemic in unimproved or unprotected districts got out of control, disaster threatened investment elsewhere in the city. Eventually improvements in the public interest were rationalized with new cost-benefit concepts which appeared to be in the economic interest of everyone. Fire insurance, building codes, fire departments, improved water distribution and sewage disposal systems, and design of streets and housing based on medical and engineering knowledge were applied throughout the city, even though such improvements imposed constraints on profit-oriented city builders.

By the end of the nineteenth century the threats of fire and epidemic abated. Major technological innovations and social changes eventually provided the means to improve and standardize public services which had been developed in the economic mode. The modern urban infrastructure maintained by regulatory city building to protect the public has also made the city more vulnerable to the threat of war. Cities in the twentieth century have been frequent targets in both world wars, in civil wars, and in terrorist actions. What makes the city attractive as a target is the apparent vulnerability of its complex systems of environmental control which are highly interdependent, technologically sophisticated, and easily disrupted at critical junctions or nodes.

Even in European and American urban centers geared toward war production but not attacked, disruption of daily services and strains on infrastructure systems were severe. To cope with wartime situations, normative city-building procedures were replaced with an improbable combination of centralized planning measures more powerful than those used by peacetime regulators and a broader degree of deregulation to permit maximum flexibility and improvisation. The burdens of war in turn inspired compensatory goals for peacetime city building which inevitably raised expectations too high, especially in housing. We shall see in chapter 6 whether the assumptions of strategists and politicians were well founded and what city builders learned about their work from wartime experience. City building is a historical process whose development has conditioned its nature

In the past quarter of a century, urban history has developed impressively as a field, but Lewis Mumford's *The City in History*, first published in 1961, has remained the only broad, chronological overview of how and why city-building practices have changed over time.[10] Although many historical studies on the built environment by specialists in the social sciences, the humanities, and the design professions have appeared in recent years, their articles and books have been scattered widely, a circumstance impeding the formulation of generalizations.

Happily, the growth of urban history has stimulated debate about the relation of case studies to theories of urban development, and about the very concept of the field itself. One of the early uses of the term "city-building process" involved an attempt to distinguish urban history from the history of "everything that happened in cities."[11] Some historians have pleaded for the integration of the social history of the city with the history of its physical development, but the promise of urban history as an interdisciplinary forum has not materialized. Scholars admit that the phenomena of urban history are too complex for any one of the many specialized, cognate disciplines to master. Ironically, this condition means that genuine integration is as necessary as it is difficult.

A historical survey of city building is worth attempting for its own sake; it also promises to illuminate the contemporary in ways that the study of the contemporary by itself cannot. This book is presented in the hope that a general historical outline of the city-building process can have heuristic value as a framework within which the search for historical knowledge and better understanding of contemporary problems can proceed.

The Urban Millennium

CHAPTER ONE

The Middle Ages

ट॰ *Urbanization in Spatial Perspective*

The revival of city life in the tenth century began a millennium of uninterrupted urban settlement during which the city has come to represent civilization itself. There is a paradox to the medieval origin of modern urban civilization that endows the medieval city with a special claim on our attention. Medieval urban patterns were inherently dynamic; the growth of cities continued long after the conditions initially favorable to their development expired. From the tenth to the fifteenth centuries, medieval city-building practices satisfied the demands of urban growth and change by adapting city space to unpredictable changes in the factors affecting urban life. Yet the medieval city did not survive. Changes in the nature and direction of medieval urban living ultimately stimulated radically new approaches to architecture, planning, and utilitarian construction, approaches which have affected urban development from the Renaissance to the present.

To appreciate what medieval Europeans accomplished when they built cities, it is useful to recall how complete had been the destruction of urban civilization during the centuries after Rome's fall. Roman power had established hundreds of new towns and encouraged the rebuilding of hundreds of preexisting ones. Probably never before had so many people lived in cities linked by roads rather than separated by frontiers.[1] The decline of Rome brought about deurbanization on an equally grand scale. Settlements in western Europe that preserved some of the political, economic, and social structures acquired from Rome nonetheless lost the physical attributes of cities.

The fate of urban settlements in southern France can illustrate the process of urban collapse.[2] Marseille is the European city with the longest record of uninterrupted settlement, having been founded in the seventh century B.C. Marseille survived the Dark Ages because a mountain range surrounding it provided natural defenses, while through its port the elements of mercantile contact, however rudimentary and limited, were preserved. But Marseille's survival did not help the hinterland cities on the plains with which it had been closely related. Today, the Roman ruins at Nîmes, Glanum (near St. Rémy de Provence), and Arles are important tourist attractions, for they contain some of the best-preserved ancient monuments in western Europe. This part of Provence, the Rhône delta south of Avignon, was once the political and commercial crossroad between Italy, France, and Spain.

Nîmes possessed a great arena, built just before the Christian era, to hold 21,000 spectators; it was twentieth in size of the seventy known Roman arenas in the world. More famous is the Maison Carrée, a small temple from the reign of Augustus, which Thomas Jefferson thought the most moving building he had ever seen. In the fifth century, the Visigoths conquered Nîmes, and transformed the arena into a fort by adding towers, filling in arches, and digging a moat around it. Every time Nîmes was besieged, its fifty-kilometer-long aqueduct (including the Pont du Gard) was damaged. After the fourth century, maintenance and repair work ceased, and by the ninth, people began removing stones to reuse in their own buildings. (The Pont du Gard was rebuilt under Napoleon III.)

Glanum was a roman town near the only rocky outcropping of the Provençal plain, Les Alpilles. It prospered in the first two centuries of the Christian era, only to be destroyed by Germanic invaders. Excavations have revealed houses, streets, canals, baths, a forum, temples, monuments, and the best-preserved mausoleum of its time.

Arles outlasted these other settlements. More loyal to the emperors than Marseille, in the third century A.D. it became the prefecture of the Gauls and a great religious center; also, it served as the great land connection between the highways, river routes, and sea traffic of long-distance commerce. Its arena, as old as Nîmes's, was converted by the Arlesians into a fort, complete with two hundred houses and a church. Its other important monuments were a theater, a necropolis, a forum, and a palace built by Constantine; by the fifth century, all but the necropolis were pillaged for their stone. When Charlemagne established the capital of Provence in Arles, the city was a shadow of its former self and lacked the means to impose its leadership on that region. The process of undoing took longer to begin in Arles, but in the end the interruption of land trade and the lack of political and military force to repel invaders left urban residents without the means to maintain city life.

The people who fled Provençal cities settled in more isolated and secure lands in hilly regions. The Provence of the Rhône delta possessed no hills, but it was marked by a chain of high (200–400 meters) mountain-like rocks in its center, known as the Les Alpilles, which offered a nearly impregnable position and a commanding view of all movement on the plains. Those who succeeded in controlling it imposed their power and taxes on the people, traders, and settlements of the plain and arrogated for themselves titles of nobility. By the year 1000, the masters of Les Alpilles ruled approximately eighty settlements from their seat, called today Les Baux-de-Provence, atop a high, long, flat and narrow rock that looked south toward the sea. At their court, they concentrated the thin strands that connected southern France with Italy and Spain, strands that once had been broad ribbons on the plain below.

In the eighth and ninth centuries, urban settlements had become as marginal and ephemeral as they had been 1,500 years before, when the Greeks established their first colonies in Italy and France. But this does not mean that the urban development of the ancient world left no residue, no foundation, for city building in centuries to come. Roman and Greek city networks had established urban settlements in places Europeans would rebuild—if only because myth and memory conferred upon these places a visibility that enhanced whatever natural, geographical advantages they enjoyed. Yet, merely the fact that a medieval city was built on the site of an ancient one does not mean the former was a continuation of the latter; ancient Paris developed largely on the Left Bank of the Seine, medieval Paris on the Right Bank, for reasons related to political and economic factors. There were fundamental differences between urbanization in antiquity and in the Middle Ages.

Feudal Christendom generated the renewal of urban life from

within itself. Although cities were maintained in the spreading Islamic and enduring Byzantine empires, and although the remnants of Roman cities in Europe continued to shelter communities, these examples did not inspire Europeans to urbanize. Europe's contacts with the cities of other civilizations influenced European urban development only after the revival of city life was underway. Several factors helped catalyze a revival of cities in Europe. That they were found together is perhaps no more than coincidence. These are not the only possible preconditions for urbanization, but the ones which were operative in Europe in the tenth and eleventh centuries.

The impact of population growth on urbanization, although indirect, affected a wider area over a longer period of time than any other factor. From the tenth century until the devastating Black Death of 1348, Europe's population encountered few natural or man-induced obstacles to its increase: the weather turned milder, epidemics occurred infrequently, warfare's terrors abated, arable land was abundant, and new farm techniques (such as plows for heavy northern soils, the horseshoe, the three-field system of crop rotation, and the collar harness) improved agricultural productivity.[3] A sustained respite from disaster not only increased the population; it must have conditioned people to expect that an investment to improve living conditions would pay dividends in the future.

Agricultural inventions allowed Europeans to substitute horses for oxen in the fields, and with horses farmers could increase the area farmed and the distance between farm and market while lowering transport costs. In many areas, farmers who used to live in isolation or in a small hamlet relocated in larger villages and even in towns, commuting daily into the countryside. The urbanization of agriculture involved an agricultural surplus which allowed increasing numbers of people to live in cities and engage in nonagricultural activities, and involved a market-based economy using barter and cash which tied farmers to cities and generated seasonal demands for labor in both urban and rural industry. Changes in agriculture occurred slowly over a long period, varied widely across Europe, and produced significant disparities in the distribution of wealth and resources among rural and urban societies alike.

Already in the ninth century, as Europeans struggled to increase the spatial dimensions of political units and religious institutions, civilized culture began to spread through the paths of least physical resistance along coastlines, river basins, and fertile plains, areas where increases in agricultural production and trade were most likely to affect population size and settlement patterns. The nascent feudal order consisted of settlements of warriors, artisans, and laborers inhabiting military camps enclosed by defense works of earth, wood, or stone. Once the warlord ceased to use his camp as a base for mobile operations of adventure, and instead chose to govern the territory he had secured for himself and his followers, then that settlement and its environs could be transformed into a town.

Coinage was one instrument that the local lord utilized to enhance his power. Money apparently antedated a demand for its use in economic transactions; it was above all an affirmation of the prestige and authority of the person who minted it. As kings grew more powerful, they preempted the rights of others to coin money and enlarged the area within which money circulated. Coins symbolized Europe's more ordered political existence, and their use probably stimulated mining and trading as well as the growth of a king's revenues. Economic activities had not created the need for money as much as the presence of money, with inherent advantages over barter (especially at long distance), gradually encouraged Europeans to invest and trade. Towns, far better than mere hamlets, provided places to coin money and collect it as revenue.[4] Increasingly, warrior-knights, ecclesiastical officials, and royal servants gathered together in protected settlements with some semblance of communication to other places; the money that passed through their hands served as the basis for a service function in town economies.

There were no models city builders could copy of cities as symbols of a more stable political order, as generators of a more active economic exchange, and as the locus of a more complex social organization. But there were monasteries in the tenth century that already performed one of the traditional functions of cities: preserving and transmitting the collective values of society. In this case, the monastery—more than the ruins of Roman settlements—continued the association among Christian aspirations, ecclesiastical organization, and cultural traditions that had been the last creative act of Rome.

Monasteries were socially integrated communities in which people who did many different things shared a common way of life. And they probably achieved, more than scattered groups of farmers could, a systematic exploitation of the land. Unlike the military camps of feudal lords, monasteries were permanent settlements which built a specialization of spatial functions into their very form.

It is historically significant that what may be the oldest surviving early medieval architectural drawing is a plan of the monastery of St. Gall. It was drawn for Abbot Gozbert of St. Gall probably because he was absent from a series of meetings held at Aachen in 816–17 at which monastic reform was discussed.[5] The drawing shows an ideal monastery complex of forty buildings for about a hundred monks and a staff of hundreds; it includes a church, cloister, refectory, hospital, dormitory, bathhouse, school, house for the abbot, guesthouse, workshop, facilities for baking and brewing, and cemetery. Not only does this document show that the ability to conceptualize architectonic space antedates the growth of cities; it also suggests that the pursuit of Christian ideals was consciously wedded to the solution of practical problems in daily living through a building program. Monasteries provided a reservoir of skills and values that could be easily transferred to the urban milieu.[6]

European towns developed political, social, economic, and cultural characteristics with little apparent difficulty and with surprising rapidity. In the nineteenth and twentieth centuries, many very small communities emerged from a thirty- or fifty-year period of growth as cities of modest size, equipped with most of the recognizable signs of urbanity such as cultural and financial institutions, transportation connections, and diversity in the retail and service sectors. Even some of the largest cities such as Chicago attained world-rank dimensions after a period of growth no longer than a generation. A similar phenomenon seems to have occurred in the formation of cities in the early Middle Ages. The transition from rural hamlet or military camp to town or city can be measured in decades, not centuries; settlements which became cities underwent changes different from those associated with mere accretion of numbers.[7]

It is characteristic of European urbanization that each city's development can be explained with only minimal reference to general phenomena.[8] In the tenth and eleventh centuries, cities came into being in response to forces and events that were experienced most intensely at the local level. There was great variety among cities in the combination of structures, street networks, and topographical features. Such variety itself was of value because each city developed in its own way, with its own identity.

Yet cities had enough in common to produce a recognizable urban civilization. The town did not yet look so very different from the countryside. It had more buildings arranged in patterns of greater density and complexity, but most urban and rural buildings were roughly comparable, many urban residents kept small plots and raised animals, and townspeople did not yet pretend to be superior socially and culturally to country folk. Cities were marked off from the countryside by walls which came to symbolize political and legal differences, because urban and rural economic activities, social organizations, and political structures were qualitatively different. Urban settlements were, in the majority of cases, very small by modern standards (2,000 inhabitants in many cases), and no more than 10 percent of Europe's total population lived in cities. The influence of cities on Europe's development was out of all proportion to their demographic weight.

Because cities developed in response to local circumstances, they were well-adapted to survive initially, but they also had to adapt as those circumstances changed. As commercial and political contacts multiplied between urban nodes and regions, new opportunities became available to some cities; others found their circumstances adversely affected. In the ninth and tenth centuries Europe turned southward: toward Rome, the Muslim threat to Christendom, and contact with unfamiliar cultures. Mediterranean Europe enjoyed a level of cultural prestige, urban development, and commercial sophistication that as yet had no equal north of the Alps. Northern lords possessed greater military power, however, and as they integrated their territories they also extended their operations south. In the middle of the eleventh century, Norman dukes conquered Sicily and parts of southern Italy; in 1085 Christians in Spain captured Toledo; and in 1095 Pope Urban II's appeal induced thousands to join the First Crusade.

The movement of men, goods, and ideas across the Pyrenees and the Alps gradually became repetitive and seasonal; slowly, like a stream of water, it cut a channel for itself in overland passes and along lowland valleys. The subsistence economy of northern Europe could not sustain either repeated or prolonged excursions of this kind, or an aristocratic lifestyle based on leisure and imported comforts, without reaching its limit. So it was that the same Italian merchant-captains who had ferried the Northerners to the Levant and who had taken advantage of the Crusades to widen the area of their control, redirected some of their surplus income northward. In turn, to pay for imported commodities and credit, Northerners began to develop a technology-based pattern of production and trade which proved so successful that by the time Louis IX of France sailed on a crusade in 1248, Italian and Spanish merchant-captains were pioneering the first regular sea route between the Mediterranean and England, France, and Flanders.[9]

Gradually urban development and long-distance commerce accentuated the transfer of political initiative from the countryside to cities and city-based rulers. To extend their control and increase their incomes, kings, landholding noblemen, and city corporations utilized city-building techniques, including the establishment of new cities. In areas of Europe where self-governing cities operated without interference from rulers trying to centralize control of a protonational territory (Italy, Switzerland, the Low Countries, parts of Germany), cities were free to respond on an ad hoc basis to threats from competing, often neighboring cities by building a suburb, a new town, or new urban facilities, as well as by using more traditional economic, political, and military means. Monarchs with claims to rule significant parts of the European subcontinent (France, England, Spain) asserted their claim through military campaigns and the administration of fiscal systems, and by establishing new cities as part of a policy of territorial control.

The new cities of western and central Europe were so conventional and unprepossessing in appearance that it is hard to see in them the new direction in which European urban civilization was heading. Most of these new settlements were, like most older ones, small agglomerations. Their size corresponded to their function, which was to control territory through trade and fiscal institutions. Necessarily, the size of the area any town could control was determined by the time it took a farmer to travel to it; converted into distance, a day or two of travel amounted to as few as ten and no more than thirty kilometers. For this reason, these settlements did not usually outgrow their early form, which in many cases has remained serviceable for centuries, even until the present.

Standardization and simplification permitted a rapid increase in the number of towns. In Westphalia, six cities were founded before 1180, twenty-seven between 1180 and 1240, thirty between 1240 and 1290, twenty-two between 1290 and 1350, and—symptom of a long decline in Europe's economy—twenty between 1350 and 1520. The timing in different regions of course varied, largely according to the political motives and capabilities of individual rulers.[10] Thus, in England new cities were more often created by landowners than the king and were established in the eleventh and twelfth centuries; but in France and Wales new settlements were founded well into the thirteenth and fourteenth centuries respectively. Their street patterns reveal concern for function and freedom from doctrinaire, preconceived ideas; they display "almost infinite variation in actual pattern, yet most are orderly and seemingly logical, possessed of a functionally effective interconnectivity of streets and rectilinearity of plots."[11]

The creation of hundreds of new cities across western and central Europe in the Middle Ages coincided with important changes in many older and much larger cities whose growth was in part a function of mercantile activities. Merchants enabled cities to escape from the limitations which self-sufficiency as an economic imperative would have otherwise imposed. At the center of international, interurban trade were great commercial staples such as wine, wool, salt, and wheat. Although many regions produced some of each, the rise in seigneurial incomes, spending patterns of the elite, and improvements in transportation regularized their use and stimulated more intensive and careful production. Certain cities came to be associated with specific products.

Specialization of commerce and an increase in the volume of production determined the outlines of a network of maritime and overland trade routes between the Mediterranean, northern Spain, western France, Flanders, England, and the Baltic. Medieval rulers and ruling groups tried to profit from commercial expansion by taxing the movement of goods in cities or territories under their control. This kind of fiscal operation was superficially similar to the taxation of farm goods in the hinterland of small cities. Territorial rulers, using administrative and fiscal institutions, tried to assimilate the areal, rural economy of small city and hinterland, and the maritime, commercial world of large port cities connected by extended trade routes, into a single political superstructure. Merchant-ruled networks like the German Hansa League also tried to establish economies of scale and monopolistic control by dominating the regions where the commodities in which they traded were produced. The organization of international trade brought the products of areas colonized with new towns to much larger and usually older urban centers in ways which benefited the latter more than the former.

Efforts at integrating two kinds of economic operations—cultivation and commerce—by combining qualitatively different kinds of cities and urban networks into a single political operation produced social, economic, and political tensions. Yet, ruling groups were hardly aware of the complexity of the problems they confronted because the nature of the emerging economic process remained hidden from those who used it; they knew how to participate in it and gain from it but not why it worked. What urban development contributed to the formation of groups with diverging economic, social, and political interests was not obvious to them; each group identified its welfare, perhaps naively, with the welfare of the city as a whole.

Attempts to make city government institutionally and juridically strong—efforts which on occasion became the source of conflict—corresponded to two goals of the medieval age: security and communal pursuit of religious standards for social life. In the name of the public good, medieval municipalities undertook to regulate economic and social activities and behavior closely, including matters affecting the environment. The authority of government expressed the superiority of the community over the individual. How power was distributed and how transfers of power were effected do not seem to have varied in fundamental ways from city to city.[12] It seems clear that merchants sought and accepted political responsibility for the social and economic welfare of the city in the same spirit as other privileged groups, not because they wanted to exploit municipal institutions for their own benefit but because, like everyone else, they saw the municipality as the legally constituted political superstructure of a hierarchical social order, united in its allegiance to the city it composed.[13]

By the fourteenth century, conditions became less favorable to urban development. As workers, markets, and production became more specialized, social fragmentation of the work force isolated some groups from each other and from a view of the city as a collectivity, a situation with obvious political consequences. At the same time, a long-term price trend began to push prices above wages. The bubonic plague of 1348 dramatically altered supply and demand patterns and transferred certain comparative advantages from some cities to some rural areas.[14] In regions where some cities declined (Marseille), others rose in importance (Barcelona); some regions declined altogether (Flanders), while neighboring ones prospered (Brabant). Given these demographic and economic checks and increased political and economic competition, deurbanization might have become widespread.

But the unexpected happened: cities, as a category and individually, continued to grow. Some cities more than made up for the losses caused by the plague. Luebeck grew from about 15,000 inhabitants around 1300 to 25,000 in the fifteenth century; Hamburg lost two-thirds of its 5,000 inhabitants to the plague, but had a population of 8,000 in 1375 and 16,000 around 1450. Marginal towns and villages provided many migrants. Unlike the Dark Ages, catastrophe in the fourteenth century did not diminish but only enhanced the attractiveness of urban living. As a category, cities possessed commercial resources, political liberties and institutions, and social attractions which widened the gap between city and countryside and facilitated the flow of men, goods, and ideas. But these advantages also encouraged many cities to look after their own interests first; cities became increasingly protectionist in economic affairs and introverted in the terms of their social and cultural life. As important in the fourteenth century as in the tenth, localism preserved diversity among European cities as the condition of their collective survival.[15]

Everything that has been said so far has been preliminary to a study

of city-building patterns as a factor in medieval urban change, and
to a study of medieval cities as a factor in the development of city
building in the cultural mode. Cities were a part of the medieval
world, but the conditions affecting urban development in medieval
Europe were never static. If cities survived and feudalism did not,
the answer lies in part in the fact that cities provided a greater measure of security from attack, political disorder, and economic loss,
not to mention greater economic and political opportunities, than
organized rural life based on the manorial regime and protection by
knights. The urban advantage owed much to a particular European
inclination toward spatial inventiveness, that is, toward relating
building and construction methods to economic, social, cultural, and
political aspects of city life. Ultimately, the process of building and
living in cities gave rise to a distinctively urban outlook on life itself.

₰ The Cultural Mode of City Building

The spatial features of medieval cities stimulated the acquisition of
cognitive and perceptual skills, essentially rooted in everyday life and
popular culture, which rendered the urban environment intelligible,
thereby enabling people to use it effectively and creatively. City
building in the cultural mode developed with the cities of medieval
Europe. Some of its characteristics were functionally related to such
features of medieval society as limited literacy, but city building in
the cultural mode survived the passing of the Middle Ages.

City building in the cultural mode emphasized environmental features which enhanced imageability. Kevin Lynch has defined this
quality as "that shape, color, or arrangement which facilitates the
making of vividly identified, powerfully structured, highly useful
mental images."[16] The primary scale for city building of this kind
was small. As a result, vernacular construction mattered more than
architecture. People distinguished buildings, spaces, and the social
status and economic activities of their users and occupants through
signs on ordinary buildings as simple as the color, number, size,
material, or decoration of doors, windows, chimneys, and roofs.
Sounds played as much a part as sights in this economy of information, especially sounds which were different yet clearly intelligible

when heard together at low decibel levels, what R. Murray Schafer called a "hi-fi soundscape."[17]

This kind of environment was highly transparent, which means that people could perceive directly what was going on in it.[18] Such an environment provided many sharply defined, recognizable, memorable stimuli to the senses, "a general frame of reference within which the individual can act, or to which he can attach his knowledge."[19] It contained many clues if observers knew what to look for; city living involved learning what to notice.[20] But no special skills were needed to understand the city, and no single professional group claimed to understand it better than any other. The result was an environment that placed a premium on perceptions, skills, and values familiar to people of all educational and economic strata.

Because the urban environment was tight, dense, and polysemous, the changes made to any building did not stand out but blended in; the shape and appearance of buildings were sufficiently rich, detailed, and varied in decorative and functional elements to permit the modification of individual units without destroying the composite architectonic relationships that gave each neighborhood, and even each city, an identity. As the city changed, it gave rise to new decorative styles, construction techniques, economic functions, and social needs; but the various kinds of structures and spaces, differentiated according to form, use, and age, coexisted. Parts of cities could grow and change without compromising the integrity and intelligibility of the city as a whole.

Cities in the Middle Ages were small enough to function well in the cultural mode. Most were no bigger than two square kilometers, and only a few were substantially larger than that. A man could walk across an average city in twenty minutes, or around it in an hour.[21] When cities began to grow in the eleventh century, few fixed, manmade features existed to block or channel expansion. Most buildings, whether of brick, stone, or wood, were small, unpretentious, and inexpensive. Adding space was a matter of building an extra story, putting a shack in a garden or courtyard, or knocking out a wall; almost any structure could be torn down, modified, or enlarged easily. Vance has called this "adaptive incrementation."[22] Because most structures could serve many different functions easily, a city's buildings changed several times in a century. Construction required very little prior investment by the community in a common infrastructure. Municipalities regulated matters of public safety such as water sources, sewage disposal, and everything relating to fires (from roofing materials to the hours when fires could be lit); but these strictures, often better enforced and more closely observed than is commonly believed, did not affect the fundamental plasticity or adaptability of the urban environment. Modifications of existing spaces and buildings, when desirable, were easy and inexpensive. The environmental consequences of change imposed few costs on the total urban order. Cities could accommodate a growing or declining population without increasing or decreasing their physical dimensions or their costs in the same proportion. No doubt this adaptability encouraged the growth of economic activities which could have a dramatic effect on city size. Cities could grow or decline rapidly and economically without compromising their ability to adjust to new conditions in the future.

This kind of urban environment did not strictly prescribe use and meaning; rather, its complexity, plasticity, and transiency allowed for multiple and changing uses and meanings. Medieval city building succeeded because it was adaptable to a great variety of local conditions as these changed over time, and because people who were illiterate and innumerate could sort out, utilize, and comprehend the urban environment using skills and values grounded in popular culture. People need not have completely understood what they were doing to have done it well. Contrasts which would shock us—as they shocked people in the eighteenth and nineteenth centuries—such as the juxtaposition of tenements and cathedrals, of wooden shacks and solid stone or brick houses, of factories, warehouses, and homes, of shops and churches, did not appear unharmonious in the Middle Ages. Although streets were often crooked and buildings uneven, the random and haphazard accretion of buildings and spaces was in fact functional, given the ways medieval Europeans exploited and perceived their cities. They were active builders and shapers; city building was a routine, normative, and popular activity.

These spatial features set the context for understanding the city as a place of production and exchange. Production of most goods and services was guild-centered. Merchants differed from guild artisans and masters in that they engaged exclusively in common transactions relevant to all stages of supply, production, and distribution, but they did not possess a monopoly on business services because guild members performed many of these for themselves. Merchants secured a role for themselves by specializing in techniques and instruments which had general value in economic affairs and which no one else offered, such as the first forms of credit transfers, lending, and insurance. Like guild members, merchants worked in their own houses. And merchants, like everyone engaged in a particular trade, tended to congregate in the same neighborhood or even along the same street.

This tendency of city-dwelling Europeans to use geography as a social matrix became an organizing element of urban form, stabilizing it, marking it in a significant way, and directing its evolution. The psychological sources of this tendency are enigmatic, but its social consequences are clear: Europeans in different cities lived in similarly structured environments. Patterns of social stratification, of the division of labor, and of social geography varied greatly in their specifics from city to city, but not in their general structure. The long-term implications of mercantile activities were not apparent to medieval Europeans, perhaps in part because their activities did not require major changes in city-building patterns. The ability of merchants to work within the existing city-building mode enabled them to exploit the latent advantages in adaptability which existed in medieval cities.

City building in the Middle Ages gave merchants an opportunity to take risks and exploit opportunities without incurring major capital expenses or inducing substantial modifications in existing land-use patterns. The inherent adaptability of medieval cities was a factor which favored the expansion of commerce and production. Economic activities were an important factor in the evolution of medieval cities at least in part because their pursuit was successfully accommodated within established city-building patterns. Cities acquired functions, services, and activities all the more readily because the environmental impact of growth involved few permanent changes. And because cities were easily and inexpensively built, scarce capital was available for more productive and potentially profitable investments outside the building sector.

Cities of intermediate or large size (over 10,000 inhabitants) reflected the greater scale of merchant activities that such cities sustained. Their activities were indirectly or directly related to technologies such as the stout and stubby cog sailing ship whose proportions and sailing gear made the carriage of bulk commodities such as wool, wheat, and wine at low cost possible, and the horizontal heddle-treadle loom introduced in the eleventh and twelfth centuries which increased the volume of production, simplified work, and lowered costs.

All the while the house remained the principal locus of production, distribution, and storage; but it, too, evolved to be more suitable for these purposes. Perhaps the most important refinement was in chimney design. Chimney stacks were first used to take smoke out of a room, but gradually they were modified so that air coming down a flue would reverse itself and draw up the smoke, leaving the heat behind to be radiated into the room. New ways of building chimneys onto houses made possible the location of a fireplace on every floor of a multistory building, and not just under a roof. By the end of the twelfth century, even poor people benefited from these advantages, which not only enhanced privacy but also increased warmth and comfort, and thus, indirectly, productivity.[23]

Other technologies with implications for city building involved mechanical and hydraulic sources of power such as mills and eventually cranks and the connections they permitted between rotary and reciprocating motions. Some of these mechancial sources and uses of power could be introduced into a building without calling for its redesign, but others required relocating certain productive activities to specific places within or outside the city.

Land use and building types related to industry and trade especially affected large cities which grew along rivers, estuaries, or the seacoast—large cities were dependent upon water-borne transport as the only inexpensive means of shipping commodities for long distances. The effort required to move goods to and from wharves was such that merchant houses where goods were stored were often built near the waterfront or on streets that ran directly to it. In Luebeck, a complex composed of the clothmakers's hall, the city hall, and the merchants's exchanges occupied an area as large as the cathedral and was connected to the streets leading to the river, not to the church-yard adjacent to it.

Typically, merchants preferred long and narrow building lots; they needed little exposure to the street. Bristol, the only English city besides London to have been granted county status, so great was its importance in maritime trade, had a dense core only two blocks from the harbor and its great bridge with towers and houses. To deepen the harbor, the course of the Frome River was diverted in the thir-teenth century. The great stone buildings serving an ecclesiastical or civil function such as monasteries, almshouses, and churches were built of stone outside the commercial center and away from the riv-erfront, which could be redeveloped easily.

The form of Bruges showed the imperatives of trade even more conspicuously. In the twelfth century a flood had created a harbor at Damme, near Bruges, and in the thirteenth century changes in the economic structure of northwestern Europe enhanced the opportuni-ties for traders in Bruges. Canals were constructed to add wharf frontage to the city, to secure silt-free passage for ships, and to cut the cost of transporting bricks from brickmaking sites. Winches were used to lift cargoes in and out of ships and barges, and water wheels regulated the flow and level of water and harnessed it for production. The new market built at the end of the thirteenth century was con-structed above a waterway such that boats could be loaded or un-loaded beneath its storerooms, under cover. Canals, quays, and re-lated facilities throughout and around the city came to replace other features as the dominant visual and topographic element in Bruges. Bruges peaked in the fourteenth century and was unable to overcome such handicaps as adverse harbor conditions, the decline in the Flem-ish wool industry, the rise of Antwerp, and political disturbances in Flanders and Brabant in the next two centuries.[24]

From the application of technology in medieval crafts and com-merce, people learned that they could modify the environment and their social and economic circumstances. A striking example is the substitution of brick for wood in construction. Bricks became more common in the thirteenth century when techniques for making them with the poor clays of northwestern Europe were developed. Municipal legislation to limit damage caused by fires in wood buildings stimulated production of bricks, especially in the Low Countries where a shortage of wood, the availability of good clay and peat, and long-term patterns of urban growth and canal networks together encouraged brickmaking. Fuel to fire kilns often cost more than labor; transport costs by land could amount to as much as 25 percent of the price of bricks, but by water freight costs were as low as ten percent. (Ships which sailed to England to bring wool to Flanders carried bricks as ballast).

Many towns had their own brickmaker, and municipalities financed brickmaking when private brickmakers could not meet local demand. In some areas brickmaking was more of a mass-production industry than a craft. A separate brickmaking factory was established for the public works of Bruges; it produced 17,501,800 bricks between 1332 and 1415.[25] Near Leyden in the seventeenth and eighteenth centuries, at least thirty kilns, each holding 600,000 bricks, were fired three, four, or even five times a year; in several urban districts total production may have reached over 200 million bricks. Such achievements were exceptional. Normal capacity elsewhere in the preindustrial era was 20,000 bricks a year per kiln.[26]

Stone and brick buildings could be built with contiguous walls, thus increasing the amount of land occupied with buildings; but in other respects the substitution of brick for wood to promote fire prevention seems to have affected only the outward appearance of buildings and land use patterns, and not the fundamental social and physical geography of the city.[27]

Rebuilding and expanding cities with brick or stone according to local supply and demand factors enabled city builders to develop several kinds of public structures such as markets, warehouses, charitable institutions, port facilities, walls, and prisons. One of the distinctive features of medieval cities was the extent to which some public works projects which would seem to us to have a single utilitarian function had at that time several functions.

Public clock towers are one example. In the thirteenth and fourteenth centuries, mechanical clocks based on a verge escapement with foliot were developed. These clocks were wedded to the existing phil-

osophical framework of the day; they told the time, but t[l]
contained the time within a theologically and scientifically o
representation of the cosmos. Their very operation transcend
ity and became an end in themselves. Because clockmakers c[c]
easily improve the accuracy of clocks, they compensated by adding
movements animating astronomical images, bells, and statues—to
the delight of city people. Until clocks were installed in cities, city
time and country time were much the same, measured by the sun
and announced by bells; clocks installed in cities changed that. Usually mounted in towers, clocks were present in Florence in 1325,
Padua in 1334, Milan in 1335, Geneva in 1353, Bologna in 1356,
Siena in 1359. Clocks were expensive, and their installation often
provoked long debates and many designs. However, cities felt the
expense was worthwhile if the clocks were big and beautiful enough
to correspond to a city's wealth and dignity.[28]

Bridges are another example. They were of obvious utility to merchants and other travelers, such as pilgrims, who might otherwise be
obliged to follow a river until a fordable passage or ferryboat could
be found. Bridges were especially important in cities along river
banks where urban development occurred on both sides. Bridges in
cities were often "surrounded and covered by towers, chapels, hospitals, houses, shops, markets, mills, and fishponds."[29] In the twelfth
and thirteenth centuries, masters of the University of Paris lived and
taught on the city's bridges.[30] Bridges must have made a strong impression, because streams and even streets were frequently named
after them, as were many towns and villages.

For the most part, bridges were built by local and central governments for the public benefit, but in some areas of France, for example, there were endowed bridges; there were also bridge-building
brotherhoods which conceived of their activity as a form of charity, a
circumstance which accounts for the presence of a chapel or hospital
on or near a bridge. Donations, of course, did not long suffice to keep
a bridge in good repair or to replace one destroyed in war or by flood.
Most bridges were supported with tolls, but their income was often
diverted to other uses, and the collection of tolls raised arguments
about free passage. The medieval bridge—as a street on piers—did
not belong to the river it crossed but to the city it drew together.

Other important public structures as diverse as markets, cemeteries, town halls, quays, and walls also combined several uses, which
today are kept separate, and were of interest to many segments of
society instead of very few specialized or professional groups as is the
case in modern times. Most public structures required few changes
in street patterns and were not distinguished by their size; they could
be modified or even abandoned without straining urban spatial patterns. Although their construction and maintenance obliged many
municipalities to borrow, sell bonds or annunities, or increase
taxes—operations which were frequent causes of friction internally
and between cities and central governments—their costs must also
be considered positively as investments in the local markets for labor
and supplies. A balance sheet would be difficult to compose when the
bottom line often included the enhancement of collective security,
social cohesion, and productivity. These facilities emphasized the totality and indivisibility of the city as an autonomous unit, and they
frequently became images or symbols of that ideal condition.[31]

Many characteristic features of medieval cities were lost in the extensive rebuilding of European cities between the seventeenth and
twentieth centuries when city walls and housing districts were torn
down, urban waterways were paved over, and many civic or ecclesiastical structures were rebuilt. Medieval city building then acquired
an infamous reputation which Camillo Sitte and Lewis Mumford have
tried to correct by describing how medieval Europeans kept cities
clean and attractive. Such medieval city-building elements as the
juxtaposition of functionally and visually dissimilar structures, mul-
tiuse public facilities, imprecise definition of the boundary between
public and private space, seemingly random street patterns, and
shacks in courtyards and on the urban periphery have survived, if at
all, in very different contexts. Typical medieval city-building elements were easily and inexpensively made, were relatively inconspic-
uous, required regular maintenance, and did not last unchanged for
a long time. Because fire or war could destroy buildings frequently
and unexpectedly, medieval city-building methods made sense.

Most buildings did not look either new or old, because style itself
remained very conservative. Few technical problems in vernacular
construction required the kind of innovation in materials, structure,

or decoration that propel stylistic change. And because style did not
change much, design did not present serious problems in understanding among owners, users, and builders. When the hospital of
San Matteo was built in fourteenth-century Florence, the walls were
specified in measurements and quantities of building materials in
imitation of several other buildings which the builders were to use as
models.[32]

Ironically, the most impressive surviving structures of the medieval
city, the great city halls and cathedrals, were the least typical. Unlike
most other buildings, they were designed to survive. Their erection
added a critical dimension to the cultural basis of medieval city
building. The construction of great Gothic churches in the twelfth,
thirteenth, and fourteenth centuries is popularly thought to have
been an expression of the collective will of the entire society. Gothic
churches probably were indeed the physical and symbolic expression
of medieval ideals. Yet, they were built not just because the people
wanted them but because church leaders possessed the imagination
and power to direct the building program from inception to conclu-
sion. The blending of elite and popular goals and needs in such a
project was not uncharacteristic of the early modern era.[33] There was
potential for conflict in this situation, but for the most part church
and state could summon the resources to execute large and costly
building projects with broad popular support.

What happened at Beauvais at the end of the twelfth century was
exceptional. Beauvais was then an important textile manufacturing
city. They tried to erect Europe's tallest cathedral, but the great
vault, 48.2 meters high (6 meters higher than Amiens's), completed
in 1272, collapsed in 1284. Having immobilized its resources and
labor in this project, Beauvais found itself with severe problems; in
1305 rioters attacked the church and pillaged the bishop's chapel,
and in the fourteenth century the city's textile industry lost its competitive position. As a result, the choir was completed only in the
fourteenth century and the transept in the sixteenth; nothing else was
attempted.

The Gothic style is identified with the rise of architecture as a
profession and with patronage as an extension of ecclesiastical and
secular power. Only architects charged with a bold program could

have posed for themselves and solved the structural problems of higher and thinner walls, vaulted and airy ceilings, larger windows, and taller towers.[34] Early in the twelfth century, hoists and cranes became available for construction; masons learned to quarry and shape regular, fine blocks of stone; and master builders gained self-confidence and control.

Architectural drawings of superior quality survive from the thirteenth century. It does not matter that architects mastered their tasks empirically, used non-mathematical techniques to derive the elevation from the ground plan, and circulated much of their knowledge orally; they nevertheless demonstrated an ability to solve structural and stylistic problems as part of an overall design. John Harvey has marshaled considerable evidence to put four myths to rest: that there were no individual architects but only groups formed spontaneously by craftsmen; that the names of medieval architects are unknown; that the people of the Middle Ages did not concern themselves with the personality of an artist; and that the aesthetic qualities of a medieval building appeared as a happy accident and not as the result of conscious intention. Largely speaking, medieval architects (and their patrons) knew what they were about.[35]

It is perhaps paradoxical that Gothic architecture did not originate in southern Europe, where building in stone had been common, but in northern Europe where it was not.[36] Gothic architecture did not emerge from a patient and progressively more perfect handling of traditional materials and methods, but rather from what the northern cultures learned among the southern cultures during and after the First Crusade. Northerners were quite simply impressed by Mediterranean cities. However, despite their greater wealth, Italians did not invest as much in building projects as northerners, who undertook projects of a scale that far surpassed anything attempted in Italy.

The Gothic style spread as princes and prelates aspired to erect churches and palaces in the new style. For the new style to have traveled so far and wide, it must have possessed an inherent attractiveness; like all great artistic movements, the Gothic soon imposed itself and made other styles seem anachronistic. Architects and builders attempted new approaches and discovered new solutions, with the result that the Gothic style became truly international: two buildings erected in France and Germany at the same time in the twelfth century had more in common with each other than either would have with another building of a different period.

Urban growth had created the need for many new churches, and the expanding economy provided resources to build them. Most new churches were small and were erected quickly because they utilized traditional construction methods. In England in the Middle Ages perhaps only a hundred large churches were built, and of these only about a quarter were city cathedrals; in Paris between 1190 and 1240 more than thirty churches were enlarged or founded, and of these only three or four were of great size. Large churches represented a modest proportion of all church construction.

It was practically impossible to complete a large church quickly. As decades passed, construction methods and architectural styles changed, so that a part of a church was contemporary only for the generation that built it. Like a sedimentary rock, the great church made the epochs of its formation visible. The great church stood above mere mortal time, but it also gave visible testimony to the phenomenon of change in human terms.

It was of the greatest importance that the majestic, monumental structures designed by architects existed in and even enhanced less systematic but efficient and productive patterns of vernacular, utilitarian construction. Until Haussmann's midnineteenth-century transformation of Paris, Notre Dame barely rose above the densely packed tenements and shacks that crowded around it, while at the same time, it clearly transcended its surroundings. In many cities the sides of great churches served as the backs of stalls and houses. In urban terms, this meant that the rest of the city kept on growing and changing in patterns that were only indirectly affected by the construction of a great building in its midst. The great ecclesiastical and civic structures of the Middle Ages exercised a centripetal power of attraction over material resources and spiritual aspirations; the rest of the city, in contrast, developed centrifugally, outward and away from them.

The construction and decoration of great buildings required specialized workmen and valuable materials whose concentration in cities probably accentuated the difference between cities and rural areas.

By erecting structures of transcending symbolic value, architects rei-
fied communal ideals, thereby centering attention on the city as the
place for realizing civilization's highest aspirations. Architecture
composed the most conspicuous aesthetic dimension of the medieval
city. The great building styles of the Romanesque and Gothic periods
must have made a great impact. Their beauty redeemed the entire
city from the more utilitarian, ordinary considerations which determined its form and appearance. If this interpretation is correct, then
a few medieval buildings of architectural value sufficed to introduce
and sustain the notion that the city itself was a chosen, favored place.

The apparent contrast between the well-conceived beauty of a
church or public hall and the seeming absence of conscious aesthetic
purpose in vernacular construction did not produce a contradiction,
as it has in city building since the Renaissance, between the ideal and
reality. Medieval city space composed a whole in such a way that
several approaches to architecture and vernacular construction could
coexist. The presence of a great building in a city did not require
part of the city to be rebuilt to conform to the aesthetic standard it
set. The medieval urban setting was composed of contrasting parts
held together by the gradual way in which they had been developed.
The results could be, and often were, quite picturesque and delight-
ful. Decorative details; street contours; the formal presence of walls,
towers, churches, and markets; and the close proximity of different
kinds of buildings with each other composed an ordered environment
which, while corresponding to no preconceived pattern, nevertheless
was visually intelligible and stimulating. To us it approaches the
sublime. E. A. Gutkind observed that "the seeming unsystematic
appearance" of medieval city space, its "manifoldness," its "unity in
diversity" was "in reality one of the most functional achievements in
the whole history of city planning."[37]

The great age of Gothic architecture had coincided with the economic, demographic, and intellectual expansion of cities in the
twelfth and thirteenth centuries. The ideals of urban life it inspired
were more difficult to pursue in the fourteenth and fifteenth centuries. It is perhaps the great paradox of urban development in the
Middle Ages that after European economic, political, and cultural
activities expanded, the city became more and more a closed society,

closed in its social opportunities, closed in its mental outlook, closed in its political role, closed in its physical shell. Because cities had not been dependent upon expensive public works projects to grow, they could remain stable or decline without incurring major expenses. The inherent adaptability of vernacular construction in medieval cities was an important factor in the survival of cities confronted by social, economic, and political problems.

City building in the cultural mode as it developed in the Middle Ages apparently reinforced patterns of social and economic interdependence among diverse groups in urban societies. The city-building process made the community visible in the organization of precincts, in patterns of social geography, in the development of public facilities and institutions, and in distinctive textures, pathways, and contours which enhanced feelings of familiarity and pride. City building in the cultural mode encouraged people to consider the city as a completely self-sufficient setting for the pursuit of social, economic, and political goals; it habituated people to manipulate the environment as a means of expression and a medium of control.

Paradoxically, city building in the cultural mode was also conducive to actions which fostered division and conflict. When unfavorable economic and political circumstances threatened to divide urban societies into exclusive interest groups and to undermine the basis for urban political autonomy, the built environment shaped the context in which debate and conflict occurred. The urban environment often aroused strong feelings, contained multiple and overlapping channels of access and communication, blurred the boundary between public and private space and behavior, and intensified experience—all factors which contributed to its politicization.

Parties to struggles used city space rhetorically, thereby dramatizing conflict at a time when the city was the sole focus of political activity for most people. Provoked by economic issues, internal power struggles, religious differences, or conflict with other political entities, urban riots and revolts were sharp reminders of the problems impeding attainment of civic virtue and communitarian unity.

The demographic, economic, political, and social causes of urban crisis in the fourteenth and fifteenth centuries have received ample attention in scholarship, but the significance of urban environments in the context of agitation has been neglected. A critical aspect of urban political action involved the formation of a crowd.[38] To assemble, the populace found certain spaces and times more suitable than others: the market square on market days, the cemetery on the anniversary of a particular death, the gallows when executions occurred, the vicinity of the town hall.

But each city also had places associated with some event or action with eschatological or political significance on a mythic level which served the same purpose. The crowd moved through streets and squares toward some goal—to persuade a city council or to vilify a tax collector. In its movement it often chose an itinerary marked by houses, shrines, statues, or places associated in the memories of the people with some event, such that the movement through the city strengthened resolve and heightened emotions. Songs, speeches, and banners added audible and visual stimulation.

Discussing late medieval crowd formation in urban insurrection, Michel Mollat and Philippe Wolff noted that violent action was generally preceded by a mass assembly where passions became heated. Public meeting places and long speeches, in their opinion, contributed to the eruption of revolts.[39] So did rumors, which spread so easily and rapidly from street to street and district to district and made violence sudden, unpredictable, and difficult to control or subdue. Urban riots and revolts occurred in several regions for a variety of reasons between the fourteenth and nineteenth centuries. Only a few generalized examples can be introduced to show the scope and importance of this aspect of city building which greatly influenced the development of architecture and planning.

After the fourteenth and fifteenth centuries, urban insurrections and disturbances which can be associated with city building in the cultural mode broke out in three distinct periods: the religious wars, the midseventeenth-century crisis, and the era of democratic revolutions. In the Reformation of the sixteenth century, Catholics and Protestants contested control over urban societies. Motivated in part by medieval and Renaissance ideals of civic virtue and Christian brotherhood, urban elites in many European cities took their social responsibilities seriously. The idea that the perfect society could be realized in the context of a given city was not dismissed as unrealistic. The rebuilding of Rome itself was an ideological act understood as such by Catholic and Protestant alike, and one that utilized cultural city building fully. In their struggle for influence and power, religious factions used city space.

Natalie Z. Davis has studied Lyon carefully, finding that Catholicism and Protestantism functioned "as two languages which, among many uses, could describe, mark and interpret urban life, and in particular urban space, urban time and the urban community. They shared some of the same vocabulary and metaphors . . .[but] their grammars were distinct. For both languages, there were areas of human experience about which they fell silent or could respond only in expletives. Yet both could be adequate to some of the needs and complexities of a sixteenth-century city."[40]

As Protestants turned iconoclastic, destroying shrines and images, Catholics multiplied processions and visual displays of dogma and history. In Lyon, Catholic processions dramatized the city's identity and sought protection for the body of the town.[41] Calvinists, however, did not conceive of streets as sacred routes. They wanted to open urban space and make it more uniform by removing religious signs. By secularizing space, they made it more available for exchange, traffic, and communication.[42] The struggle between Catholicism and Protestantism in cities from Spain to Scandinavia included urban conflicts shaped in part by environmental features.

Cities were often the locus of insurrections and disturbances because they housed institutions and leaders presumed to be responsible for or capable of redressing some alleged grievance. In addition, because cities contained supplies of food and water needed in any conflict between local and regional or national authorities, their population swelled whenever food supplies were short or political conditions insecure in rural areas. They also provided numerous places for people to hide while organizing, to carry out schemes of revenge, and to celebrate success or succor defeat.

Until late in the seventeenth century, cities were viable political units able to control their own affairs or negotiate with other authorities, because the small size of armies enabled cities to compete with states. Cities could also afford to pay tribute to avoid pillage when besieged. The siege of La Rochelle in 1627–28, although more spec-

tacular and protracted than most, revealed how much easier it was
for a city to revolt against a king than for a king to suppress such a
revolt. The centralizing, absolutist governments of nascent nation-
states gained enough power to change all that by maintaining larger
armies, but not before urban revolts broke out in numerous cities.
The causes of these revolts have been the subject of considerable inquiry and debate, but their consequences for cities were clear.[43]

Marseille, which grew from 45,000 to 65,000 inhabitants between 1604 and 1660, contested extensions of royal power and revisions in its fiscal and judicial systems. After one rebellion too many,
the young Louis XIV entered Marseille with 6,000 troops, installed
judges from Marseille's political rival Aix-en-Provence, ordered the
destruction of the old royal gate and part of the city wall, and directed Nicolas de Clerville, a royal engineer, to refortify the city. The
new forts commanded the maritime approaches to the port from locations which were visible from the city. De Clerville also planned to
build a port for the king's galley fleet and double the size of the city
by creating new districts. (The city in fact did double its population
between 1664 and 1789.) The political symbolism of such plans was
not lost on the city fathers, who argued that the cost would inhibit
commercial investment. Costs reached £1,200,000, of which
£700,000 became part of the city's debt. Louis's political strategy
used city-building projects to humiliate his enemies, celebrate his
power, and create new patterns of financial and political dependency
between cities and the state.[44] In the cultural mode of city building,
forts, monuments, public squares, town halls, and the like figured
in political struggles, to be erected or destroyed for maximum effect.

Paris in the era of the French Revolution provides a third example
of the relationship between politics and city building in the cultural
mode. Richard Andrews and Richard Cobb have described the importance of the urban environment as a factor in organizing or re-
pressing political action, in Paris and in smaller provincial cities; but
the significance of Paris in the Revolution is reason enough to look
more closely at that city.[45]

According to Andrews, the sheer compression of Parisian life vastly
facilitated political mobilization.[46] With very high population densities, practically every district of Paris contained a complete cross

section of the urban society. In Paris, social life was intensely public, the streets and squares congested with people of all social categories "distinctly recognizable by dress and gesture" yet intermingled. Promiscuity, human compression, and abrasiveness exacerbated social tensions and gave them form; these conditions also made people suspicious "of any person or groups perceived as alien, dissimulant, furtive, unattached to a neighborhood or to a 'respectable' trade."[47]

Ordinary people, whether literate or not, were familiar with and exploited the city's social and physical geography in all its detail; the police used a similar kind of knowledge to gather information and pursue suspects. Popular classes used the threat of disorder and violence as a political weapon and, as in eighteenth-century London, expressed their disapproval of a person or policy in more acceptable ways "by staging some sort of street theater: Rough Music, effigies, burlesque costumes, mocking songs, and pantomimes all played their part."[48] People were spectators and participants in organized and improvised public rituals which involved games, processions, feasts, and masquerades in carnivalesque events. Such events were relevant to political disorder not only because riots often had carnivalesque overtones, but also because they familiarized people with highly complex, ritualistic, politicized uses of public space.

The social and cultural center of Paris was the Palais-Royal, "perhaps the consummate site of that intense 'brassage' (abrasive rubbing) of all classes" because of its unique combination of gardens, cafés, salons, boutiques and gambling dens."[49] The Palais-Royal was a "sanctuary where intellectuals could turn from speculation to organization, . . . the point through which new ideas broke into the power elite of the old regime, . . . a living link with the underworld of Paris and with the new social forces that had to be mobilized for any revolutionary victory."[50]

In late eighteenth-century Paris, rumors spread rapidly and could generate a crowd spontaneously. The urban environment made people acutely aware of social behavior and political opinion, and easily aroused them to action. Their experience of life in the city habituated them to certain patterns of thinking and feeling which enhanced the political value of space.

As Charles Tilly and R. A. Schweitzer suspect of London, one reason why nineteenth-century politics differed from eighteenth-century politics may have been the greater degree of residential segregation by class which destroyed the intense intermingling of social groups characteristic of the earlier period. Tilly and Schweitzer are mapping events to see "why and how people got there, what they did next, what started and stopped the action, and so on," the better to identify "such connections as exist between the changing character, geography and repertoires of contention and the shifting distributions of population and activities within the city."[51] Their approach focuses upon the relationship between urban space and politics as a topic as important as the issues of political action themselves. This relationship has not received the attention it merits.

City building in the cultural mode produced an environment which favored certain kinds of political action and amplified the threat of disorder. The conscious use of the urban environment for political action was a function not only of the cultural, social, and political characteristics of particular urban societies but of their urban environments as well.

The transformation of architecture and city planning from the Renaissance to the eighteenth century was conditioned by urban politics. Elite groups, anxious to reduce the incidence of violent, disruptive behavior which weakened the ability of cities to resist encroachments by the state and the position of elites in their own society, appreciated changes in city building which, they believed, offered a way to control popular behavior. The visual complexity of the medieval city became in their eyes a symbol and cause of intellectual, political, and social disorder.

The gradual withdrawal of elites from participation in popular culture in early modern Europe had its parallel in the pursuit by elite groups of architectural and planning styles which owed little or nothing to vernacular construction. The Renaissance approach offered new options and gave city building a rigorous theoretical basis it had lacked. Notwithstanding the differences between medieval and post-medieval styles, the latter retained, indeed revalued, an essential feature of medieval city building: an unshakable reliance on the immediate, direct, intuitive perception and comprehension of the urban environment in its manifold aspects by people of all educational and social levels. Architecture and city planning between the Renaissance and the nineteenth century changed the content of the message, not the medium. Cultural skills, perceptions, and values would continue to dominate city building as they had since the revival of city living in the early Middle Ages.

CHAPTER TWO

Architecture and Urban Growth

⟨⟩ The Early Renaissance

Debates about the spatial, temporal, and conceptual boundaries of the Renaissance continue to animate scholarship, but broad agreement can be found for the proposition that cultural changes originating during the second half of the fifteenth century in Italy provoked some Europeans to explore their world in radically new ways. The Renaissance, like most great transformations, had its source in an earlier time and influenced later generations; and, like most, it can be stretched to cover too much. Nevertheless, particularly in terms of urban history, the intense and imaginative pursuit of knowledge which was grounded in the Renaissance stands apart.

Renaissance ideas about cities and architecture in Italy were both a reaction against medieval city-building patterns and directed toward possibilities in the medieval city which had never been perceived before. By any measure, Italy was the most advanced country of the fifteenth century: Its commercial systems were sophisticated and intensely developed; its civic life was concentrated in politically conscious, city-dominated provincial states; its culture was associated with Europe's oldest and most numerous universities. Italian city-states were small enough and sufficiently numerous to compose a political chessboard on which the balance of power could be pursued, securing small states against the designs of large ones, and distributing power among them as the condition of their collective independence.

This political system fostered a commitment on the part of the upper classes to sustain and enrich the city-state. Changes in economic and social conditions raised risks, costs, and anxieties in Italian affairs, in much the same way as they affected life across Europe, but with this difference: Because Italy was so urbanized, and because Italian culture and politics focused upon the city to an unusual degree, economic and social problems were perceived acutely in an urban dimension.

A desire for order and control found its finest expression in a new architecture. Two circumstances made changes in architecture more probable in Italy than elsewhere: First, Italians were less attached to medieval ideas and forms, and were more aware of ancient culture; second, the number of easily accessible cities, rivalry among patrons, and a reservoir of mobile artistic talent made it likely that fruitful experiments in building would take place, and could be replicated.

Artistic ideas provided the catalyst for architectural change. These ideas have long fascinated scholars, yet much will always remain a mystery about them because some of the most precious documents—drawings by Brunelleschi, for example—have been lost. Nevertheless, the essential story can be reconstructed. It begins in Florence in the 1420s, when Filippo Brunelleschi (1377?–1466) invented linear perspective in pictorial representation by placing all objects and figures within a spatial frame in relation to a geometrical, abstract superstructure dominated by a vanishing point.[1]

The theory which made linear perspective plausible stated that visually perceived space is ordered by an a priori, abstract system of linear coordinates. Linear perspective was not thought to be an artificial device to give the optical illusion of reality on two dimensions but a two-dimensional version of reality, a key to the spatial organization inherent in the world. It was believed that the real space before one's eyes can be understood in the mind and transferred onto canvas because it is structured according to divinely composed, geometrical laws of nature: There is truth in what one sees because God has constructed space according to true, natural laws.

This theoretical statement did not exist until Leon Battista Alberti (1404–1472), of whom more later, set the rules of linear perspective into print in the mid1430s; but Brunelleschi's experiments must have been guided by some of these ideas, which were not particularly new or original. What was inventive was the artistic technique, which linear perspective provided, to give them precise visual form.

The composition of a painting based on linear perspective involved using a geometrical grid to determine the location and proportion of the details. Once the grid technique and linear perspective were linked, their use became generalized, with consequences for both architecture and city design. In the absence of linear perspective, a map or drawing of the spatial layout of a medieval city did not appear to have a logical structure which could be determined abstractly, but instead appeared as an agglomeration of parts whose internal connections did not require objective graphic description or verification to be understood.[2] Thus, artists who could not use linear perspective reproduced buildings from several different vantage points, notwithstanding the visual contradictions this produced in a two-dimensional work: Some buildings were shown from one vantage point, others from another; many buildings were rearranged in the same city, or combined with buildings from two or more cities.

Renaissance artists must have felt a tension between actual city space and theoretical notions about space as constructed according to eternal principles and divine laws. Brunelleschi demonstrated that the grid could be used to copy buildings to scale, and he incorporated it as well as a compositional element in some of his buildings; and Alberti used the grid to make more accurate city views. By the end of the fifteenth century, the grid had become the theoretical design model for city squares, and even more significantly for entire cities.

At first, buildings of a style we now identify as Renaissance were conceived by painters (Ghirlandaio, Pinturrichio, and Botticelli, among others) working from imagination, because no buildings had yet been erected which could have served them as models. The imaginary space in their paintings was composed of ideally shaped buildings, streets, colonnades, and the like, which were subordinated to the entire composition through symmetry, perspective, and proportion. The characters placed by artists into such settings were given a stage for moral, historic action which placed them outside ordinary living experience. The self-imposed task of the first great Renaissance builders was to transfer that setting from canvas to the real city. Artists became architects.

Between the end of the twelfth and thirteenth centuries, the population of Florence had at least quadrupled, with most new housing provided by building in open spaces and courtyards and by adding on stories to existing structures. Florence appeared as a "mass of tenements, towers protruding everywhere, . . .[with] little overall organization . . . and few points of focus to pull parts of it together visually."[3] Then the spirit of a new political order inspired Florentines to insist on a greater assertion of civic values against the centrifugal forces of a corporate society and to give more coherent shape to communal government.[4]

A fire in 1304 destroyed 1,700 buildings, a flood in 1333 everything along the Arno River; rebuilding gave Florentines an opportunity to start afresh. The cutting down of the towers of factious families, plans to enlarge the city and rebuild its walls, and legislation to give some order to urban expansion were "informed by a consciousness of public space and inspired by the desire to make a distinctive mark on it."[5] Uplifted by a sense of their uniqueness and superiority, Florentines developed a collective vision of their city which provided a civic context for public and private building.

The transformation of medieval into Renaissance Florence involved the construction of civic, ecclesiastical, and patrician buildings by artisans with little academic training.[6] Height and mass more than purely artistic features distinguished newer from older structures. So long as styles were traditional, architects encountered few problems in communicating their intentions to craftsmen, who in turn enjoyed some scope for their own talents. (Even after architectural style departed from tradition, architects were still paid at a foreman's rate for the amount of work they did, not for their ideas.)

Brunelleschi, the first to compose a painting according to linear perspective, was also the first to deal with the problem of designing a building according to the new aesthetic in an existing urban setting. A century before, Giotto had erected a campanile next to Florence's cathedral, but the dome over the cathedral still remained to be completed. Brunelleschi's design for the dome has been interpreted to symbolize the evolution of art since Giotto. Giulio Argan's discussion of Brunelleschi's dome brings out the protean consciousness of early Renaissance architectural design which conflated architectural form, urban space, and the universe and implied that a single, systematic, rational, homogenous order structured them all.[7] Argan

makes clear that Brunelleschi's achievement represented the suprem-
acy of the liberal (intellectual) over the mechanical (artisan) arts:

> From the point of view of the technical construction, the dome is a
> completely new thing which transformed not only traditional meth-
> ods of work but the very social organization of the building trade as
> well. It is well known that before undertaking the technical problem
> of construction Brunelleschi went to Rome to study the fabric and
> proportions of the ancient city walls. However, it is clear that, al-
> though the dome of Santa Maria del Fiore implied a familiarity with
> ancient methods, it was not built in a traditional manner. It is thus a
> modern invention based on historical research. Evidently Brunelleschi
> thought that a new technique could not be derived from the past,
> but must come from a different cultural experience, from history. In
> this way he refuted the old "mechanical" technique and created a new
> "liberal" technique based on those typically individualistic actions
> which are historical research and inventiveness. He abolished the tra-
> ditional hierarchical form of the mason's lodge where the head was
> the coordinator of the specialized work of the various groups of
> skilled workers who made up the lodge masters. Now there was only
> one planner or inventor; the others were merely manual laborers.
> When the master mason rose to the status of sole planner, whose ac-
> tivity was on a par with the other humanistic disciplines, the other
> members of the team of masons fell from the rank of *maestri* in charge
> of various aspects of the job to that of simple working men. This
> explains the impatience of the masons and their rebellion against the
> master mason who had become an "architect" or "engineer."
>
> The consequence of this—its importance also in the field of city
> planning—could be seen already in other works by Brunelleschi. He
> used the classical architectural morphology of equal, repetitive ele-
> ments almost in series and eliminated the abundant Gothic decora-
> tion that had generally been carried out in the masons' workshop.
> Architectural elements such as columns, capitals, cornices, and so on,
> could now be constructed outside the shop and then put in place ac-
> cording to the architect's design, just as prefabricated elements are
> used today. This saved an enormous amount of time, both in the
> planning and in the execution. . . . Even with delays caused by un-
> foreseen circumstances, the construction could be carried out accord-
> ing to the plan of the original architect; a great construction need no
> longer be the work of successive generations, but of a single artist. If

it became possible in the Renaissance to think of the city as a unified form (in a utopian but not absurd manner), willed into being by a prince and created by his architect, this was due to the changes in the methods of planning and execution begun by Brunelleschi, which made it theoretically possible to construct a city within a man's lifetime.[8]

The key word in the last sentence is, of course, theoretically. Construction of private mansions and civic structures recycled wealth into art, generated demand for decorative arts of high quality, and stimulated the enjoyment of lovely things. Conspicuous consumption of this kind, however, did not generate new wealth. Given the deteriorating economic and social circumstances of late fifteenth- and sixteenth-century Italy, the demand for new construction could not be sustained long enough to transform the medieval city completely.[9]

Leon Battista Alberti (1404–1472) was the first to test the applicability of architectural design to city planning. Pope Nicholas V, having restored unity to the church and determined to safeguard its doctrines and institutions, elevatd the Vatican as the seat of the Papacy, initiated the construction of St. Peter's, and adopted the arms of Peter as the papal seal. With Alberti's guidance, he also undertook to rebuild and restore the city of Rome to is rightful position as the greatest city of Christendom. This was no mere propaganda effort; the ideology behind midfifteenth-century plans for Rome was grounded in a vision of a city whose appearance would make manifest and visible the power, purpose, and primacy of the church. Alberti understood what Nicholas wanted.[10] He undertook to do two things: first, to formulate a theory to justify the reconstruction of Rome (published as De re aedificatora, in different editions between 1443 and 1452); second, to conceive of conspicuous architectural, spatial forms which could express the historical and contemporary significance of Rome, and to make a hierarchical order visible.

Alberti and Nicholas intended to design the entire district enclosed between the Vatican, the Castel Sant'Angelo, and the Tiber River, and a new piazza further along the Tiber; but their plans never advanced far enough for us to know what individual elements would have looked like. It took one century to complete St. Peter's, and another to integrate the Vatican into the structure of Rome; in the meantime, the city's demographic growth determined the shape and scale of most construction. Nevertheless, Alberti's conceptualization of a reconstructed Rome included all the features which characterized Renaissance city planning: the revision of existing urban space by opening it up with new streets and wide squares; the enlargement of a city by adding new, planned districts; the erection of monumental buildings whose presence and qualities would generate development around them.

Nicholas's plans exceeded the means available for their realization, but Alberti combined theoretical and practical considerations more satisfactorily in his other building ventures. More than anyone else, Alberti developed the idea, through his writings and designs, that a building's stylistic qualities, spatial form, and architectonic placement in the cityscape should integrate that building into the daily lives of the citizens. This dialectical approach toward the erection of churches, patrician palaces, and social welfare and public institutions—the kinds of buildings patrons of Renaissance architecture commissioned—emphasized respect for the total urban environment in all its manifestations as the setting for cultural, social, and political life.

Realizing that only a few buildings in the Renaissance style would be built in any city, Alberti did not require the destruction of large parts of existing cities as a precondition for rebuilding along fundamentally new lines. Rather, he wanted to maximize the visual and ideological impact of every project in the belief that a few Renaissance buildings, by their very presence, could revalue their surroundings and stimulate changes in the quality and meaning of urban life. This conservative, practical approach to construction, which preserved a balance between beauty (*voluptas*) and usefulness (*commoditas*), recognized that Renaissance styles were not appropriate for all kinds of buildings. It also contained within it an idea which, however, could not be restrained by utilitarian, quotidian considerations: that architecture, unifying all the arts with philosophical thought, could bring life to the medieval ideal of a community harmoniously integrating social order and moral action.

From this perspective, it appears that Renaissance architecture, for all its differences with medieval building, remained in the cultural mode to the extent that it emphasized the immediate and direct apprehension of space, and reaffirmed the power of spatial forms to influence people. In their attempts to make order in cities by promoting civic values that would engage people in socially responsible activities, Renaissance designers articulated a higher purpose for city building in the cultural mode. To clarify architecture's message and eliminate any ambiguity, complex and polyvalent spatial features which created many layers of meaning were cut.

The moral imperative of Renaissance architecture implied that the medieval urban world was morally corrupt and aesthetically inadequate, and hence could not provide the outlines of forms for a vision of the world as it ought to be. To penetrate the consciousness of city dwellers, Renaissance architects required styles which could symbolize, by directly embodying, the transcending reality behind appearances. Rudolph Wittkower has described how Renaissance artist-architects, starting with a revival of the Roman Vitruvius and an archeological search for classical buildings, produced a style in which proportion, harmony, and classical derivatives had unquestioned status as the most immediate and intuitive expressions of form and content. The result was a new humanistic, metaphoric architectural vocabulary which evoked a remote golden age in order to open up an imaginative vision of a future society immeasurably closer to divine and natural law than the present one.

Classically inspired ideals emphasized the city as the unit to be governed, produced the need for a new kind of public space as a forum for political action, and commanded architecture to visualize the secular and religious uses of power.[11] Although Renaissance architecture referred to a time sequence, it was nevertheless profoundly antihistorical, designed not so much to resemble antiquity as to point up the anachronisms in medieval urban culture. Renaissance artist-architects did not know, however, that their break with the past would inspire, and indeed compel, their successors to break with them. After all, they believed quite sincerely that their designs, which symbolized eternal values, would endure and would hasten the commencement of a new enlightened age for man.

In the 1490s the rise of genuine religious anguish and the destruction of the Italian city-state cut short the ambitions of artist-architects. Yet, they continued to pursue the visual representation of the ideal society without recognizing that their assumptions were illusory or impractical. Reaffirming their faith in imagination, and rejecting the real world as an unsatisfactory model for art, they persisted in the search for the perfect expression of truth, beauty, and goodness in architectural form. They did not reconcile themselves to the fact that their influence on cities was limited to the design of palaces, civic and ecclesiastical structures, fortifications, and public works, or to the fact that they often competed with traditional crafts- men even for these commissions.

Until the eighteenth century, vernacular, utilitarian construction evolved satisfactorily along established lines, enabling cities to grow and change with little direction from architects and planners. Traditional city-building methods thus preserved the latent adaptability of the urban environment to change, and thus kept the cost of providing and maintaining that environment low. For this reason, in that large part of the city that continued to evolve in the vernacular tradition, visible differences over time were much less striking than in that small part of the city affected by architecture, even though both parts might be rebuilt extensively in every century. Such change as took place usually did not affect the size and shape of the city but only land-use patterns and individual structures in ways that were easily assimilated into the city as a whole.

The role of vernacular, utilitarian construction in city building was largely lost on artist-architects, who continued to pursue their ideals. To the high-minded designers, for whom design was a principled intellectual activity, the coexistence of architectural masterpieces and ordinary dwellings, workshops, and public facilities was intolerable. The consequence of this situation for the history of the city was enormous: At a time of rapid urban development, those most able to speak, write, draw, and design ideas about and for cities were often unable to provide practical solutions to urban problems. Having placed theory before practice, artist-architects at the end of the fifteenth and the beginning of the sixteenth centuries contributed to a division in urban culture. This division separated those with ideas about urban affairs from those responsible for the everyday needs of ordinary people. There has been no turning back from the notion that architecture can restore order to society and dignity to man, but each generation from the sixteenth century to the present has recognized the failure of its predecessors to imagine architectural projects and city-planning schemes which successfully combine beauty with practicality and artistically designed structures with quotidian, vernacular ones.

ᔒ The Evolution of Architectural Style and the Concept of Urban Growth

Perhaps no other period of western civilization has been as free to invent and appreciate architectural style as the early modern era. Like literature, architecture became even more exclusively an urban form during the early modern era than it had been before. Like literature, architecture belonged to a print culture which developed a mass audience, stimulated a phenomenal increase in vocabulary and expressive power, and demanded the codification of rules to govern its systematic use. Like literature, architecture amplified the widening economic, social, and political differences between city and countryside, and it placed value judgments on those differences. Like literature, architecture enabled individuals and social groups to develop a conscious awareness of their identity.

The literary qualities of design as it evolved in sixteenth-century Rome had great consequences for the concept of architectural beauty. The cleverness and scholarship which went into the formulation of design ought to be compared in importance to the synthesis of vernacular languages and their refinement into powerful rhetorical instruments, which occurred at the same time. The parallel extends in fact very deeply. For example, Roman architects placed especially great emphasis on the wall as a facade or sculptural unit and rather less on the plastic possibilities in space, almost as if architecture, like language, were created on the two-dimensional surface of the page.

The codification of style largely involved both drawing and printing, and enormous technical and artistic advances were achieved in both, especially in the first half of the sixteenth century when Raphael and Antonio de San Gallo, both chief architects of St. Peter's, strengthened the consistent use of correct orthogonal projection to represent aspects of a building on paper; and Sebastiano Serlio produced a volume of fifty fanciful doorways and published the first architect's manual, a multivolume work which combined classical models with commentary. The first printed map of Rome designed to be sold by itself appeared in 1551. The architectural drawing, for the architect's own use, and the architectural illustration, for public consumption, reinforced the evolution of style in the direction of a contemplative, cerebral notion of beauty.

The two-dimensional exposition of architectural design facilitated comparisons between architectural forms and styles and between ideas and concepts which had nothing to do with architecture per se. Is a style or form arbitrary, or does it correspond to a natural law of proportion? Should physical man or reason provide an ideal model for architecture? How literal or metaphoric is the correspondence between a symbolic idea and an architectural form? Questions such as these made architecture important to nonarchitects, while at the same time helping to give architecture the critical content it had lacked as a purely decorative art. Printing gave that theory the widest possible geographical and intellectual dimensions. As a result, the evolution of style became not a professional prerogative of architects but a public matter. Architects considered questions of style according to new choices and conflicts in ideas and politics. The results, as in Rome, were often very beautiful.

Like the Catholic reform movement itself, the rebuilding of Rome had been a long time in coming.[12] The Rome in which artists and architects worked throughout most of the sixteenth century still appeared largely as it had in the late Middle Ages, a city as unlikely to change as the hierarchy of the church itself. In 1480, Sixtus IV composed the first of a series of legal injunctions controlling construction and public hygiene, and compelling absentee owners to look after their properties or risk losing them; and in 1574, Gregory XIII reformulated these texts into a document which remained in force until 1870. Most new buildings had been erected either in older areas of the city (often at the expense of gardens) or in newer districts; individual popes had conceived of new streets to facilitate the movement of pilgrims or armies, but these, like most buildings, had been inserted into the city without being related to each other. Construction per se, even buildings by Raphael, Michelangelo, and other architects of stature, had not provided Rome with a vision of what it might become.

It was Sixtus V (1585–1590) who made Rome a Renaissance city, advancing the construction of St. Peter's (the cornerstone had been laid in 1506) and undertaking to subordinate construction in the rest of the city to a comprehensive spatial framework. New streets were created to orchestrate pilgrimages into a complete urban experience and to orient Romans toward the city's hills, which they had failed to develop for industry and housing until then. Within five years, ten kilometers of streets and several industrial and residential compounds were constructed to enlarge the city and to integrate the new and old parts into a single spatial frame. In all, Rome acquired fifty-four new churches, about sixty grand mansions and twenty aristocratic villas, housing for fifty thousand people, thirty new streets, three aqueducts, at least thirty-five fountains, and some new fortifications.

Renaissance architects were ill-prepared to meet the demand for palaces, churches, and other important buildings in sixteenth-century Rome. Until the end of the sixteenth century, Rome lacked the kinds of streets and squares architects thought essential to good design. To achieve a scale which isolated their works from the rest of Rome, architects either had to inflate their projects to grandiose proportions or insert them into the city as aesthetically self-sufficient structures whose stylistic integrity was complete.

Like Brunelleschi and Alberti, sixteenth-century architects from Bramante to Palladio turned to classical models, but with this difference: The novel conditions in which they worked required a more thorough understanding and a more complete repertoire of classical models. In sorting out the literary and archeological evidence from antiquity, architects began to standardize, simplify, and codify stylistic elements into their constituent parts. These parts they then reused imaginatively to meet the specific task at hand as they imagined classical architects might have done. Because architectural works were isolated from each other in Rome and stood in contrast with their immediate surroundings, architects needed an externalized set of stylistic values as an objective standard against which their buildings could be designed and evaluated. Reliance upon an architectural code tended progressively to narrow the range of stylistic variety and to emphasize superficial elements of style at the expense of its spirit and method. Yet this situation did not stifle creativity; because no building either approached the ideal of perfection posited by the architectural code or appeared to exhaust the structural or decorative possibilities latent in it, architects were willing to experiment. Vacillating between dogmatism and skepticism, architects were often inspired to push their art into new forms.

Perhaps Alberti and Brunelleschi would have approved; perhaps it was only the logical unfolding of the flower that bloomed in fifteenth-century Tuscany. But it would be a mistake to say that the development of architecture in sixteenth-century Rome merely carried forward the early Renaissance program. Not only did sixteenth-century architecture specialize the architectural vision and make it more selective; it also enlarged the cultural context in which architecture was designed and appreciated. Had Rome not grown so spectacularly and its spatial features not imposed special limitations, and had architects in Rome not felt the historical importance of their opportunity, the evolution of architecture might have been different.

Perhaps the greatest (and least noticed) contribution of architecture to urban development in the sixteenth and seventeenth centuries was to normalize the phenomenon of urban growth in terms that elite groups understood. To grasp this, let us remember that the cultural paradigm of city building had lost none of its vigor since the Middle Ages. High architecture remained a virtuoso art which coexisted but had little in common with popular, vernacular, utilitarian construction. Although architecture was grounded in the assumption that people respond instinctively and intelligently and without conscious, rational analysis to the spatial phenomena of the environment, architects qualified this theorem by eliminating most ordinary construction from having any salutary or positive influence on ideas and behavior. On the contrary, in their eyes ordinary buildings were badly designed and corrupt, a symbol and perhaps even a cause of social, political, and economic problems of urban life. They believed that only proportion, geometry, symmetry, and style—aspects of design that appear in utilitarian construction fortuitously—create beautiful forms and communicate important messages about power, authority, morality, and obedience.

The presumed moral superiority of architecture and associated city-planning techniques was attractive to elite groups. They could understand and appreciate the design process for its own sake precisely because it provided a means of channeling, shaping, and controlling urban growth in spatial terms. (Around 1500, only four cities in Europe had over 100,000 inhabitants; by 1700, as many as twelve had crossed that threshold, among them Paris, London, Naples, and Amsterdam.) The cultural impact of architecture and planning on attitudes toward urban growth was in fact much more profound than their impact on the actual form and shape of cities, as measured by the number of executed plans. Using the techniques of architecture and city planning, Europeans came to see urban growth as a normative process that need not threaten to bring on a collapse of political institutions and social order.[13]

The architectural imperative offered Europeans in the sixteenth and seventeenth centuries, in larger and smaller cities alike, a way to keep change orderly—or, at the very least, to keep the appearance of being orderly. They began to adopt a new attitude toward city space which accepted urban change as a natural, if unpredictable, process. As a result, elite social and political groups which otherwise might have abandoned the city and its problems accepted the responsibility of coping with urban affairs. The buildings and institutions they endowed, constructed, and administered—the hospital, prison, granary, poorhouse, market hall, church, city hall, bathhouse—made manifest a code of values for daily life, a system of reward and punishment, a distribution of power. Whether these facilities functioned as intended, whether urban life was as orderly as the governing classes wished it to be, is beside the point. These structures corresponded to a set of attitudes toward urban life and urban change that originated in the architectural ideas of the age.

Descartes set forth the idea that a well-ordered environment acted unconsciously on those who use it, teaching them by example to order their own lives by reason, its most famous formulation. In the *Discourse on Method*, Descartes proclaimed his belief in the inherent power of visual forms to express ideas and values. He found superior those buildings which reflected one architect's comprehensive, ordered vision. To cities which reveal the many stages of their growth in the crowded, disordered layout of their streets he preferred "the regularly constructed towns which an engineer has planned according to his fancy, on an open plain," concluding that new cities which visibly illustrated "the will of a few men using reason" were superior to older ones built by "chance."[14]

Descartes perceived the relationship between political and spatial order. Harmoniously constructed districts would call to mind the power of their author, standing out by the degree to which reason and reason alone determined their features. City building of this kind was an example of good government in action that would induce and inspire good behavior in people. From the Italian Renaissance utopias of the sixteenth century to the end of the French Enlightenment, philosophical and psychological concepts explaining how the environment acted this way inspired and rationalized imaginative plans for scores of ideal new cities and hundreds of projects to rebuild parts of existing ones. In these plans, as in Descartes's text, the street took on an importance in architecture and city planning it had previously lacked.

Modern city-building practices such as uniform street design and comprehensive planning were introduced across Europe as several developments converged. During the late sixteenth and the seventeenth centuries, surveying and engineering methods advanced rapidly. Graphic artists learned to depict topographical and spatial features in map or plan form with greater control; mathematicians undertook the study of probability and statistics, analytic geometry, and advanced algebra, among other topics; and political and philosophical thinkers applied themselves to a consideration of society in geopolitical perspective.

Except for civil and international warfare, from which no country was spared, conditions favorable to these developments varied according to local circumstances. These were: in England, the enclosure movement, and inflationary trends that encouraged landowners to look after their property more closely; in Spain, colonization of America and the rebuilding of cities in Italy and Spain; in the Netherlands, reclamation of land from the sea, and urban and commercial growth; in the Baltic, colonization and warfare associated with the rise of the Swedish empire; and in France, an urbanism of royal grandeur designed to make French cities as productive as the size and power of France suggested they should be. City-planning techniques were abstracted from diverse scientific, political, economic, and cultural sources as new city-building practices were promoted by landowners eager to maximize returns on investments, by municipalities concerned about public order, and by members of the upper classes with a newly acquired taste for larger houses, carriages, parks, avenues, and other amenities provided by a well-ordered cityscape.

Geometrical principles of order, harmony, and proportion gave Europeans the feeling they had gained mastery over urban space. Reduced to the two-dimensional page, the random and the ordered and the actual and the proposed features of the city lost their height and mass and became abstract elements to be measured and cut to size, like the statistics of a hundred voyages on the pages of a ledger or like the mathematical coordinates of planetary and stellar movements. Indeed, in a fundamental sense, in early modern Europe the development of transoceanic commerce on a regular basis, the study of astronomy, and the reconstruction of cities according to city-planning techniques all shared a common view of space as quantifiable, measurable, and knowable.

In this regard it is important to refer, as Descartes did, to the work of military engineers. Although the fortifications of the early modern city became obstacles to the expansion of cities in the nineteenth century, their construction was once a creative, even exhilarating, enterprise. Fifteenth-century city walls were too thin and too well-integrated into the physical texture of city and suburb to provide an effective defense against artillery siegecraft. Engineers preferred to clear an area around the city on which they could erect low, blunt, triangular bastions, outerworks and walls precisely coordinated to permit defenders to concentrate fire power on attacking forces at little risk to themselves.[15] To be sure, the cost of refortification deterred many cities from looking after their defenses so long as enemy armies rarely exceeded 10,000–15,000 men, operated episodically, and would lift a siege if paid a tribute. Prolonged conflict in the seventeenth century and the organization of standing armies of 20,000 or even 100,000 men, stationed in garrisons, compelled states to modernize the defenses of cities.[16] The construction of urban forts and defense works, intended to protect nations from invasion and to break domestic insurrections, profoundly affected urban design.

Refortification, a highly technical process, stimulated the growth of a new professional group: military engineers employed by the state bureaucracy. The relationship between civilian and military practices was closer than is often realized. Idealized fortifications were infused with the same aesthetic principles as formal civilian design, and suggested how entire urban districts could be planned. Critical to both aspects of design was a mathematical approach to space itself, as can be seen in their shared appreciation for straight streets and formal squares. Just as the conduct of siege warfare improved the ability of staff officers and bureaucrats to organize labor, food supplies, and production, so did the construction of fortifications improve the ability of engineers to design and execute large-scale projects.

The scale of refortification can be illustrated by Vauban's citadel at Lille. It was built in 1670 by 5,000 workers, cost £1,409,702, and used 60 million bricks and equally huge quantities of other materials.[17] Within were facilities for 1,800 soldiers, including prisons, an arsenal, nine wells and an underground aqueduct, bakeries, barracks, officers's quarters, and a chapel. Because so many of the workers came from the region of Lille, much of the construction reflected local materials and techniques; because the concept came from Paris, the ensemble reflected the implacable logic, simplicity, and order characteristic of the absolutist state. The fusion of potentially conflicting traditions actually evoked something positive, indeed pleasing, about the builder's art; massive forms, crisp lines, appropriate materials, and articulated contours have a visual richness and interest which cannot be denied, although civilian architects have frequently shown disdain for the work of their military colleagues. The streets built to connect the city and the citadel, the new districts laid out between the old city and the new fortifications, and renovations in the old city gave new opportunities to builders who still pursued traditional, artisan approaches. Building innovations proliferated in Lille in the generation following construction of the citadel. Throughout Europe, military construction often stimulated urban development, suggested how the parts of a city can be subordinated to an overall design, and proclaimed political and social imperatives—all goals of early modern civilian architecture and city planning.

Underlying both the theory and practice of early modern architecture was the notion that by changing the urban environment, the ideal city would emerge and the social, economic, and political problems of urban life would abate. Europeans did not know that mastery was elusive, but neither could they foresee that urban development of the kind they fostered would itself nurture political and economic revolutions at the end of the eighteenth century.

The Crisis of Architecture and City Planning in the Eighteenth Century

The commitment of elite groups to urban living was critical in the seventeenth and eighteenth centuries when many cities were massively refortified, grew substantially, and assimilated major spatial changes by increasing the number of squares, streets, gardens, and public facilities. That architecture and city planning claimed to be able to control the spatial and influence the social consequences of urban growth and change contributed not a little to this commitment. Yet, the more cities grew, the less able were architects and planners to keep up with the social, political, and economic changes affecting urban development—with consequences for the originality of design in the eighteenth century. Since the limitations of architecture and city planning, however, were not apparent either to most practitioners or to their public audience, the nature of the crisis in design and its implication for the ability of cities to cope with growth and change were not appreciated.

By the eighteenth century, many local building traditions were under pressure across Europe, to survive only as a romantic manifestation of culture. Local building traditions represented one way a city could maintain its own identity, use local materials effectively, respond to local needs, and mark its distance from the centralizing state; but such traditional approaches were unable to meet the challenge of modernizing water systems, roads, and fortifications, projects usually handled by engineers employed by the state or at work as consultants in several regions.

Nîmes, in southern France, grew from around 17,000 in 1700 to 36,000 in 1765 and 50,000 in 1788. Most of the newcomers were active in silk manufacturing. As the city grew, most of the new residences and workshops were located in the suburbs. The old city core had no room for growth; the ancient arena still housed 2,000 people in Louis XIV's age. In the eighteenth century, only 10 percent of the inner-city population was in manufacturing, compared to 30 percent of the population of the suburbs. Few street changes were introduced in the urban center, where renovation was a matter for private investors and was limited to the rebuilding of upper-class houses and of Catholic churches damaged in the wars of religion. As the suburbs were built up, gradually a new entity emerged composed of suburbs and center as subordinated parts of a larger whole.

The silk manufacturers needed much more water than was available to the old city of Nîmes. Jean-Philippe Maréchal, a military engineer, using the Fontaine spring, developed a network of water mains and canals which deliberately tied together newer and older areas of an enlarged Nîmes. In 1785 the walls of Nîmes were demolished because they were no longer needed and were too costly to maintain. Their removal had symbolic value, transforming Nîmes from a closed into an open city; it also realized a political objective, permitting the suburbs to be fully integrated into the municipality—and property in the suburbs was taxed thereafter at the same rate as property in the old city.

The urban projects of 1780 in Nîmes included development of the esplanade into a royal square as the end point of several new streets; communication and transport routes were more important to commercial Nîmes in the eighteenth century than they had been before. The transformation of Nîmes was largely the work of state engineers working in response to local conditions. In the newly emerging Nîmes, people began to reassess buildings and monuments they had not considered before. To attract tourists and enhance the city's reputation, plans were made to restore the arena and demolish houses in and around it. In the urban culture of Nîmes, ancient history had an appeal that medieval and early modern structures lacked.[18]

New attitudes toward architecture were emerging as social groups, political factions, and economic interests which had survived, and indeed often prospered, in provincial cities opened up their cultural horizons to the light of the Enlightenment and made their peace with the social and political authority of the central government and the nation-state. The architect's choice whether to follow rules and precedent, or to break with the past and discover his own destiny, seemed to be a paradigm for the choice society was making about itself.

This debate created a climate for architectural culture which was more cosmopolitan—more broadly based in social terms, more widely diffused geographically (from Russia to Virginia), and freer of prejudice—than any other since the thirteenth-century Gothic. Vernacular, local, creative architectural traditions could not match the appeal of cosmopolitan design, which was associated with the principal intellectual currents and the social trends of the age; these traditions soon disappeared—awkward, parochial, and anachronistic baggage to their contemporaries. Within a generation or two, many buildings in local styles were remodeled beyond recognition or allowed to decay, while those who knew how to build them properly learned to do something else.[19]

Yet, architects were unable to produce a single style which, like the Gothic, consummately expressed the spirit of the age. Notwithstanding what architects intended, style became increasingly ephemeral and transitory. This is surprising, given the enormous advances in architectural training and in the accumulation of knowledge since the early Renaissance, an investment of artistic capital of inestimable value. Yet there were probably fewer architects of the first rank at work in the eighteenth century than in the previous three centuries. Among the greatest architectural ensembles of the century was Thomas Jefferson's University of Virginia, the work of an amateur.

Architectural historians have carefully dissected into periods, categories, and trends the diverse architectural styles which proliferated during the eighteenth century, but neat distinctions and careful formulas miss the point; architecture was confused and directionless because it was caught up in the crisis of the old regime itself.[20] The nature of the crisis was neither contained in Enlightenment ideas per se nor in the disparate and often mediocre styles architects produced. It lay in the irrelevance of Enlightenment concepts of truth, beauty, morality, and experience—and consequently of much of eighteenth-century architecture—to the urban and social changes which sharpened political conflict and transformed the scale of economic activities.

Cities needed modest, easily erected buildings in great numbers and plans for new districts that required little prior investment; but architects believed that cities ought to undertake projects commensurate in complexity and scale with their size, growth, and prospects. In the eighteenth century, more cities grew larger than at any other time in the early modern era, but architects had not yet begun to understand the forces sustaining such growth. Many of them still held to the utopian view that when cities reached a certain size, their development could be capped and new cities created, as if such factors as migration, seasonal employment, demographic trends, and the relative costs of basic commodities had less influence over growth than state officials with decree powers. Governments, of course, were concerned lest urban growth affect public health and food supplies adversely, giving rise to violent, destabilizing political action. Regulations inhibiting urban growth were impotent, however, especially because once national frontiers were fortified, many cities no longer needed fortified walls. Improvements to harbors, canals, naval architecture, and inland waterways enabled cities to expand their resource base and productive capacity economically.

Advocates of urban growth argued that the expansion of the urban economy generated national economic growth, that efforts to limit the size of cities only added to rural unemployment, and that the process of urban growth itself was manageable. Those who held contrary views argued that only rural property and agricultural improvements provided the basis for sustained economic development; cities, they insisted, encouraged unproductive investments and the wasteful consumption of luxury goods. Architects tended to view urban development in static terms, engineers in dynamic terms.[21] The architect's image of the city as the visual representation of a hierarchical, stratified social order corresponded to a static vision of urban space as the setting for monumental buildings as works of art; engineers were more interested in the movement of goods, services, and people throughout the city and hence with a city's growth.

The roles of engineers and architects were still poorly differentiated from each other in the early eighteenth century. Engineers who built fortified towns and interurban roads came to design churches, houses, and civic buildings in the course of their duties; architects on occasion designed markets, bridges, and even military structures. Gradually, however, engineers became increasingly capable of doing some things that architects did not learn to do.

When Bernard Forest de Belidor published *Science de l'ingénieur* in 1729, scientific testing of materials became possible. As engineering became more scientific and mathematical during the second half of the eighteenth century, engineers were able to construct larger buildings and bridges according to precise estimates of materials and costs. The mastery of the engineer was consummated in public opinion when, between 1768 and 1772, Jean-Rodolphe Perronet designed and built a bridge across the Seine at Neuilly, outside Paris, by calculating the size of the piers according to the loads to be carried, thereby reducing the width of the piers to half what traditional architectural methods would have specified. Of course, such knowledge was not needed for the majority of urban buildings and public facilities, which could still be designed by rule-of-thumb methods.

Two of the main concepts propagated by engineers were the rectification of street outlines (*alignements* in French usage) and master plans governing several projects simultaneously for the addition or modification of city space (*plans invariables*).[22] Both concepts used refined methods of surveying and emphasized the geometric qualities of space; both lent themselves admirably to cartographic representation; both articulated the utopian vision of the Renaissance, as interpreted after Descartes by Voltaire, that straight streets are the symbolic embodiment and reflection of good laws. The selection of sites in the city where major public buildings should be erected and private development encouraged became a function of planning on maps, which facilitated analysis of the relationships between buildings and districts on a large scale.

Could the projects and methods of engineers and architects be reconciled? Engineers and architects alike assumed that the existing urban fabric was inadequate functionally and aesthetically. They reviewed each other's designs and shared a common vocabulary, but I wonder whether the same words had identical connotations for them. There was a fundamental difference in their approach and philosophy. Engineers were increasingly called upon to provide solutions for urban problems because investors and administrators recognized that they possessed valuable expertise. To generalize, engineers were bet-

ter able than architects to consider whether government should spon-
sor a lot of construction or achieve redevelopment through regulation, whether urban services should be centralized or diffused
throughout the city, how much of a city's physical plan should be
predetermined, what the relationship of important buildings to the
street plan should be, and how the costs of urban development could
be amortized.[23]

Some architects, unwilling to let engineers gain so much influence
and prestige, learned more science and mathematics themselves, but
nonetheless still claimed that only the architect could infuse a design
with an indefinable aesthetic and spiritual essence. They implied that
the engineer, presumably a slave to his calculations, produced aesthetically pleasing results fortuitously. Architecture, some architects
asserted, combined rationality and beauty in forms and styles which
would direct and shape the social and moral stature of individuals
and collectivities. They designed primarily for aesthetic effect, as if
style possessed an almost mystical power to affect sentiments and
values, and as if the architect himself possessed an unquestioned right
to dictate the shape of the environment.

But society was no more willing to defer to architects than architects were to engineers. In the eighteenth century, many well-
educated persons discovered that appreciation of style enabled the
connoisseur to proclaim his social superiority through his exercise of
discriminating judgment. Architecture's claim to arbitrate between
the beautiful and the ugly, which had never been so forcefully asserted, corresponded perfectly to the social needs of well-to-do and
well-educated patrons who could point to an external authority as
proof of their good taste. Different social groups could therefore indicate what they thought of other groups through the conscious acceptance or rejection of a style, while masking their social motivation
by discussing style as if it were a purely intellectual matter. This
phenomenon was not limited to architecture, of course, as anyone
who could borrow, earn, or inherit wealth could purchase luxury
goods in unprecedented variety. A society which distinguished between individuals and groups according to their manners, customs,
appearances, and origins was confounded by duplicity and pretense
in a matter critical to its organization.

Architecture could not cope with the consequences. As more people wanted to use architectural style as a means of indicating their social position, architects confronted a contradiction they could not solve, the contradiction between architecture as the expression of universally valid perceptions and concepts, and the public's desire to link architecture to fashion. Thus, the irrelevance of architecture to the problems confronting municipal authorities did not diminish the demand for architects and planners; rather, commissions and competitions for private mansions, commercial and residential structures, and public buildings of all kinds confused the architectural profession about its mission. Architectural style suffered.

Two of the most important stylistic developments of the eighteenth century reflected architecture's new ambivalent role in urban society. English design of naturalistic gardens and French preoccupation with the decorative and structural possibilities of interior residential space, whatever their positive literary and intellectual associations may have been, emphasized the architectural experience as a luxurious, private, personal affair, *in* the city but not fully *of* it. Typically, many French cities (e.g., Besançon, Nîmes, Montpellier, Dijon) structured the development of a new part of the city around a garden landscaped in the latest style. Thus, in the eighteenth century, to look at the city as a beautiful place was not to see it as it was but rather to distort reality—in the same way as when one looks through the wrong end of a telescope, one misses those things one really ought to see.

Not surprisingly, architects were frustrated. They did not understand that architectural beauty, as with so many other things bought and sold in the city, was in the process of becoming a commodity. Realizing that society limited the range of buildings and styles they could design, architects remained committed to architecture as an art form by producing drawings that were finished, figurative, visual representations of buildings outside the conventional range. Buildings by Gilly, Walpole, Ledoux, Boullée, Blondel, and Piranesi have had far less of an impact than their drawings of buildings which were never constructed. For the first time, architects published to advertise their talents, as when Robert and James Adams's *Works in Architecture* appeared in 1773. (Someone must someday undertake a study of the eighteenth-century architectural printing trade, whose paper suppliers, printers, and booksellers drew architectural style into the cash nexus.) It proved to be only a short technical step from the consumption of style as an art form to the production of style as a commercial object, to be bought as if from a catalogue; the architectural publishing trade of the eighteenth century was the prototype of the architectural design industry of the nineteenth.

Public interest in architectural design and beauty corresponded to a significant cultural movement which interpreted the outward appearance of urban beauty to be an external, but by no means superficial, sign that its society and government conformed to the laws of reason and nature. This movement, which was a legacy of the Renaissance, had spurred elite groups to take a serious interest in the evolution of cities. In the eighteenth century as in the Renaissance, however, aesthetic principles dominating elite perceptions implied that the real city of everyday life was inadequate in visual and spiritual terms. Most structures were still erected in the vernacular tradition, utilized familiar skills and materials, and resembled similar buildings of earlier periods. Yet, literary and artistic images of cities in topographic views and books did not focus upon them. Well might Dr. Johnson comment about London in 1763, "If you wish to have a just notion of the magnitude of this city, you must not be satisfied with seeing its great streets and squares, but must survey the innumerable little lanes and courts. It is not in the showy evolutions of buildings, but in the multiplicity of human habitations which are crowded together, that the wonderful immensity of London consists."[24] Rather than appreciate cities as they were, the educated audience that delighted in literary or artistic impressions sought pleasures which the existing environment could not always provide.

With this in mind, it is interesting to note how Arthur Young (1741–1820) recorded the impressions which French cities made on him during his travels between 1788 and 1790. As England's foremost proponent of scientific agriculture, Young could examine a countryside anywhere, comparing its resources with what he knew could be done to make the most of them. But he could not transfer this critical power of description and analysis to cities. Perhaps he was simply caught in a trap created by aesthetic notions: A well-cultivated landscape was indeed as pretty as a picture, but a beautiful cityscape usually had little to do with commercial or industrial productivity. Young liked cities with good air, promenades, grand buildings, and straight streets; but above all, he liked cities that were as pleasant to be in as they were beautiful when viewed from a distance.

> The view of Brive from the hill is so fine, that it gives the expectation of a beautiful little town, and the gaiety of the environs encourages the idea; but on entering, such a contrast is found as disgusts completely. Close, ill-built, crooked, dirty, stinking streets, exclude the sun, and almost the air from every habitation, except a few tolerable ones on the promenade.[25]

If Brive disappointed, Reims did not:

> The first view of that city from this hill, just before the descent, at the distance of about four miles, is magnificent. The cathedral makes a great figure. . . . Many times I have had such a view of towns in France, but when you enter them, all is a clutter of narrow, crooked, dark, and dirty lanes. At Reims it is very different: the streets are almost all broad, straight, and well-built, equal in that respect to any I have seen. . . . You enter and quit Reims through superb and elegant iron gates; in such public decorations, promenades, etc. French towns are much beyond English ones.[26]

Comments about Brive and Reims could be multiplied for a score of other cities, all of which Young apparently evaluated against an abstract aesthetic standard. It was the function of architecture and urban design to transform a city into an aesthetically satisfying ensemble, a work of art to live in.

Young admired magnificent architecture for its own sake; he also used it as a standard to measure the social and economic vitality of a city. In the eighteenth century, theaters, opera houses, cafés, parks, promenades, art galleries, and smart shops became common in provincial and capital cities. (The relative ease with which they were inserted into cities speaks directly to the inherent adaptability of city space at that time.) Increasingly, after 1700, these facilities and buildings were taken to be the measure of a city such that even a small provincial city could be considered open to modern, cosmopolitan currents. In Nantes:

> Go to the theatre, new-built of fine white stone, and has a magnificent portico front of eight elegant Corinthian pillars, and four others within, to part the portico from a grand vestibule. Within all is gold and painting, and a *coup d'oeil* at entering, that struck me forcibly. It is, I believe, twice as large as Drury Lane, and five times as magnificent. . . . What a miracle, that all this splendour and wealth of the cities in France should be so unconnected with the country! . . . The town has that sign of prosperity of new buidings, which never deceives. The quarter of the *Comédie* is magnificent, all the streets at right angles and of white stone.[27]

But in correlating building with prosperity, Young ended, as did Defoe two generations before, by criticizing those areas of the city which were most thoroughly given over to trade and manufacturing. Thus, when he found that Bordeaux's fine theater, new squares, and streets stopped short of the waterfront, he commented about the quay, "of which I had heard most":

> [It] is respectable only for length, and its quantity of business, neither of which, to the eye of the stranger, is of much consequence, if devoid of beauty. The row of houses is regular, but without either magnificence or beauty. It is a dirty, sloping, muddy shore; parts without pavement, encumbered with filth and stones. . . . Here is all the dirt and disagreeable circumstances of trade, without the order, arrangement, and magnificence of a quay.[28]

Why should Young have cared to judge a waterfront by aesthetic or stylistic criteria that were derived from notions of sensibility and beauty having nothing to do with maritime affairs? Apparently, his perspective on cities made it impossible for Young to understand how those other complex uses of urban space (which could not be justified by apriori aesthetic criteria) functioned.

The pursuit of beauty through architectural and urban form, despite all the good design and brilliant architecture it produced, failed to provide the measure of order and reason in urban affairs that was its self-appointed mission. Architecture as an art form introduced qualitative distinctions between different kinds of urban spaces that corresponded to and reinforced the political and social power of some groups at the expense of the rest of society; and in so doing, it contributed to the polarization of urban life and to the aggravation of political and revolutions at the end of the early modern era. Architectural trends, like the tip of an iceberg, rode above the mass that was really in motion.

CHAPTER THREE

The Development of the Economic Mode

ᔥ Port Development, Engineering, and the Economic Mode

Although statistical knowledge was inadequate, governments in the Age of Enlightenment knew, as accurately as they needed to know, that cities were growing. Cities grew at a faster rate than Europe's total population. London increased tenfold in two centuries to a size of at least 800,000 by 1800, the first city in Europe since ancient Rome to have attained such size. Amsterdam, Madrid, Berlin, Vienna, Moscow, Paris—all capitals—increased four or five times in the same period. Lyon, Bristol, Manchester, Liverpool, and other cities grew significantly.

Some countries had more cities and more larger cities than others. The Netherlands and Italy were still more highly urbanized, and eastern Europe much less, when compared with France. Yet, the degree of urbanization was no guarantee of economic growth, as both Italy and the Netherlands did not make the transition to industrialization as rapidly as England. Early modern urban growth involved changes in size which signified changes in kind. The very existence of large cities was fraught with risk and uncertainty. Governments were concerned that uncertain food supplies, a sudden increase in the price of basic commodities, or high unemployment would spark an insurrection. The survival and growth of cities in early modern Europe represented the conquest of material, spatial, and temporal limits.

Most cities which grew to any size over 50,000 inhabitants before railroads were port cities, built on the seacoast, on estuaries, and on rivers. What distinguishes port cities as a generic type, in the past and present, is their potential for enormous growth and for contact with distant cultures, societies, and economies. Only port cities could free themselves from the inelastic production capacity of a rural hinterland and from the high cost of overland transport. Although the social structures of small and large cities were equally complex, diversified, and stratified, their spatial worlds were qualitatively different. All cities, of course, depended upon a zone of immigration and a zone of agricultural production. While these two zones were never precisely the same, the degree of overlap was much greater for the small city than for the large one. The spatial environment of cities included a variety of fiscal, commercial, and cultural networks that linked it to its neighbors and to continental, even global, partners; but whereas the small city participated in the widest networks only through intermediaries, the largest cities often had their own agents acting abroad.

The multiple spatial worlds of early modern cities were limited by several factors: the time it took to send and receive messages, familiarity with dialects and accents, ethnic differences, and everywhere a fear of the unknown—a not altogether irrational fear considering the frequency of highway brigandage, shipwreck, wild animals, and war. Nevertheless, the macro spatial worlds of cities changed during the sixteenth and seventeenth centuries as Europe's maritime commercial domain expanded, and during the eighteenth century as the construction of highways, bridges, ports, and canals—and improvements to existing facilities—shortened travel times and lowered freight costs

The connection between an expansion of maritime trade and speculative urban development was made in northern Europe for the first time in sixteenth-century Antwerp. The growth of Antwerp has been well documented. As part of the refortification process common to many early modern cities, plans were made in 1543–45 to erect a new wall outside Antwerp on land where many small industries and houses stood. This led to a feverish search for land and buildings within the city, a situation conducive to profiteering at the expense of those who had to relocate. Social tension, economic dislocations, and the slow rate of progress in constructing the wall gave Gilbert van Schoonbeke his opportunity. In 1548 he convinced the city to

adopt a plan which called for development of land beyond the walls
to the north of the city to form a new district connected to the harbor
and to the old city by canals and bridges. The initial costs of developing this district were to be recovered through the lease and sale of
property in it. Van Schoonbeke's systematic approach succeeded; he
made great profits on increased land values in the new district and
old city alike, which he then invested in businesses (such as brickmaking and brewing) that the larger city needed. By consolidating
larger parcels of land, Van Schoonbeke constructed manufacturing
facilities which realized lower costs and achieved a greater volume of
production because lower building costs more than compensated for
any increase in the cost of land itself.[1] But sixteenth-century Antwerp was not a satisfactory model for capitalistic land development,
not only because its economy declined precipitously during the wars
of religion, but also because conditions were not yet as favorable elsewhere for similar forms of speculative investment.

As much can be said for Amsterdam. To Europeans, Antwerp,
Amsterdam, and Venice all appeared to owe their prosperity, growth,
and distinctive water-oriented spatial features to a unique constella-
tion of circumstances. The three rings of canals built in Amsterdam
according to a plan of 1607 expanded that city's waterfront in ways
which allowed development to proceed incrementally as trade and
population expanded. Amsterdam's canals provided for the integration of the parts of the city into a whole, and for the progressive
extension of the whole through the parts at the same time. But engineers and statesmen who copied the urban forms of Dutch cities in
the hope that cities which looked like Dutch cities would enjoy
growth failed to appreciate the extent to which urban forms favoring
maritime commerce were inseparable from other social, institutional,
and economic factors. For this reason, whatever else economic growth
in eighteenth-century France and England owed to earlier forms of
mercantile capitalism, the conscious development of eighteenth-
century port cities owed little to Venice, Antwerp, and Amsterdam.

The great series of paintings of French ports which Joseph Vernet
executed for the French state in the middle of the eighteenth century
represents the European port city on the eve of decisive changes in its
spatial order.[2] Looking at Vernet's tableaux of Marseille, Nantes, Tou-

lon, La Rochelle, Bordeaux, and many other ports, we see that early modern port districts were the central spatial and social unit of the port city: the place where people came to work or to find employment, to learn the news or exchange information, to greet travelers, to send or receive shipments, or simply to observe with pleasure the animation that came from concentrating so many activities in such a well-defined space. To one side of the waterfront, there was a wall of ships; to the other, the city's buildings. Both were densely packed, richly varied, familiar, and directly accessible to the pedestrian. To be sure, there is an air of unreality to Vernet's paintings; he cautiously rearranged what he actually saw to make a better composition, and he treated the conduct of sailors on shore leave and the problem of dock pilferage in a more lighthearted way than did most shipowners and merchants. Nevertheless, Vernet's images, which associate the primary economic and political function of ports with the domesticated civilized virtues of urban life, ring true. The waterfront of the early modern port city centripetally attracted everything to it.

In most port cities before the eighteenth century, the port infrastructure was modest: a quay, not always of stone but sometimes just a muddy embankment; a minimal breakwater that might have to be rebuilt every year; only rarely a lighthouse. Severe tidal flows, changing river beds, and ensilted harbors hampered the development of many port cities and made the work of the pilot far from easy. Port cities before the eighteenth century were often poorly connected to inland cities, even in nearby regions; they were semiautonomous and tended to look after their own affairs. The amount of money that could be raised locally for port construction, as well as the skills needed to improve ports and the political will to see projects through, were inadequate. Yet, in England by 1830 at least thirty harbor and dock trusts and commissions were functioning, and at least sixteen joint-stock companies were engaged in a dock and harbor business.[3] Because port cities were ill-prepared to enlarge harbors and improve waterways to keep pace with the growth in shipping in the eighteenth century, governments either assumed this responsibility or tried to nurture institutional and financial conditions favorable to private investment.

Engineers had access to the state bureaucracy and to politicians—

in other words, to the money and enabling legislation needed to promote port improvements. With these resources and their desire to
prove themselves useful, engineers often took the initiative in pro-
posing port projects (as in France); alternatively, they were retained
by municipalities or syndicates anxious to advance the commercial
prospects of one port over another (as in England). To succeed, an
engineer had to master the skills of the lobbyist, the promoter, and
the financier. The merits of scores of proposals for established port
cities, small trading towns, and previously undeveloped coastal sites
from the Bay of Biscay to the Baltic often involved the publication of
books, articles, and pamphlets and became the subject of public debate. In this climate the *feasibility* of large-scale port, canal, and river
improvement projects went unchallenged; people argued over what
ought to be done at a given site, *not* whether improvements were
necessary or feasible.

Decisions about port districts were increasingly subject to purely
technical criteria. Advances in the state of the civil engineer's art were
codified, sanctioned, and publicized by the leading scientific authorities. Of course, that knowledge was imperfect and incomplete. On
many occasions engineers giving advice or drawing up proposals con-
tradicted each other; sometimes a project advanced in one decade as
"state of the art" was found to be seriously deficient in design ten or
twenty years later. (Both circumstances occurred in the development
of Glasgow and the Clyde.)[4] As a consequence, efforts were made to
improve cartographic techniques and administrative and accounting
procedures to generate better information. Instead of abandoning
port improvements altogether when plans were conceptually deficient, people doubled their efforts, believing that technical and scientific progress was only a matter of time.

The better to control port projects and limit dockside pilferage,
engineers tended to treat port improvements as completely self-
contained, integral units.[5] Using graphic techniques of great clarity
and refinement, engineers designed port districts on paper whose
symmetry, proportion, and geometrical order expressed mastery of
scale and space in forms of high symbolic potency. In this way, projects for ports enhanced the legibility and clarity of urban spatial patterns in the same way as post-Renaissance projects by architects for

palaces, churches, and great civic squares. Within a walled perimeter, the multiple tasks of shipbuilding, outfitting, and freight handling were broken down into their component parts, each of which was assigned its own space. These tasks were then coordinated and integrated in terms of their spatial relationships.

The design of port facilities was also linked conceptually to changes in the design and construction of ships. Large ships then (as today) were among the largest structures built. In the eighteenth century, warships carried upwards of a hundred cannon and a thousand men, and cargo vessels also reached unprecedented size; yet, sailing ships possessed better sea-handling characteristics than ever before and could undertake longer, more arduous voyages in greater safety.

To build larger ships in greater numbers, a new kind of shipyard was designed in the context of port projects.[6] Its origins can be traced back to French attempts of the 1730s and after to evaluate shipbuilding materials and methods scientifically. These experiments led to the standardization of designs, parts, and methods and, eventually, to the prefabrication of ships. Working in the 1770s at Thunberg, near Karlskrona, Sweden, Swedish and French engineers designed an arsenal in the shape of an octagon with about thirty basins disposed around most of its sides two or three deep, so that several ships could be constructed assembly-line style in a limited area. Borda, a French naval engineer, then conceived of partially building ships and storing the unfinished hulls in a warehouse, to be completed when military or commercial circumstances dictated. (Thomas Jefferson asked Benjamin Latrobe to design a facility of this kind for Washington, D.C., but Congress never funded it.[7])

Many skills and concepts of value to city building were developed in these efforts to improve ship design and construction, and to plan new port districts. The great ambition of many port planners was that a modern, rational port district would determine the street outline in much of the rest of the city. But many well-designed port improvements were never executed, due to political and financial factors outside the engineer's control. In many cities, an ad hoc, improvisational approach, characterized by a failure to coordinate development of port districts with other kinds or urban spaces, replaced planning, thereby giving rise to unsanitary living conditions, to polluted waterways, and to congestion in harbors and in streets servicing dock areas.

The example of eighteenth-century port development suggests how the process of urban growth began to effect qualitative changes in the city-building process. As it became apparent that the volume of shipping could keep pace with urban growth, the possibility of a city without spatial limits became conceivable; and the image of national territories as coherent, integrated economic and social systems took hold.[8] The attractions of trade also made cities more vulnerable to powerful and sudden changes in regional, national, and international economic conditions.[9] The timing and financing of public works projects therefore mattered at least as much as their design characteristics, but the sheer cost of harbor and river improvements was such that only an assumption of uninterrupted strong growth promised the eventual recovery of the initial investment. On the one hand, cities became concerned lest a failure to undertake such projects and other forms of improvements more generally compromised their prospects, to their rivals's benefit; on the other, nothing prevented cities from duplicating facilities needlessly.

With hindsight, we see that city builders were groping toward answers to such questions as how municipalities could retain control over development if they lacked access to capital for improvements; how plans that looked attractive and even practical on paper might be assessed, not only for their financial cost, but also for their relation to demographic and economic trends; who should determine what should be built, and where; what costs and benefits to the city as a whole derived from developments which promised great profits to a few investors, and how a city could tax those profits. The development of city building in the economic mode made some problems easier to solve but gave rise to others.

What changed between the seventeenth and eighteenth centuries was not so much the formal design vocabulary of architects and engineers as the relative weight of certain issues that lay behind stylistic trends and design techniques. On paper, projects from the seventeenth and eighteenth centuries do not look so very different, but this apparent similarity is deceptive. Straight streets had once been a symbol of political and social order; they became an instrument to facilitate tax assessments and improve the movement of intraurban and interurban traffic. Architectural styles had once proclaimed certain values and ideas in a visual rhetoric; they became a means of attracting investors and defining the social composition of neighborhoods. Buildings and districts had once been shaped over time by their occupants and users; they came to be erected in large numbers by speculators and investors according to standardized designs, to be sold for profit. Municipal regulations had once made many matters of urban hygiene and maintenance the responsibility of individual residents; the responsibility became increasingly assumed by public authorities and private syndicates, with gains in administrative control and uniformity in standards.

The changes that occurred in city building to reflect and exploit economic criteria more completely were most visible in the largest cities, an instance of a change in size producing a qualitative difference. Paris and London exemplify changes in city building. As contemporaries were quick to note, the two capitals had much in common. For the purposes of this study, what matters is the impact of city building in London and Paris on the development of cities across Europe. This impact was significant because whatever happened in the great capital cities enjoyed enormous prestige and because other cities encountered similar problems which gave new city-building techniques immediate relevance. The importance of economic criteria in new city-building techniques reflected and magnified changes in social and economic affairs, changes which called for different emphases in urban perceptions and values. The urban development of Europe as a whole gave innovations in Paris and London the widest possible impact.

ह City Building and Economic Development: England

The transformation of city building from a cultural to an economic mode was a measure of the high latent adaptability of the urban environment at that time. Like many historical developments, the rising importance of economic criteria was a function of many incremental steps taken on relatively simple matters. The transitional nature of city building in the eighteenth century—one set of techniques and criteria mutating and evolving into another—and the interrelationship between urban phenomena in dissimilar cities can be seen in the English inn. Alan Everitt suggests that the English inn preserved its traditional identity while assimilating itself into a new economic era.[10] While their numbers were scattered across the countryside—by the end of the seventeenth century nearly two hundred towns and villages in Wiltshire boasted at least one inn— their presence was heaviest in the larger towns and along the principal highways.

Inns were often grouped together around the market square, in some other prominent location in the city or town, or in its immediate suburbs. They provided, of course, lodging and food for travelers and their horses, requirements which made some of them by necessity the largest private structures in their districts; but, in addition, they sheltered a variety of other commercial and social functions which became increasingly important in the seventeenth and eighteenth centuries. In England, agricultural seed merchants and dealers in commodities such as hops, wheat, malt, and cloth conducted business in inns; and farmers often stored their products in rooms built by innkeepers for that purpose. Traveling salesmen and professionals (surveyors, surgeons, etc.) used the inn as a base of operations, making contacts there, receiving clients, and departing from it into villages and countryside. These activities enabled innkeepers to act as bankers and brokers in a rudimentary way before banking was established. Their volume of business also enabled innkeepers to undertake more elaborate social activities requiring some capital and imagination, such as dinners and meetings of a formal business, social, or cultural nature.

The English inn was a variant of a European type that had come into being to serve the local trading economy of the hinterland market town, and not the long-distance commerce of the metropolitan city; without losing its recognizability as a familiar and traditional institution, it developed into the local branch or outlet of commercial and administrative networks which drew their energy from, and were centralized in, the metropolis. The inn provided a point of contact between newer and older social groups, between local trade and long-distance commerce, between business in one place and in another, and between the metropolitan city and an ever larger and more remote hinterland. In England's case, that city was London, which grew at this time to be larger than any other European city had been since ancient Rome.

The English urban experience in the eighteenth century shows how urban development projects had a multiplier effect. This suggests the need to look at the linkages among agricultural improvements, transport development, and the growth of trade—trade connecting market towns, new industrial cities, and great metropolitan centers. A recent study by E. L. Jones and M. E. Falkus underscores the continuities between preindustrial and nineteenth-century phenomena and the contribution of eighteenth-century urban development to the transformation of the economy as a whole.[11] Better market facilities, wider and straighter roads, new and enlarged bridges, paved and lighted streets, new kinds of urban facilities such as retail stores, and the substitution of brick and tile for more flammable building materials transformed cities, modified administrative structures, increased social and cultural expectations, and enhanced the productivity of capital compared with labor. Some of these changes were introduced earlier than others; some required more time; some were tied to other changes external to the building economy; and some were interrelated. Notwithstanding such qualifications, the broad outlines are clear.

Many of these changes could be implemented by skilled craftsmen with an existing economy of skills and supplies, a modest approach which capitalized on existing strengths in the vernacular tradition. The number of administrative bodies set up as commissions to undertake improvements in England meanwhile rose from 4 in 1749 to 164 in 1799, mostly for paving, cleansing, watching, and lighting town streets in response to local conditions and to the growth of interurban traffic. Much of the capital to pay for these changes was local—from greater specialization, from gains in efficiency in traditional sectors, and from the introduction of new products and processes. Many of these changes simply allowed existing towns and cities to perform established functions as the tempo of the economy increased; but cumulatively they gave a fillip to economic activities in general and to the development of a consumer-oriented economy in particular, with large, long-term effects.

The commercialization of novelty, change, and fashionable style permeated urban culture, stimulated demand, increased the variety of goods and services available, and promoted new forms of advertising, wholesaling, and retailing.[12] As Jones and Falkus conclude, "the changes of the period made a permanent mark. There was a ratchet effect to improvement. . . . Savings became more productive, consumption went up, and urban improvement fed back impulses to the economy at large."[13] Living standards, incomes, and expectations all rose. As Everitt has written, what "was remarkable about the English country town of the Hanoverian period was the concentration of so many varied functions within it, and the range, the scale, the scope and the quality of the facilities it afforded."[14]

Jones and Falkus emphasized the degree to which improvements were made not only in London but also in modest market towns whose population size remained stable or increased moderately. The diffusion of improvements across entire regions exposed many towns to national economic and cultural trends to an unprecedented extent. But the growth of London, Jones and Falkus acknowledge, was in many ways qualitatively different. E. A. Wrigley wrote a seminal essay about how the growth of London accelerated economic change in England as a whole.[15] The transformation of city building from a cultural to an economic mode was a part of that process.

Focusing on the period between 1650 and 1750, Wrigley explained why "London was so constituted sociologically, demographically and economically that it could well reinforce and accelerate incipient change." Wrigley did not examine the role that construction played in London's growth and development, but each of the ten changes which he listed as having succeeded in dissolving features of the agrarian and commercial economies of the preindustrial era were either affected by, or affected, changes in London building: (1) the creation of a single national market for a wide range of goods and services, so that specialization of function and economies of scale could be exploited; (2) changes in agricultural methods which increased farming productivity and changes in the work force; (3) the development of new sources of raw materials; (4) the provision of a wider range of commercial and credit facilities, so that the latent strengths of the economy could be more expertly, quickly, and cheaply mobilized; (5) the creation of a better transport system, to foster the above changes; (6) the securing of a steady rise in real incomes; (7) a population growth that is not too rapid; (8) environments that socialized individuals to behave "rationally" rather than "traditionally"; (9) the promotion of upwardly mobile groups who did not share the same priorities, or use wealth and status in the same ways, as the upper levels of traditional society; and (10) awareness that a change in one's pattern of life is possible.[16] Wrigley did not limit the impact of London's growth to London alone; it is one of the merits of his essay that he considered how London's growth may have affected growth and change throughout England, a process he described as "indirect, springing from the changes which the steady growth of London provoked elsewhere."

In the seventeenth century, London's growth upset people because it disrupted established ways of doing things. A proclamation of Elizabeth in 1580 banned construction of houses within three miles of the city gates in places where no houses had stood within living memory; moreover, the number of families in houses already built could not be increased in the future. Injunctions were repeated in 1593 and 1602.

In 1605 James I issued a proclamation decreeing that all new houses should be built with fronts of stone or brick to minimize the use of timber, to impede the spread of fire, and to achieve greater uniformity in the appearance of the city. This proclamation was reissued in 1607 with the additioinal stipulation that new buildings could only be erected by special license, on payment of a fee of £2,000. Obviously the wealthy, such as Frances Russell, fourth Earl of Bedford and developer of Covent Garden, could afford to build and still pay a fine; but because most people could not, most buildings were erected in defiance of the decree and did not conform to the building standards explicit in it. Attempts to restrict construction in London only exacerbated the poor living conditions which had alarmed the authorities in the first place. Proclamations issued in 1620, 1622, 1624, 1625, and 1630 only revealed the impotence of the law.[17]

The fire of 2 September 1666—or rather the rebuilding after it—
helped to bring London's growth under control in ways that magnified not only the impact of economic factors on city building but also
the city's potential for growth. The fire destroyed 13,200 houses, the
exchange and customs house, the halls of forty-four guild companies,
and St. Paul's and eighty-six other churches.[18] The fire started inno-
cently, but went out of control when a strong wind from the south
drove the flames over the conurbation. It was stopped only when
King Charles II, his brother, and great landholding noblemen rallied
troops and citizens to destroy buildings in advance of the fire, which
subsided for lack of anything more to burn.

The fire made a savage mockery of political boundaries. The city
fathers wanted rebuilding to begin quickly, lest people resettle on
vacant land at the edge of the suburbs. The Crown also wanted London to be rebuilt, but unlike the City, it possessed the power to
determine the nature of the rebuilding process. Through proclamations and acts of Parliament, starting as early as 13 September 1666,
builders were enjoined to use only brick or stone, and were forbidden
to use wood widely in interior scaffolding or exterior decoration. In
addition, major streets were to be widened to act as fire gaps, and all
streets were to be widened to permit traffic circulation. Before any
building was to commence, maps were to be drawn showing all property lines, so that owners whose property had to be reshaped to modify the street network could be fairly and expeditiously compensated.
The maps were never made.

Owners were unable to comply with the September 1666 law or-
dering them to provide a perfect survey of their property within two
weeks. In general, urban application of surveying techniques, an essentially rural practice, had long been retarded by the physical difficulty of taking accurate measurements of numerous, small land parcels in a congested space (property units were not accurately mapped
in smaller European cities until 1720–50, and in the largest cities
only after that); but the physical difficulty imposed by the post-fire
chaos of London was insurmountable. Further, while owners could
not supply separate property surveys, neither could work wait for
new overall schemes; reconstruction of London could not be delayed
while the merits of plans for a completely redesigned street network
by Evelyn, Hooke, Wren, and others were debated.[19]

It took three months to clear the rubble, and three more to reach the end of an unusually harsh winter, and by then tens of thousands of displaced Londoners were more than anxious to see their city rebuilt quickly. Amazingly, that task was completed in less than six years. However, no miracle redesign was implemented. A few new streets were laid out, and many old ones were straightened as they were paved and widened; but, for legal, political, and practical reasons, an entirely new street plan was simply impossible.

Builders at first simply lacked the skills and resources to undertake the reconstruction of a city of a half-million inhabitants. Under the traditional system of exploiting London property, the different operations involved were divorced from each other, making the task of correlating land size and value with building costs to establish a property's potential nearly impossible. The builder, for example, paid for materials and workers as they arrived on the job site. Inigo Jones, who was the first English architect to design complete buildings on the drawing board, may also have come upon a novel way of paying for buildings: With the complete building designed and drawn out in a "plat" before work began, the actual amount of masonry, brickwork, roofing, and so on which went to make up the completed building could be estimated beforehand, permitting the developer to contract with various craftsmen for the work they were to undertake. The Fire brought this practice into temporary widespread use because it facilitated construction when time and money were in short supply.

William Leyburn, one of the six officials appointed to survey London after the fire, published a treatise in 1667, "intended for persons concerned in the letting, selling or building of or upon ground then in the Ruins of the City of London." Stephen Primatt published a similar treatise that year "for the Determination of the Differences touching Houses burnt down, or demolished by reason of the late Fire in London," called *The City and Country Purchaser and Builder*; it included a series of estimates of the cost of rebuilding according to the London Building Act (1667).[20] No doubt there were many other pamphlets and books which attempted to formulate principles that craftsmen, builders, developers, lessors, and owners could use conveniently. The diffusion of such techniques, of course, meant that no professional group monopolized information valuable to everyone.

The London Building Act greatly facilitated the tasks of all involved in the building process by establishing four categories, or classes, of buildings, which related the height and number of stories of buildings according to their location; it specified the dimensions for each of the four categories and how materials were to be used. And it also ordered surveys of all property to be made as part of the building process. This act standardized London building to a remarkable degree, and went the furthest of any sixteenth, seventeenth, or eighteenth century act toward harmonizing and unifying London's appearance. It also included a provision allowing the City to receive an indirect tax on coal, to help with the cost of public improvements.

The improvements contemplated by the authorities, which included streets, and the Fleet and the Thames Canals, might have cost in excess of £1.5 million had they all been undertaken. The normal debt carried by the City of London was £40,000, and its income less than half that amount; its debts exceeded its assets at the time of the Fire. The revenue from the coal tax amounted to just under £740,000 in the next ten years.[21] Clearly, the scale of London's reconstruction far exceeded the ability of the City to do very much, except at such a slow rate that its projects would be completed only after the rest of London had been rebuilt (its canal schemes were commercial failures, probably for this reason). Thus, many costs, such as those related to street improvements, were passed on to the public at large. The rebuilding of London succeeded because the laws affecting building made sense to the thousands of people who wanted to get on with the task at hand.

This was the situation that the large-scale developer, and in particular one of their number, Nicolas Barbon, could exploit to his own advantage. Building in London after 1666 allowed many people, including many artisans, to go into business for themselves. The building boom launched by the Fire did not die out when most people were rehoused and buildings rebuilt because London itself continued to grow in population and in area with fewer restraints than before, and because the wealthy wanted a higher standard of housing.

Barbon (c. 1640–1698), more than anyone else, explored the possibilities in private finance to develop building on an unprecedented scale. Barbon used all the techniques of landowners, builder-speculators, promoters, surveyors, and financiers, selecting the combination best suited to the situation at hand. Sir John Summerson has told his story well. Barbon "was active all over London, building here a square, here a market, here a few streets, or chambers for lawyers. When we read in a contemporary letter that he laid out £200,000 in building it certainly does not sound like an exaggeration. He completely grasped the advantages accruing from standardization and mass-production in housing. . . . The houses he built were all very much alike, economically planned to the point of meanness, with coarse ornaments which repeated themselves over and over again."[22] Barbon's greatest skills were in promoting his schemes, finding credit, buying up properties which he wanted, getting builders to construct on his terms, and selling. He often fell into trouble and made enemies, but he also was elected to Parliament, and he knew better than anyone else what he was doing, and how. He died in debt, but the amount of money that passed through his hands may well have been exceeded only by the tax receipts entering the Treasury. It was Barbon who applied insurance to building for the first time, insuring 5,650 houses between 1686 and 1692 alone (premiums were 2½ percent for brick and 5 percent for wood houses). His most enduring legacy, besides his debts (which he specified in his will were not to be paid), was a book, *The Discourse of Trade* (1690), in which statements on the relation between use and value, between value and price, and on the significance of currency, credit, and interest, anticipated eighteenth- and nineteenth-century thinking. Karl Marx quoted from Barbon at the beginning of *Das Kapital*.

And where did the poor live? East London has always been renowned for its slums. Between 1600 and 1700, the population of the area that extended below the Tower along the Thames grew from 21,000 to 91,000. Like the rest of London, St. Katherine's, Spitalfields, and Smithfield became more orderly in their street pattern, and by 1700, were lined by brick houses instead of wooden ones; but houses in these districts, unlike those for the middle and upper classes of the kind Barbon built, were most likely jerrybuilt. A pattern revealed itself in East London that was to characterize English cities throughout the industrializing era: high density and extreme concentrations of people along alleys and around inner courtyards. A late seventeenth-century census recorded 892 persons living along eleven alleys off Whitechapel Street, as against 544 along the street itself; densities reached 200 rooms per acre near the docks, a figure that can be compared against today's norms for cities of 65 per two-story and 85 for three-story buildings per acre.[23]

London was rebuilt after the Fire of 1666 in such a way that the city-building process itself changed, and changed more profoundly than the study of the street network would otherwise indicate. Perhaps the greatest difference in city building was its enhanced sensitivity to external economic factors such as the availability and cost of credit, labor, materials, and land. As people learned to think of building in purely financial terms, the architectural, social, and utilitarian aspects of buildings all found their place on the drawing board and in the account book.

Throughout the century, books appeared reproducing architectural details, patterns for structural and decorative elements, and instructions for the standardization of building. From the builder's point of view, taste was something to exploit to maximize profits and lower costs. Manufacturers of architectural elements, such as George Coade, who molded an artificial stone to mass produce decorative and structural elements, developed the market. Coade provided every builder with a ready-made, fixed-price selection of fireproof materials, ranging from an ornamental satyr at just over £2, to a river god with urn measuring 2.74 meters high (adapted from an etching by Blake), for £105.[24] Standardization and mass production did not eliminate variety, as the Coade catalog and London's facades survive to demonstrate how dissimilar the details of nearly identical houses could be.

But economic incentives were not yet strong enough to provide sufficient housing for London's growing population. The wealthy landowners of large estates developed land too slowly, and speculative builders for the most part worked on too small a scale.[25] In 1774 a new act was passed setting aside many of the provisions of the act of 1667. Its principal features were a classification of buildings into seven classes (or rates), for fiscal purposes, and the repeal of a statutory limit on heights at four stories. As the seven rate categories enabled the authorities to classify any kind of building according to its cubic capacity and cost of construction (techniques already in use in shipyards), the visual anarchy of London could still be sorted into some kind of administrative order. The 1774 act remained in force until 1845, when London's population had risen to 2.25 million inhabitants.

The growth of cities in provincial England took off in the second half of the eighteenth century from a very small base, whereas London was already one of the half-dozen largest cities in Europe. Nevertheless, many of the same phenomena visible in London building were also present in provincial cities.[26] London's growth had been related to changes in national economic and social conditions such that the transformation of city-building practices in the capital and in provincial cities were complementary aspects of a larger process.

Manchester, Liverpool, and Birmingham together had fewer than 20,000 inhabitants in 1700, but about 400,000 in 1820; Sheffield, Leeds, Hull, Nottingham, Bath, Portsmouth, and Plymouth all grew at a rate more than double that of England as a whole. There was no shortage of land on which to build: innumerable yards, gardens, and closes were absorbed, small old buildings were replaced with larger ones, and cities grew outwards. When the New Town of Edinburgh was developed through a land drainage scheme by the city council between 1767 and 1783, £14,910 were spent leveling and paving streets, providing drains, and laying sewers over a fifty-acre site. To purchase land, the council spent nearly £6,000. By 1802, Edinburgh had spent £70,000, yet earned only £66,000 from resale and leasing of land in this district.[27]

In England, most improvements cost much less. Capital could be raised locally for projects which cost a few hundred pounds, involved a small block of houses or tenements, and represented a sound, steady, and secure income. In this way, about 5,000 houses were erected in Birmingham between the 1740s and 1780, and about 5,000 more between 1784 and the mid1790s. By around 1815, residential building in provincial England was worth £6.5 million, and public building another million, or nearly three percent of national income. This sum can be compared with the £15.5 million invested in all canal construction between 1764 and 1820. The process of city building, abstracted from the various factors that make one city recognizably different from another, was critical to the accommodation of more people in, and the formulation of new attitudes toward, urban space, regardless of the size of the city involved. In England, the transformation of city-building techniques from a cultural to an economic mode was directly related to other forms of economic and social change.

⇥ *The Role of Cartography in Urban Development: France*

Notwithstanding the obvious differences in the economic and political histories of England and France, many of the changes in city building which occurred in English cities can also be seen in France. The use of maps to rebuild, administer, and expand Paris in the eighteenth century accompanied and facilitated a transformation of city building from an economic to a cultural mode. The relationship between cartographic techniques and city building in the eighteenth century has not received the attention it deserves. What follows is the first comprehensive overview of this topic.

As cartographic techniques were improved, the role of maps in urban affairs became more important. The characteristics of urban maps conditioned urban growth, encouraging a rationalization of fiscal structures, a transformation of street networks, and the construction of large, sophisticated public works. Like some of the British city-building techniques (already introduced in the previous discussion of English patterns), the pursuit of better maps became widely diffused and generalized. And like so many of the English examples, improvements in cartography show how an older kind of urban environment could be transformed into something else.

There are reasons why significant advances in cartography occurred in eighteenth-century France. Beginning in the 1660s, French scientists and engineers executed the first published national map survey according to a triangulated, geodetic matrix; completed in 1744, it was revised and enlarged with additional fieldwork between 1747 and 1789. These surveys provided a valid scientific framework for detailed, local-area maps. (The English lacked such a framework until the Ordnance Survey of the nineteenth century.)

French military and civil engineers working for the state performed numerous manuscript surveys of regions and cities in the eighteenth century, diffusing better cartographic techniques and modern attitudes toward map usage in the process. The preference of engineers to pursue planning through the rectification of street outlines (*alignements*) and master plans (*plans invariables*) encouraged mapping. Standard techniques to present proposed changes included color codes to differentiate buildings to be destroyed, to be built, and to remain unchanged. Paris was also the center of the printed map trade in Europe. Frenchmen were proud of their cartographic achievements, and many of their techniques and uses for maps were taken as a model by other Europeans.[28]

If Paris instead of London had burned in the 1660s, maps would have been as scarce and useless. Maps frequently combined bird's-eye perspectives of the most important buildings and horizontal tracings of the street network at different scales. They were designed to glorify the city, its leaders, and its history as emblematic icons; they were to be framed and displayed, not consulted. This genre of cartographic image conformed to the cultural mode of city building. Maps of this kind were designed to arouse certain moral and aesthetic feelings and ideas. On small-scale maps of provinces or nations, symbols next to a city's name indicated whether that city had a law court, college, cathedral, or the like; municipal privileges and institutions qualified the importance of a city far more than population size or wealth.

The first steps in making better large-scale maps to show street networks and topographic features in detail were taken incrementally and sporadically, as local conditions dictated. One of the oldest maps appropriate to city building in the economic mode was of Valenciennes in 1693. It combined a census, an inventory of productive resources, and a map. Every street and church was given a number on the map; an accompanying list gave the name for each number and a corresponding page in the census text. The document had been made to determine how much wheat was needed to feed the population of Valenciennes, to calculate whether there was enough wood for fuel and construction to meet local needs so that any surplus could be sold elsewhere, to determine whether the city was growing or declining by counting the number of empty houses, and to consider whether army requisitions might induce hardship. Clearly this report was based on the assumption that only if data could be understood as corresponding to persons, buildings, and resources distributed spatially could the desired analysis be performed.[29] Although similar examples remained rare in the eighteenth century, a relationship gradually emerged between the content of maps and city building in the economic mode.

Like London, Paris was so big that city-building techniques evolved earlier there than in provincial cities and made people more aware of what was changing. Paris grew impressively during the reign of Louis XIV; the city walls were replaced with boulevards, and new projects such as the Invalides and the Place Vendôme encouraged development in areas of low density. In 1674, the government placed boundary markers in the suburbs to indicate the new outer limit of urbanization, but people interpreted these markers to mean that the authorities sanctioned construction to that limit.

The government, however, remained ambivalent about Paris's growth. Because laws and administrative decrees limiting Paris's growth were ineffective, the administration sought through the application of maps a more effective instrument. In 1724 a census and survey were decreed for areas immediately surrounding Paris. The object of the 1724 decree was to produce a list and a map of what existed on the city's periphery, so that henceforth any *new* construction could be identified in an annual survey—and ordered demolished.

The first maps and enumerations following this decree were made between 1724 and 1729, and covered eleven suburbs and 188 streets. Buildings were identified by a common number on the map and in the text. The text contained the names and professions of occupants, information on whether a given property was rented, the area of a property free of buildings, and the length of street fronts. In addition, floor plans of 1,417 houses were made. Finally, the positions of 294 ground markers indicating the new limits to Paris's expansion were indicated on the maps.[30]

In 1728, Abbot Delagrive drew and published a map of Paris and its suburbs showing the location of these markers (symbolized as a fleur de lis), which were connected by a dotted line on the map to strengthen the impression that they formed a continuous, linear border.[31] Delagrive's map was the first to abandon oblique, perspective drawing of buildings. By concentrating on the street network at the expense of the city's three-dimensional, architectonic patterns, he emphasized Paris's growth as territorial extension.[32]

Pierre Patte, an architect and author active in the 1760s, was one of the first to conceptualize what the application of better maps to urban development could be.[33] Paris, after all, kept growing. Patte accepted this growth as a given. He understood that the city's growth involved the transformation of parts of the city that were already built, as well as its outward expansion, and he wondered how what was new and what was old could be tied into a totally new pattern. Patte suggested identifying on a detailed map of the street network buildings or blocks to be preserved or demolished. Such a map could be printed and distributed widely so that people would know where to build or not to build, and so that architects could design appropriate structures for development sites. The street network, Patte believed, was important to emphasize because it provided the linkage among districts and between the center and the periphery.

Patte wanted the government to invest £4–5 million over ten years to redevelop part of Paris, beginning with the Ile de la Cité. The city should purchase land, redevelop it, and then sell it for a profit. Sales of property in that area would generate funds to purchase and redevelop another district. After the same operation had been repeated several times in half a century, Paris could be entirely rebuilt. Patte knew that maps good enough for this kind of planning did not exist. He was familiar with the map made in 1676 by Pierre Bullet and François Blondel at the request of the government so that all projects for improvement such as quays and street changes could be visualized. Their map measured over four meters square, presented the street network more accurately than any previous map, and displayed plans for boulevards around the city, street extensions, and the future Place de la Concorde. But it could not be revised.[34] Patte was also familiar with a map (in forty-seven sheets) of Paris's street network, begun around 1750 but never completed by Philippe Buache, a famous cartographer.[35] But the cost of making a proper planning map was such that only the government could commission one. With modest funding from the civil engineering corps in 1776, Edme-Sebastien Jeaurat, a civil engineer and teacher of mathematics, began to make a map according to scientific standards of geodesy. He made slow progress, however, and abandoned the task when he realized in the early 1780s that Edme Verniquet, with far greater resources at his command, was at work on a similar map.[36]

Edme Verniquet (1727–1804) purchased the municipal office of Commissioner of Streets for £100,000 in 1773 with capital accumulated from his architectural practice in Burgundy.[37] His functions included rectifying street widths and lengths and eliminating parts of buildings overhanging streets. In the course of his duties, Verniquet realized how obsolete and useless older maps were, and began to make maps of particular areas as he needed them. Dissatisfied with half measures, he began to map Paris systematically, and actually covered five-eighths of the city's surface within the boulevards of Louis XIV by 1783.

In that year the government extended the boundaries of Paris for tax purposes, making them more congruent with the built-up area. (A new map of the new boundaries was made.[38]) In a decree of 10 April 1783, the government also provided several new urban regulations: All new streets were to be 20 feet wide, and existing streets were to be widened progressively to 30 feet; no construction along a street was to commence until plans had been submitted to and approved by a municipal office; the height of buildings was fixed at 50 feet if in stone, 48 feet if in wood, on streets at least 30 feet wide; building heights were fixed at 48 feet on streets between 14 and 29 feet wide, and on narrower streets, heights were limited to 35 feet; buildings already in violation of these limits were to be reduced in height to conform; parts of buildings projecting over the street were to be removed; and fines would be imposed as a means of enforcement. As in London, such regulations had the positive effect of encouraging construction, so long as a few simple rules designed to facilitate traffic, prevent fires, and increase tax revenues were observed. Moreover, these regulations, like those of the 1774 act in London, had the effect of treating buildings as cubic containers whose stylistic embellishments mattered far less than their taxable value.

The government also announced its intention of having a new map of Paris made for the purposes of monitoring compliance with these standards. All projects were to be evaluated on the new map, the better to coordinate new construction with the existing street network and building stock. In fact, three maps were to be made: One of the city itself at a scale of 1:1,720 was to show every street, passageway, public square, market, and quay; the second, just of the river and its embankments, was to be less detailed, at a scale of 1:56,400; and the third was to show city and suburbs altogether at a scale of 1:172,000. Verniquet was invited to submit a bid to undertake this unprecedented mapping venture. On 8 July 1783, an agreement was reached between Verniquet and his superiors; apparently no one else submitted a bid.

Verniquet, then, was to make a set of maps the likes of which had never been made for Paris or for any other large city. Such a venture was costly: Between 1780 and 1791, Verniquet received £610,000 from the government, a sum nearly as large as the budget for the second national map survey of France between 1747 and 1789. Originally each owner was to pay a fee per *toise* of street front to have his property mapped (one *toise* = c. two meters), but such a fee would have been difficult to collect and would not have provided Verniquet with working capital. Verniquet approached the controller-general on several occasions for major subsidies, and these were always granted, despite the perilous condition of France's treasury.

Verniquet employed a professional staff that averaged thirty-two in number as well as up to seventy-five manual laborers, many of whom worked at night on geodetic fieldwork for additional pay.[39] Verniquet's map was based on a dense, strong triangulation network. The distance from every prominent building and street crossing to the Paris meridian or to a line intersecting it at the Observatory was measured carefully. Verniquet published a geodetic chart so the public could see what had been done to establish the map so accurately; as the map was to be used to determine the price of expropriated land and the value of tax assessments, public confidence in it was essential.

Verniquet understood fully the implications of cartography for Paris's development, and he undertook to make his maps with an energy and vision worthy of a Balzacian character. In 1785, a colleague, astonished at how rapidly the mapping was advancing, sought approval for plans for about 400 street and building changes on the

Right Bank near the Ile de la Cité. Tables had been prepared with columns showing the length of each street, its present width in the middle and at each end, its average width, and its ideal or proposed width. This official wanted to know whether changes in streets could be worked out on map sheets Verniquet had already finished or whether the entire survey had to be completed and approved first.[40]

Verniquet understood that by providing a sound cartographic base for others to work from, his map would enable changes in Paris to be undertaken more rapidly. Working on such a scale, Verniquet knew that his maps would facilitate measurement of the street surface area and of the gradient of the earth; that his maps would facilitate the coordination of such functionally related features as markets, quays, and public buildings; and that his maps could be used in conjunction with an enumeration of the building stock and a census of property owners. Verniquet claimed as well that his maps would facilitate the making of new maps of Paris in the future to take account of the very changes which, he hoped, his maps would stimulate.[41]

Verniquet wanted to popularize knowledge about Paris in map form. Maps would show owners exactly how much of their land was to be expropriated if a given renewal project was approved. He believed that property owners would welcome renewal and street widening because the government permitted higher buildings on wider streets. To encourage private investment, he recommended that taxes be suspended on building materials for six years and levied at a reduced rate for the next twelve. In Verniquet's mind, there was no conflict between comprehensive planning for public works and massive private investment: If certain major renewal projects were traced on maps that were readily available, investors, looking to their own self-interest, would then be guided to make decisions which would conform to the government's intentions.

When the Revolution brought forth many proposals for urban monuments and utilitarian facilities and released large ecclesiastical and aristocratic landholdings for development, at least one set of Verniquet's maps was used by the Commission des artistes to display all the projects for improvements submitted to legislative bodies.[42] The Verniquet maps, when spread out on a table in the Bibliothèque nationale, measured approximately 4m × 5m. The Commission used color codes: red for street improvements related to the sale of nationalized property, yellow for street improvements for the benefit of public health and traffic circulation, and blue for improvements as part of a beautification project. The intent was to execute red projects first, then yellow, and finally blue ones. Only a few of these projects were ever implemented; in any case, it seems that the committee working on the map made little effort to eliminate potential conflicts between various proposals.

The successor to the Verniquet map was the cadaster of Paris made by the finance ministry. Until the cadaster was finished, the ministry used the Verniquet set of maps to assess property values. To make the cadaster, the Verniquet set was enlarged from a scale of 1:1,720 to 1:200, and additional surveys were made to show the outlines and structural parts of buildings. Work began in 1809 and was completed, some 30,000 sheets later, in 1836.[43]

For the sake of convenience, maps of Paris as a whole have been discussed first, separately from thematic maps of particular aspects of its spatial order. Both kinds of maps in fact evolved simultaneously. Most specialized, thematic maps of eighteenth-century Paris dealt with the city's relationship to water, including the Seine as a port, a source of drinking water, an obstacle to be bridged, a terminus for canals, a cause of floods, and a space to be beautified. The city's relationship to water, a matter of general public concern, brought problems of urban growth into focus.[44]

One of the earliest thematic maps was of Paris's water mains. A map by de Fer in 1716, typical of several from the pre1740 period, showed just the network of mains leading to fountains. Because streets were omitted, this map showed the network as a highly schematic abstraction, an independent qualifier of urban form rather than as a dependent variable. Three symbols were used to distinguish public fountains, fountains at which there were water concessions, and openings in the pavement where there were spigots to drain the mains.[45] Abbot Delagrive presented a more comprehensive map of the city's water mains in 1737.[46] This map showed the water system in relation to the street network so that people would know where to look for water in case of fire. The streets along which water mains ran were highlighted by a shaded or hatched border, and a line indicating the water main was placed to the right or left side of the street, according to its actual position. Several symbols further differentiated municipal water mains from those belonging to the Crown, as well as mains carrying water from wells, from the river, or both. Symbols also indicated the locations of fountains, wells, and street-level and subsurface taps.

Delagrive had commented in the legend of his map that Paris's traditional water supplies were inadequate, but the best means of increasing the supply was not obvious. Pierre Patte suggested dividing the Seine into a main navigable channel and two peripheral canals, one for clear and the other for dirty water.[47] If the Seine became more important as a source of water, conduit of wastes, and navigable pathway, it would be necessary to locate more of the larger public facilities such as hospitals, lumber yards, prisons, and abbatoirs close to the river. To prepare for such an eventuality, Patte suggested building up the river's embankments, dredging its bottom, and clearing its bridges of houses; he also suggested placing separate water and sewer pipes under each street and rebuilding the street surface to separate pedestrians from vehicles. Pierre-Louis Moreau-Desproux, while serving as Superintendent of Buildings, made maps between 1762 and 1769 showing where new bridges and permanent, broad, and straight embankments could be built.[48]

Others who saw disadvantages to very high density in Paris's riverside center preferred a more even distribution of public facilities across the city, an objective which meant some way of increasing the water supply and distributing water throughout the city had to be found. This issue involved the difference between capital-intensive and labor-intensive public works.[49]

Expansion of Paris's water supply required more detailed knowledge of the city's topography and subsurface structure. A beginning was made in 1740, after a devastating flood on 26 December. The Seine rose 7.3 meters above its normal height and remained abnormally high for fully six weeks. Philippe Buache made a map showing the extensiveness of the flood and its relation to the city's subsurface structure. He used two shades of hatch lines, dark to indicate areas flooded through the sewer system, and light to indicate areas flooded through basements.[50] Buache published another version of this map, modified by the addition of cross sections of the city.[51] He called for comprehensive water maps of the city to include depths of wells, the highest point in each district, information on water mains, and descriptions of the current and of the navigable channel of the Seine. Buache also made surveys of the Seine from above Paris to its mouth in 1766, so that a low-water navigable channel could be identified, and nonnavigable sections of the river could be distinguished from navigable sections. He even developed a bar graph—perhaps the first of its kind—to show the monthly variation in the river's depth in Paris, and the minimum depth necessary for navigation.[52]

The final steps to making comprehensive topographic and hydrographic maps of Paris were taken during the Napoleonic Empire, and produced the first contour map of the city (if not the first of any city). The problem with previous field-survey measurements of Paris's topography, wrote the civil engineer P. S. Girard in a book accompanying these maps, was that they had not been made with or recorded on a single, standard outline.[53] Taking as point zero for elevation a level of water 1.5 meters deep in the canal basin of La Villette, Girard and his colleagues mapped Paris's gradients by making measurements at numerous street crossings. First they divided Paris into four zones, measuring elevation along an east-west and along a north-south line. Then they made detailed measurements within each zone. This work, begun in 1807, lasted for several years. All readings were transferred to Verniquet's map. All measurements of the same value, corresponding to an identical elevation, were connected by lines, as much as possible at one-meter intervals. A map was then engraved (at a scale of 1:28,000).

Girard also published maps showing the distribution of water from aqueducts and pumps along the Seine. Such maps, Girard believed, were essential to the selection of the best places for reservoirs, aqueducts, water and sewer mains, and canals. (Maps of sewers lagged behind maps of water mains, however. Between 1800 and 1812, statistical tables and charts were made showing the emplacement and carrying capacity of sewers but without any map, cross section, or measurement of subsurface depth. The first detailed map of Paris sewers appeared in 1833.)

These examples highlight the importance of Verniquet's maps to other, more specialized efforts. Before the Napoleonic Era, when nothing like the Verniquet maps existed, projected canals along Paris's outskirts, both to drain land and to provide new transportation routes, were drawn crudely on small-scale maps. These merely illustrated a proposal but provided no information either to evaluate or execute it. The Verniquet maps were triply valuable to canal engineers: as an overall record of all public works projects, as the basis for detailed topographic mapping, and as a detailed planning document.

Copies of Verniquet maps used to plan and build canals have survived.[54] They show how engineers traced several projected canal routes across buildings and streets without moving a single paving stone or demolishing a single wall. By redrawing lines on the maps, engineers could modify their projects. The same maps on which they planned could also be used to estimate expropriation costs and to execute the final design. The colored lines and shadings drawn by engineers transformed entire districts according to a new image of urban space. They saw a canal not as a conduit connecting two remote points, but as an agent of change whose presence would create new opportunities for commerce and industry along its banks. Plans for canals functioned for engineers as part of an even larger plan to transform Paris into a commercial city attached by improved waterways to the ocean. Enlarged canals in Paris were to be considered in relation to plans for a canal connecting Paris directly with Dieppe and the coast or to plans for improving the Seine. Such plans were important vehicles for land speculation in Paris in the prerailroad era.[55]

As Paris became an important commercial center, building types and land uses became more specialized. People searching for certain commodities and services were at a loss; the old pattern of geographic specialization brought tradesmen in a given line together in certain districts, but as the city grew some businesses were redistributed over a larger area. Parisians could no longer rely on memory, personal knowledge, and word of mouth alone for information. In 1808, Maire published one of the first practical guidebooks to Paris. It contained an alphabetical listing of street names, bridges, public gardens, churches, government buildings, theaters, hospitals, and the like, together with a series of maps. The user was guided from list to map with cross-references, as in any modern gazeteer.

In 1821 Maire brought out an atlas of fourteen maps, each show-ing the distribution of one category in the entire city: cab ranks, fire stations, hospitals, quarries, markets, streets illuminated after dark, etc. These maps, which enabled people to see that the distribution of services across the city formed distinctive patterns and networks, re-flected the diminishing importance of socially significant architecture in determining land-use patterns. They form the antithesis to the map views of the seventeenth and early eighteenth centuries.[56]

Provincial cities in France were also affected by changes in cartog-raphy. After a fire that began on 13 December 1720 and lasted for six days destroyed 945 buildings in Rennes, the capital of Brittany, the intendant called on Isaac Robelin, director of fortifications at Brest, to take charge of the city's reconstruction. Without consulting the city fathers, who wished to rebuild Rennes as it had been, Ro-belin worked on a plan for over a year. In the course of his work, Robelin made exact surveys of each house destroyed or damaged by the fire, so that reapportionment of land to conform to new lot sizes and street patterns would be feasible.

Fortuitously, a surveyor named Forestier had made a manuscript map of Rennes and its environs in 1718. The Forestier material relat-ing just to Rennes within its walls was enlarged in 1723 so that Robelin could draw new streets and property lines on a general map to be attached to the decree of 12 April approving these changes. Finally, in 1726 Forestier printed a map of Rennes showing the new district, with an insert showing the street pattern in the burned area as it had been before 1720. Both the 1723 and 1726 maps also showed a projected new channel for the Vilaine River in the middle of the city superimposed onto existing built-up areas, and a rectilin-ear grid extension to carry the new street pattern over all the land within the fortifications on the far side of the proposed river channel.[57]

In improving Strasbourg, the architect J. F. Blondel used maps in a more complex way to identify projects in the order in which they were to be executed.[58] Because Strasbourg was a garrison city with about 6,000 soldiers, the city had to keep fortifications; within a defense perimeter there was little room for new barracks and parade grounds, or for enlarged commercial facilities. Moreover, the medie-val street pattern interfered with the swift movement of troops as well as with the passage of heavier and wider carriages and wagons. At the request of the city and the military authorities, Blondel visited Strasbourg in 1765; his projects were approved three years later.

Blondel worked with a series of maps made for his task in 1764–65 in two formats: one a set of maps of Strasbourg made by an engineer using triangulation, the other a more detailed set about properties and proposed changes made by a surveyor. Expropriation costs could be calculated by consulting the second set of maps with a series of fiscal registers. Blondel used these maps to design several circulation corridors between the city's center, garrison, and gates, some for the use of the military (red on the map), others primarily for travelers and residents (colored green). Blondel considered that construction of military projects might last twenty years; this construction would precede the widening of streets and quays for commerce, the cleansing of polluted canals, and the building of stone bridges, tasks which would last until 1800. Conflict between the city and the government in Paris over expropriations and changing economic conditions affected the choice of particular projects for construction, and only a few of the projected improvements were ever undertaken.

Marseille provides a final example. It seems that a map had been made of corrected street outlines in 1720 which was supposed to be modified thereafter only with the approval of the intendant and controller-general, but pressures of growth, which inspired projects to move cemeteries, to change the city's walls, and to create new avenues, aroused conflict. The map was constantly referred to by landowners eager to have its provisions enforced or modified. By the mid-1770s, landowners appealed to have a new general map made. Some landowners, principally from traditional mercantile groups who wanted a moratorium on new construction to expand the city until the new map was made, used mapping to block development; others, in the aristocracy and state service who urged development, hoped that a new map would give them the initiative. But the real issue was not over whether development should occur but over the extent to which the costs of development and profit to be gained should remain in private hands or be transferred to the municipalities or other levels of government.[59]

Maps for planning purposes conditioned people to look more closely at detailed microstructures in the urban tissue. In the process, a traditional way of looking at city space emphasizing verticality in important buildings and the dense, clustered bulky mass of ordinary street fronts became anachronistic. The older way of looking at cities emphasized compression: the newer way, extension. On small-scale maps of regions and nations, cities had been represented by clusters of towers, walls, and buildings. Crudely, such symbols were enlarged or diminished according to the importance of a given city. By the late eighteenth century, it became desirable to describe cities by their size measured by area and population, instead of by the age, number, and beauty of their monuments and the jurisdictional authority of their institutions.

An understanding of urban density proceeded through the study and use of maps. Charles René de Fourcroy (1715–1791) was a marshal in the French army, director of fortifications, and military attaché at Versailles; he was also interested in natural history and was an associate member of the Royal Academy of Science in Paris. In 1779 he wrote a report on Le Havre for the army which made the ratio between population size and urban area explicit.[60] Le Havre's population, he estimated, was 22,000 persons; its area (exclusive of fort and port) was fifty-two arpents. This gave a population density of 420 persons per arpent, a density Fourcroy considered excessive. He proposed that Le Havre's area be increased to at least sixty arpents. In his report, Fourcroy stated that he was already engaged in research on the optimal ratio between population size and urban area. Thanks to the efforts of François de Dainville, Fourcroy has been identified as the author of a study, published anonymously in 1782, on the ideal size of cities.[61]

Fourcroy, inspired by requests for information from the government on the size of cities whose fortifications were being enlarged, began to make a comparative study of population density. He determined the area of cities by studying manuscript and printed maps, measuring their area with a metal divided scale, and converting the results into a common unit, the *toise* of Paris. Fourcroy, of course, had access to the large stock of printed and manuscript maps held by the fortifications engineers. He recognized the difficulties in using maps of questionable accuracy and acknowledged the problem of defining the limit of a city.

Nonetheless, he was able to reduce his results to several classes of cities, by area: very large cities in excess of 2,000 arpents, such as Peking or Rome, or between 1,000 and 2,000 arpents (5–15 km²), such as Lyon or Florence; large cities, 300–1,000 arpents (1.5–5 km²), such as Brussels, Strasbourg, and The Hague; medium cities, 70–300 arpents (0.35 km²–1.35 km²), such as Liège, Cadix, and Amiens all the way down to Tournai and Bastia; very small towns, less than 25 arpents (or under 0.12 km²), such as Belfort and Monaco.

To calculate population size, Fourcroy used a variety of published sources as well as estimates submitted to the government in Paris by its officials; these, too, he evaluated critically for their probable accuracy.

From estimates of urban area and population size, Fourcroy calculated ratios of population density. Paris, he found, was not excessively dense with an average of about 200 persons per arpent; but Fourcroy realized that this varied considerably according to the district within Paris, dropping to 100 per arpent in the suburbs and rising to 300 per arpent in the areas of the Halles, the university, and the Ile de la Cité. By discriminating among districts, Fourcroy revealed differences according to the age of the building stock, spatial structure, and social and economic conditions. In Lille, he found that the third of the city which was newer had lower densities than older areas. By his measures, some cities were underpopulated: Milan, Parma, Calais, Douai, even Lyon. Others were overpopulated: Marseille, Le Havre, Toulon. Paris, Lille, Dunkerque, Naples, and Turin, Fourcroy thought, had tolerable densities.

To summarize his findings on area alone for about two hundred foreign and French cities, Fourcroy composed a chart; to summarize population density ratios, he drew up a list of cities grouped into size categories and then ranked in order according to density. Others extended Fourcroy's concepts to cover larger areas than cities; their work formed the background for debate before and during the Revolution over whether administrative units should be of equal area or population size.[62]

Outside France, maps were used with increasing frequency and sophistication, especially in Germany, Italy, and Spain. After an earthquake destroyed much of Lisbon on 1 November 1755, engineers were organized into teams to make maps with measurements of grades on which different street plans could be traced.[63] In England, however, the structure of the engineering profession and of the state bureaucracy inhibited the development of costly systematic mapping ventures. Perhaps the first English map equal to the best French ones was of land use in Greater London, made in 1800. Based on trigonometric surveys of 1795–99, Thomas Milne's map covered 673 square kilometers and distinguished twelve major and five secondary types of land use.[64] But well into the nineteenth century, the average London map printed for sale was not revised consistently, and it omitted thematic displays of social and economic patterns.[65] However, when Charles Booth gathered maps in 1889 for his *Life and Labour of the People of London* (1892), he was able to code streets with seven colors according to the economic status of residents, ranging from the wealthy (yellow) to "working-class comfort" (pink), "standard poverty" (blue), "very poor" (dark blue), and "the lowest grade . . . occasional laborers, loafers, and semi-criminals—the elements of disorder" (black).[66] In America, maps were used as early as the 1790s to determine probable causes of yellow fever and other diseases by plotting the address of sick people in relation to such features as sewers and docks.[67]

The ultimate impact of maps on urban development came in Europe and America as cities were laid out in a grid pattern to make them easy to map. This meant that, practically speaking, any person with some education, under proper supervision, could survey property, calculate area, and lay out streets. The simplification of procedures involved in laying out cities this way was economical, provided landowners with clear titles, and facilitated the imposition of real estate taxes.

The emergence of a grid pattern of streets in Glasgow in the 1770s and 1780s was prophetic. Streets were laid out without any indication of the nature of the buildings to be erected along them, the implication being in any case that the street front would be a continuous, unified sequence. The grid implied that the city lacked both a center and an outer limit, and was no respecter of topographical features. Adaptable to changing land use and unpredictable patterns of demand, the grid pattern enabled the city to determine the street network, and investors the shape of buildings and land-use patterns, without getting in each other's way. The Glasgow grid was essentially expansionary, and absorbed most social and economic needs.[68]

The preceding discussion of urban cartography has illustrated one aspect of the transformation of city building from a cultural to an economic mode. Better maps were not critical to this process, but they became more important because city building in the economic mode elevated the importance of spatial variables that could be mapped more easily than they could be analyzed and recorded in other media. Like the collection of statistics, which accelerated after 1750, the production of better maps significantly increased the amount of information available about cities. Better maps, like other techniques which facilitated public and private investment in land development (such as fireproof construction, paving, street widening, and more rational methods of administration), represented incremental improvements within an established technological framework. Taken together, these techniques had a far greater impact than if each had occurred in isolation. By the end of the eighteenth century, city building had been transformed in its fundamentals. The appearance of cities changed more profoundly in the nineteenth century than in the eighteenth, but city building techniques in the nineteenth century represented not something radically new but a further evolution of trends already manifest in the eighteenth.

As the example of Arthur Young from the end of the previous chapter illustrated, the extent to which city building had been transformed in the eighteenth century was not apparent to most people. They did not understand, simply by looking at cities, how much had changed. As a result, the ideals of social order, civic virtue, and municipal authority transmitted by city building in the cultural mode remained potent. One of the tasks of the French Revolution was to reimpose communitarian values on an urban society that was in the process of losing them. James Leith's valuable studies of architecture and planning in the 1790s are full of splendid projects for new monments, civic buildings, and pageants; and for the selective destruction of Old Regime structures which functioned rhetorically, as propaganda instruments and ideological agents.[69]

The grandiose scale which many artists and architects adopted was a measure of the size of the crowds to be assembled and influenced. But in the larger city of the eighteenth century, growth had begun to induce changes in social and political behavior that broke decisively with the small scale of civic life inherited from the Renaissance. Did artists and architects understand intuitively the nature of the modern anonymous crowd? Should their projects be compared to designs favored by late nineteenth-century national-romantic and twentieth-century fascist governments, or to projects for squares and civic buildings which elite groups had favored since the Renaissance? Clearly, they believed that both the environment and society were highly plastic, for underlying their projects was the assumption that if the environment could be changed, a new social order could be nurtured. This claim also attributed to the artist or architect the role, if not the right, of leading society into the future. Architects designed structures which provided for maximum control over inmates of prisons, asylums, and hospitals, and over workers in Owenesque or Fourieresque utopias, but their methods were ineffective on the scale of the city and its society.

In the French Revolution, decrees called for the numbering of all buildings and obliged each resident to mark his name, age, and occupation at the entrance to his house or apartment building for policing, for census taking, and to help people move about in a city where economic and social relations were increasingly characterized by anonymity.[70] The more personal, familiar environmental features which had structured the urban experience in the past and which had provided the cognitive basis for city building in the cultural mode were being replaced by other features which had to be mapped, listed, and tabulated to be visualized, analyzed, and manipulated. The rhetoric of city building in the cultural mode still possessed great attraction, but the more the urban environment has changed since the 1750s, the more architecture has struggled with the issue whether or not it should accept cities as they are and acknowledge its impotence to affect deeper social, political, and economic forces at work.

CHAPTER FOUR

The Nineteenth Century

੩ଈ The Conservative Evolution of City Building

In the 1820s, people who had heard about or visited Manchester began to realize that the nineteenth century might produce a new kind of city. They recognized Manchester as a city of the future and viewed it with a mixture of fascination and revulsion.[1] Manchester's problems were not simply a function of rapid growth.[2] Manchester's population had increased from 29,000 in 1774 to 110,000 in 1811, 155,000 in 1821, and 228,000 in 1831. Although most of these people lived in misery, Manchester's builders had increased the number of houses from 3,450 in 1775 to 22,450 in 1831. They had also managed to erect the first railroad station in the world and such remarkable structures as a frame factory in Salford, which stood seven stories high, was heated through hollow cylinders in central columns, and was illuminated with gas. In Manchester, factories and warehouses (designed by men whose names have not survived in written records) were built on a scale previously reserved only for churches and civic monuments.[3] Utilitarian structures of such size had rarely if ever been built in such numbers. Their arrangement in Manchester was elaborated without regard to anything except efficient and economic construction and use.[4] For the first time, the European world recognized that an important city could take shape and function without any building of aesthetic distinction.

After Manchester became a great city, the trappings of culture were added: the first English exhibition of pictures gathered from private collections, the first free library in a large city, a large assembly hall, and a resident orchestra. Manchester's greatest cultural legacy, however, was the set of ideas associated with its political and economic interests: that active competition fostered the strength of the middle class; that such competition and the middle class were, in the long run, in the workers' interest; and that international trade and competition were good for the world.[5]

It was easier to *see* that Manchester was different than to *describe* what made Manchester different. Léon Faucher and Alexis de Tocqueville struggled vainly to condense Manchester's unprecedented spatial features and social conditions into "intelligible generality."[6] Tocqueville saw, in Steven Marcus's words, "the absence of government and the prevalence of the Irish, the crowded and dreadful housing, the unclean and unpaved streets, the absence of sanitary conveniences, the disastrous separation of classes, the enormous factories, the bad and unhealthy appearance of the working people."[7] Tocqueville's finest phrases referred, however, not to Manchester in its visible aspect but to an abstract representation of the city in its global extension: "From this foul drain the greatest stream of human industry flows out to fertilize the whole world. From this filthy sewer pure gold flows. Here humanity attains its most complete development and its most brutish; here civilization works its miracles, and civilized man is turned back almost into a savage."[8] But this kind of writing, which failed to incorporate the specific into the general, was as ineffective as the picaresque or traveler style that emphasized visible details at the expense of abstract analysis and conceptual thinking.[9]

Friedrich Engels, in *The Condition of the Working Class in England*, set forth with unprecedented precision and compression the connections between Manchester's physical and social structures. His first paragraph about Manchester is three pages long, a literary parallel to the city's scale. He described the spatial separation of classes in Manchester, overcrowding, unsanitary conditions, and landlord profiteering in clear, plain language devoid of hyperbole and metaphor, graphically heightened by maps, drawings, and floor plans of typical working-class dwellings. Engels presented the shape of the city and the social conditions of its residents as complementary manifestations of a single reality. As Steven Marcus has written, Engels saw Manchester as a "concrete, complex and systematic whole, each one of whose parts has a meaning, and more than one meaning, in relation to all the others. These meanings begin to come into view when we realize that this total whole is, naturally, more than the sum of its parts, that it is made of its parts and their histories, and that the entire elaborated and coordinated structure is in motion."[10] Engels was correct to see that the environmental conditions of Manchester were a reflection of profound economic and social forces, relationships, and ideas.

In its early phase, industrialization did not have major environmental consequences for cities. The first factory complexes such as New Lanark, Scotland, and Le Creusot, France, were in remote rural areas; there, factories and housing were brought together to form ensembles which recalled the small town or military camp of the preindustrial era rather than the great commercial centers of the day. The transformation of city building in the economic mode began independently of industrialization but contributed to its development. In the eighteenth century, the transformation of city building generated new goods and services, more efficient commercial and transportation networks, additional capacity in the construction sector, and stronger administrative mechanisms to regulate and plan expansion and change.

Perhaps commercial and technological innovation and improvisation were easier to pursue in eighteenth-century Glasgow and Birmingham, for example, given the effects of city building in the economic mode. Industrialization in the eighteenth century grew out of and in response to broader changes, of which the transformation of city building was both cause and effect. In the eighteenth century, industrialization owed more to city building than city building to industrialization. Their roles were reversed in the nineteenth century. To grow, industrialization exploited many features of city building in the economic mode; but in the process, it appears to have remade city building in its own image.

Manchester showed what might happen. In the past, cities had been established with political and social institutions as the basis for attracting traders, entrepreneurs, and workers. This sequence was reversed in the development of cities of the Manchester type. These grew to be very large without many of the institutions and characteristics that people thought were indispensible to cities. In the Manchester-type cities, the economic function was free to shape social, spatial, and political patterns.

City building in the economic mode enhanced the sensitivity of cities to trade cycles, tariff policies, commodity prices, technological change, and demographic trends—circumstances over which business leaders had little control. It also enhanced the impact of economic factors on the shape of the environment itself. Economic factors determined land-use patterns, the supply of housing, and the provision of public services within the city. Decisions about what to build were not taken by thousands of workers and investors who considered only what kind of city they wanted to live in. Such decisions were made in a larger context in which opportunities for urban development and construction had to compete for labor and capital against other opportunities for investment.

Given "*the competitive sorting of land uses* by a highly speculative land market, . . . the maintenance and enlargement of urban areas were always competing for resources by the returns they might offer *relative* to those alternative courses undertaken outside the city milieu."[11] Perhaps at earlier moments in Europe's economic development, city building offered comparatively secure and easy opportunities for investment because the vehicles for speculative capitalism were altogether so few. In the nineteenth century, however, that was no longer the case.

The biggest profits in city building were made by those who first developed an area, buying land cheap and selling at the crest of a price rise.[12] Ninety percent of building in Victorian London was on speculation, in anticipation of demand.[13] Conditions favored large landholders (such as English aristocrats whose rural estates on the edges of older cities were converted into urban space)[14] and large building firms (employing hundreds of men) which were better able than small operators to withstand the swings of boom-and-bust building cycles. Nevertheless, "the accretion, repletion or piecemeal replacement . . . of artifactual parts of cities were paid for out of the savings (or borrowings) of hundreds and thousands of punters and plungers in the course of everyday transactions. . . . Each venture depended at any time on some enterpriser's expectation—more or less informed—of its *net* earnings potential as conventional accounting might disclose."[15] Most of these decisions were taken "wholly outside the purview of local authorities," who at best limited themselves to matters involving street networks.[16]

Private investors provided most public amenities; many services were left to private initiative or to the efforts of voluntary or charitable societies. Market mechanisms provided a modest infrastructure in commercial districts and in upper-class residential neighborhoods, but could not meet the basic needs of millions of residents who could not afford them. Notwithstanding differences among property law, patterns of urbanization, investment mechanisms, and rates of economic development between various countries, the nature of city building in the economic mode did not vary in its fundamental aspects from country to country.

Yet the warning signals which were so easy for some to read in Manchester were ignored by many. Engels might have seen the relationship between environmental conditions and social and economic structures, but most people preferred to look at the unpleasant aspects of cities as of no lasting consequence or significance. Not that it mattered. The outlook of the nineteenth century prevented all but the radical fringe from considering any fundamental restructuring of society or redistribution of wealth as a means of treating social and environmental problems.

Critics saw cities as unnatural growths which threatened traditional values and political order; apologists for cities argued that trade and growth would, in the long run, solve urban problems.[17] Both critics and promoters of cities advocated a laissez-faire approach, the former out of a concern that public intervention would only stimulate further growth, the latter out of a belief that intervention was unnecessary. As a result, little was done to reform municipal politics or the relationship between cities and states during the early phases of industrial, urban growth.[18]

Failure to grasp what the growth of cities implied for their future highlights one of the most remarkable and little-noticed aspects of nineteenth-century city building: its conservatism. The economic model of city building was improved in the nineteenth century; its fitness was not questioned until late in the century, notwithstanding the widening differences between eighteenth- and nineteenth-century urban conditions. Concepts and techniques inherited from the eighteenth century were improved and adapted until the 1880s and beyond.

Ideas and techniques in city building did not evolve as rapidly as the economic, demographic, and social aspects of urbanization. City builders, anxious to exploit the opportunities urban growth provided, mastered the design and construction of specialized, utilitarian building types (many of an unprecedented scale or functional purpose) by applying already proven techniques to labor, land, and capital. Ironically, city-building techniques that emphasized economic criteria produced environments ill-prepared to adjust to many of the changes accompanying urban development.

Perhaps contemporaries believed few changes were needed in city-building practices because they did not understand the dynamics of industrial urban development. In any case, from their vantage point, these practices seemed to work well enough. Builders, landowners, and users managed to enlarge cities and to insert more specialized building types into them without engaging in any fundamental rethinking of how urban space should be organized. Visionary images, as for a Crystal Way in London, remained just that, the architectonic equivalent of science fiction, balanced precariously between fantasy and plausibility. In an age of invention, when technology transformed economic production and commercial distribution several times over in a few decades, city-building practices changed very little. No doubt the conservative evolution of city building facilitated urban growth to the extent that cities could be built with established, labor-intensive, common skills. But the adaptation of existing city-building techniques to nineteenth-century cities aggravated conditions that those techniques could not alleviate.

The railroad station and the slum illustrate different aspects of this theme. Frequently the largest private or public building open to the public, railroad stations displayed architectural styles and mechanical inventions without restraint, blending functional requirements and aesthetic concerns in imaginative and often masterful combinations. The particular virtues of Hittorf's Gare du Nord in Paris or of Cubbitt's Euston Station in London are not what concern us here; instead, we want to know what railroad stations reveal of the nature of nineteenth-century city-building practices.

The scale of railroad building can be easily grasped. In England, by 1890, the principal railroad companies had spent over £100 million—more than one-eighth of all railroad capital—on the provision of terminals. Railroads owned up to 8 or 10 percent of all central city land and indirectly influenced the utilization of an additional 10 percent. Initially, railroad builders did not anticipate the contribution railroads would make to urban growth by increasing the efficiency of urban production and distribution and by transferring population from less densely to more densely populated regions. They underestimated the expense of terminal facilities, the likelihood that such facilities would need to be expanded, and the rise in urban land values. With foresight, railroad companies in the 1830s and 1840s could have set a complete railroad infrastructure into place; instead, they sought the easiest ways of entering cities, making property deals with monopoly landlords or owners to simplify land acquisition. Competition between railroad companies for advantage had more influence upon the location of railroad facilities than an imaginative, rational assessment of how best to serve the passengers and shippers of a given city.[19]

London was the worst served; its railroad stations remained outside the central city, requiring an extensive surface transfer network of taxi cabs and omnibuses. When the South Eastern Railway built Charing Cross Station in central London between 1850 and 1864, the railway built seventeen bridges (including one over the Thames), 190 brick arches, an iron viaduct, the station, and its hotel; it removed 8,000 bodies from a dispossessed graveyard and demolished parts of several neighborhoods.[20] Railroad schemes put forward for metropolitan London in 1863 involved raising millions of pounds, laying out 174 miles of track, building four new bridges, and scheduling one-fourth of all lands and buildings in the City for compulsory purchase and demolition. By 1900, Glasgow's urban lines, terminals, and suburban trackage occupied an area equal to three-quarters of the built-up acreage of the whole city in 1840; in Liverpool and Manchester, the lands owned by railroads were half as large as the built-up area of each city sixty years earlier.[21]

Only a building mode receptive to frequent change could have facilitated the entry of railroads into cities. If the railroad had depended upon a totally new building technology and a totally new method of dealing in property, even the most adventuresome investors might have been reluctant to assume the added risks of railroad building. The impact of railroad building on cities was profound; while it quickened the connections between them, it divided cities internally and provided city dwellers with unforgettable and unavoidable sights and sounds. But the social and environmental costs of railroads were not calculated until their undesirable consequences (including inefficiencies in the railroad systems themselves) threatened to get out of control. Much remains to be learned about the reciprocal influences of the property market and railroad building. (However, in England, documents which "could give a closer insight into the mechanisms of urban growth are still largely unused, and indeed, are being destroyed at an alarming rate."[22])

The existence of slums provides another example of the conservative direction in city building. Building practices applied to middle- and upper-class residential districts were frequently modified to produce cheap, easily erected structures of brick and stone for the poor. Slums had taken shape, not because people thought the poor deserved to live in slums, but because feasible alternatives were not available given the appallingly low incomes and the high incidence of unemployment of poor people. The Victorians could not bring themselves to attack private ownership of urban land and its exploitation for profit; even philanthropic reformers who sponsored the construction of improved dwellings for the poor wanted to prove that such buildings could be erected *at a profit*. Nothing could oblige the investor to build housing for the poor when he thought his money would earn a better return elsewhere, and no public agency yet existed to supplement his efforts.

Many factors made the removal of slums difficult, including lack of money for expropriation, failure to provide alternative housing elsewhere for displaced residents, and the need of many poor people to live close to their place of employment. The first public housing sponsored by London government dates from 1895, at a time when over 55,000 two-room and 24,000 three-room flats in London were overcrowded. One of the worst areas of Liverpool housed 32,000 persons in partly-underground rooms in the 1840s. The Liverpool Sanitary Amendment Act gave that city the power to buy and clear any court, alley, or house unfit for habitation or prejudicial to health; but with a budget ceiling of £6,000 per year to compensate owners, this well-intentioned law was ineffective. A generation later over 10,000 people were still confined to prelegislation housing.

The housing structure of nineteenth-century cities, characterized as it was by an ever more rigid spatial segregation by class and income, nevertheless provided moderately decent housing for more than half the population, no mean achievement. But the economic and social forces that made success possible also made the Victorian slum possible.[23]

Laissez-faire worked to establish transportation and manufacturing on a modern technological basis; it appears to have had the opposite effect on city building. Innovative building technologies were simply not applied to most building projects. The economic mode of city building was obviously quite successful at erecting many new kinds of industrial, civic, and residential structures on an unprecedented scale, but its very success may have made innovative city-building techniques too risky and unattractive.[24]

The Crystal Palace (1850) was no doubt the most famous "modern" structure built in the period between 1800 and 1880; 608 meters long, 124 meters wide, with 293,635 panes of glass, 4,500 tons of iron, and 38.4 kilometers of guttering, it took but sixteen months to design and build, and cost half the estimate for a comparable masonry structure. The Crystal Palace was to have been dismantled after six months, but it survived for eighty-six years, only to be destroyed by fire. Paxton's exhibition hall was not revolutionary for having been built of iron and glass, because small conservatories, medium-sized markets, and large railroad sheds had all been built of these materials after the second decade of the century. What justifies Paxton's fame, as Pevsner aptly remarked, is that "in designing and detailing his building he virtually created the method of pre-fabrication—i.e., members to standard sizes, production of these on manufacturers' premises, and only assembly on the site."[25]

The greatest impact of prefabrication was not felt in England but overseas; its characteristics—flexibility, portability, low cost, interchangeability of components, ease of erection, standardization—advertised themselves to emigrants whose new cities in America, Australia, and Africa rose overnight. Cellular, multistory cast iron buildings, assembled out of factory parts, were produced in several countries and exported as needed; for example, cast iron houses were sent to Hamburg after its devastating fire in 1842. The oldest house intact in San Francisco is probably a simple Greek Revival farmhouse, now surrounded by other buildings; it was prefabricated in New Orleans and shipped around the Horn. In 1853, 6,368 prefabricated houses were imported into Victoria, Australia; the next year, 30,329 units arrived, mostly from Great Britain.

Houses and commercial structures, even banks, hotels, and churches, were all designed by prefabricating firms. The catalog of the Walter Macfarland Company ran to nearly 2,000 pages, giving the buyer complete latitude over selection. In the United States, the large mail-order houses such as Sears and Montgomery Ward included houses at several price levels in their catalogs. The technology of prefabrication was equally adaptable to new and old materials. Even Paxton's Crystal Palace combined both wood and iron technologies more than it supplanted the former with the latter; wooden elements, for example, were joined by quick-fastening systems of bolting and ingenious metal clamps and fasteners.[26]

The high point of prefabrication innovation occurred around 1850; from then until the 1890s, the potential of prefabrication was so far neglected that the state of the art actually regressed to an early nineteenth-century level. Outside of Europe, prefabrication allowed large numbers of buildings to be erected in ways that did not inhibit radical changes in land use and construction patterns in the future. But in Europe, prefabrication never became an important influence on urban form, presumably because the building industry could provide labor and materials relatively cheaply and in response to demand.

The conservative trend in city-building practices contributed to the creation of an urban environment that was more difficult to renew and modify later in the nineteenth century. Victorian building created problems for the future that have proven difficult to solve. Despite continuities in city building in the economic mode from the eighteenth to the nineteenth centuries, there was a significant difference between them. Usually that difference is expressed in social-demographic terms that call attention to the size of cities and the rate of urbanization, circumstances which overwhelmed the improvements city builders had achieved in the eighteenth century. Attention has not been drawn to another contrast: the declining margin of flexibility in the urban environment of the nineteenth century.

Most cities in the early modern and early industrial eras made few demands for a capital-intensive infrastructure, and were easily adapted to changing circumstances. In the economic mode, buildings and areas could be demolished and rebuilt if more intensive, more specialized, and more profitable uses could be substituted. But such opportunities were available far more frequently in certain areas of the city than in others. We shall see in the last section of this chapter that, ironically, economic factors gradually encouraged a reduction in the latent adaptability of city space, with consequences that increased the cost and complexity of city building.

Prefabrication might not have been the answer; but cities, like Vancouver or Johannesburg, that grew very rapidly and used a combination of prefabricated and temporary, wooden structures to accommodate nearly all their needs were able to rebuild almost completely after their initial growth had been consolidated; this at a time when English cities were encountering the Victorian heritage as a cumbersome obstacle to growth and change.

City Planning in the Nineteenth Century

Could city planning have imposed more order and control over urban development? Or did planning, at least as practiced in the nineteenth century, make little difference? These questions turn our attention from England to France, where the directing political energy of the central state influenced urban development. In England, select committees, commissions, trusts, and boards investigated conditions and undertook improvements, usually limited to only a single facet of urban life (such as public health, sewers, paving, or building codes). As Anthony Sutcliffe has pointed out in the (perhaps exceptional) case of London, no metropolitan authority had been able to bring London's environmental problems much closer to solution by 1914 than they had been in the 1850s.[27] English institutions and traditions inhibited government from direct participation in the urban land market and so limited government to regulatory intervention; as a result, the people with the technical skills needed to comprehend and redirect urban development patterns were mostly in the private sector.

By the midnineteenth century, French government on both national and local levels had accumulated considerable experience in construction and some forms of planning. The work of Baron Haussmann did not represent something new in France; had urban planning been as uncommon in French as in English history, it is unlikely that the French government would have initiated massive city planning schemes. In France as elsewhere, conservatism was a paradoxically critical factor in the nineteenth century.

The interest of the French state in city planning can be traced to Henri IV, but his assassination in 1610 created a gap that was not filled in this area until his grandson Louis XIV came to power in 1660. Although Louis XIV had abandoned seditious Paris for his father's hunting lodge at Versailles, he allowed a high-level committee to recommend improvements in the city's administration in 1666; and in March 1667, he appointed a chief police magistrate for the entire city. In their efforts to improve Paris, Louis XIV, the administration, the bourgeoisie, and financiers found that, more often than not, they shared common interests and assumptions. Improving the quality of life by enhancing the city's housing, circulation, public order, and economic activity was as important to the monarchy's urbanism of grandeur as the more formal monuments to the ruler himself. Three of the most important epochs in French city planning occurred when rulers perceived that a rival state possessed commercial advantages that threatened France: Louis XIV's reign (the Netherlands); Napoleon III's (England); and, recently, the Fifth Republic of Charles de Gaulle and Georges Pompidou (the United States).

The processes of industrialization and urbanization were by no means so uniform that cities in every country resembled each other closely; techniques of construction and design in the first industrial age evolved slowly and conservatively, thus preserving some parochial, localized, and individualistic characteristics in city building. Nevertheless, the problems of providing housing, water and sewage facilities, larger markets, cultural institutions, and political centers on the scale of industrialized urban growth were sufficiently similar across Europe that a common interest in problems and solutions could have developed. In fact, it appears that very little effort was made to circulate information about problems or solutions. Travelers and commentators, like Tocqueville and Engels, informed continental audiences about English conditions, and some English writers performed the same service in return. Authorities in London and Paris were aware of the other's police, sanitation, and transportation services, but an international concert of informed opinion and expertise was never organized to study and propose solutions for urban problems. With this in mind, let us consider how Baron Haussmann transformed Paris's spatial order.

Baron Georges Haussmann (1809–1891) was born in Paris, and studied law there; he left the capital when he entered the civil service in 1831, rising through the ranks to become a prefect in the provinces (1843–53). In 1853, he returned to his native city with the rank of Prefect of the Seine *département*, serving in that post until 1870. The Prefect of the Seine was not only the chief administrative officer for Paris; in the French state this prefect was the most powerful political figure in Paris after Napoleon III himself. After his enemies secured his dismissal in 1870 (no one as powerful as Haussmann could operate without alienating influential people), he became a deputy in the National Assembly (1877–81) for Corsica—one of the most rural and rebellious *départements*—but he no longer had any direct influence on the capital's administration or development. By then, complacency, inertia, and local politics prevented the renewal of planning. Haussmann had not been brought to Paris by its citizens but by the country's ruler; he depended upon the state, not the city, for his authority. What was it like to build in Paris before Haussmann?

Since the Middle Ages, the central market district for Paris, *les halles*, occupied a prominent site on the Right Bank. Despite the construction of new buildings in the eighteenth century, the market was too small. Napoleon I decreed in 1811 that within three years a new market be built on the site of the old. Delays ensued. In 1839, the city established a commission to examine several related issues of city growth. This commission examined both population growth and mobility within the city, and concluded that the market should be rebuilt and relocated to a Left Bank quay, where it would not generate so much traffic congestion and where it might stimulate desirable development. This proposal, like the very condition of the market itself, provoked controversy. Another commission, impaneled in 1843, adopted an alternative plan of 1842: to triple the size of the market. The Municipal Council received this proposal in 1844, and approved it in 1845. Royal consent was granted in 1847. Victor Baltard and Felix Callet were chosen as architects in 1845; Baltard and two administrators then traveled to England, Belgium, Holland, and Prussia to study markets.

The Revolution of 1848 then intervened, reopening several issues already settled, such as whether the market should be centralized or dispersed, and whether it should be wholesale exclusively or retail as well. The outlines of the 1845 decision were reaffirmed, but the architectural conception was reopened: Baltard's plan for pavillions had to be compared with others, most significantly with Horeau's proposal to realign the market on an axis perpendicular to the river, extend it from the river inland, and connect it to the river by streets and underground railway. Newspapers described this plan in detail, and land speculators began to act as if its selection had already been decided. More commissions deliberated, and in 1851 rejected all alternative proposals but Baltard's; Horeau's fell for lack of legislative appropriations to acquire new land (43 million francs would have been needed).

Work was begun, and then terminated in 1853 on Napoleon III's orders because the first building lacked adequate lighting and ventilation, and resembled too closely a fortress blockhouse. Forty-two new projects were submitted in 1853, revealing great indecision about construction design and methods: whether to use cellars or not, how to illuminate, whether to leave the pavillion sides open, whether to let certain products be sold in the open air. All the proposals were shown to the Emperor, who did not favor any of them.

Haussmann, the new prefect, who knew Baltard from school years and as a fellow Protestant, told Baltard that the Emperor wanted "Iron, iron, nothing but iron," a material Baltard had despised but which many of his competitors admired. Baltard worked up his masterful, third project for fourteen glass and iron pavillions, each serving a different commodity, connected by tunnel-vaulted avenues; it was approved enthusiastically. The markets were built in two sections, starting in 1854.[28] The reason for telling the story of *les halles* is not to moralize on the power of a Haussmann as the great decision-maker as much as it is to highlight two things: first, the length of time separating the apparent need for a new market (c. 1810) and its realization (c. 1860); second, the extent to which architectural design, and administrative and political practices, were ill-adapted to each other and to the city's problems.

Haussmann presided over a city that needed and wanted to build.[29] He began by making a map of the city; enlarged, it was mounted on a frame on wheels in his office, where it remained throughout his tenure. He also undertook to study Paris's historical development, so that he might know the origins of contemporary phenomena. However, Haussmann, like most of his contemporaries, had no sense that urban textures and districts from the past merited preservation; only individual buildings received protection. Haussmann concentrated on certain aspects of the city, such as traffic and sanitation. In so doing he reduced complex features of the city to manageable variables; urban administrators try to affect those parts of city life that are most amenable to treatment by them.

The broad outlines of Haussmann's achievements and methods are well known, but historians will still be busy for a long time studying both specific and general features of Paris's rebuilding. Between 1817 and 1827, fewer than 2,500 houses were built, meaning that at a time when the population increased by 25 percent, the housing stock grew by only 10 percent. These averages of about 250 new houses a year lasted until 1850. Then from 1851 to 1860, the average soared to 1,240 yearly in the city, and 3,500 in the suburbs; between 1852 and 1870, the value of constructed property rose from 2.5 to 6 billion francs. Four times as many buildings were erected as were demolished.

Slums were cleared, new streets were laid out, parks were planned (although rather more open space was destroyed than was created at the same time), water supplies were increased (from 112,000 m³ in 1852 to 430,000 m³ in 1869), and wide sewer lines were lengthened (to a total of 560 kms; by 1869, only 15 kms of the old, narrow lines were left). But housing densities and urban amenities were still very uneven, and were still heavily determined by economic, social, and biological inequities; and whatever improvements were made were only for the city of Paris itself, and not for its suburbs. Paris's population rose from 1,053,000 in 1851 to 2,714,000 in 1900, while the population of its suburbs increased from half a million around 1850 to a million in 1900. Haussmann was prefect of a region that included both Paris and its suburbs, but he distributed improvements unevenly throughout that region, thus abandoning the suburbs to develop according to the same forces that had made his presence and methods indispensable in Paris, a point to which we shall return.

How did Haussmann facilitate changes in Paris? The answer involves a detailed study of private and public decision-making which the destruction of documents, largely in the Commune fires of 1871, renders difficult. Remaining records reveal a careful coexistence between regularization (simplification to enhance rapid construction) and older, established building and property-holding patterns (which survived in such things as the placement of courtyards).[30] The Haussmannian period did not so much invent new building patterns as borrow selectively from the past.

Haussmann changed Paris through the scale on which he worked, by destroying entire districts (such as the wood and plaster tenements on the Ile de la Cité, which became a government office district, a project first proposed in the 1770s), and by developing entirely new areas on the city's circumference. On the macro level, these operations were stunningly successful; on the micro level, the penetration of new streets through old districts—necessary to Paris's spatial and functional integration—involved builders in problems of property change and building design for which no master plan or strategy could be elaborated in advance. Haussmann's revisions of the street network produced visible contrasts between new and old streets (the former straight, broad, and long; the latter short, narrow, twisting), and between property units of very regular shape and—especially where the two street networks crossed or overlapped—some peculiarly odd-shaped ones.

Architectural aesthetics reconciled the arrangement of interior space, which reflected the geometry of property lines, with the place of the building in the city (and hence with the value of its land) by disguising the true outline of a building. Because in Haussmann's Paris the facade conferred value on a property, the number of secondary streets was increased to augment developers' frontages. Rather than respect the peculiar shape of property units and their inner organization, architects applied repetitive, homogenous, monotonous styles to street facades that gave the lie to the true shape of a building and its inner organization. Although the architectural styles favored in each decade changed, the relationship of style to street did not.[31] Architectural style gave street fronts an artificial unity, and conferred a visual, aesthetic prestige on newer buildings and streets, emphasizing the difference between them and Paris's older buildings and streets, frequently just around the corner.

The architecture and city space of Paris were very adaptable to midcentury ideas about city life, but in this adaptation there were inherent contradictions not apparent at the time. On the one hand, the spirit of the nineteenth century was so clearly inventive; on the other, Haussmann (and almost everyone else for that matter) acted as if inventions would have little impact on either architecture or city design in the future. For example, the mechanization of bathroom plumbing and the vertical conquests of elevators first made their appearance during Haussmann's years; the term elevator was first used in 1853, radiators date from 1855, and American hotels had bathrooms from around 1850. Yet, none of these became common in the better class of buildings in Europe for another thirty years, when most of the buildings erected in the 1850s were still standing. Innovations in heating, plumbing, and mechanized motion had great implications for land density, structural design, and the arrangement of interior space; yet, no one foresaw that these innovations would become standard.

Similarly, great social mobility, which had such profound effects on land-use patterns and on architectural design, was not applied to a vision of the city's future needs. City builders lacked the critical distance to see that cities which reflect the values of the present would have to change as society changed. Ironically, it would seem that the Paris of the 1850s and 1860s was built such that it was considerably less adaptable to future ideas about social life and organization, public health, economic process, and political order than the suburbs, which were left untouched by Haussmann and his agents.

Consider the evolution of the Avenue de l'Opéra.[32] The idea of an avenue in that area antedated any project to build an opera house at one end, but only when the decision to build the opera house was taken in 1860 did the project for an avenue advance rapidly. By 1870, when the opera house was nearly finished, construction of the avenue had been completed only at its two ends. In the middle, there remained a dense network of older streets whose very existence had given rise to the vision of a grand avenue in the first place. Although the problems of indemnifying tenants and owners in the 1870s were complex, the street was finished between 1876 and 1878, and new buildings were erected rapidly. As the avenue aged, its social character changed, for it became less a place of residence (as originally intended) than of business; but almost all the buildings erected in 1878 had been apartment houses, and so needed to be reconverted. (At least the exterior architecture had little to do with internal spatial organization or activity!) This sumptuous, monumental avenue that had cost tens of millions of francs to complete slipped in rank in the city as social and economic conditions in the city—and the city's own spatial development—attracted the upper bourgeoisie elsewhere. There is little to be learned of the original urban vision that inspired the Avenue de l'Opéra from a walk along it today.

We can see that Haussmann's intention to modernize Paris produced in turn a problem that affected city building after his time. There was no room in the planned Haussmannian city for the simple, easy-to-change spaces and buildings that had contributed so much to the growth and development of cities since the Middle Ages. Because so much more was of brick and stone than before, and because so much new construction visibly was cut off from the older parts of the city around it, the evolutionary process of city growth itself changed. The creation of new districts and the remodeling of old buildings to provide flexibility for growth took the place of the more organic development of buildings and blocks that had been possible before with widespread use of temporary building materials. The only way Paris could grow easily after Haussmann was by extending the suburbs and the city further outward, creating new districts of permanent materials that modified the uses of older ones (some of which might be only twenty years old). Yet this problem did not loom large in the eyes of ambitious and energetic contemporaries of Haussmann. Indeed, Haussmann's rebuilding of Paris was taken to be a signal achievement, and in the 1850s and after, Haussmann's methods and visions were applied to other cities.

Lyon was one of the first to be rebuilt in this way. There, too, a prefect, Vaisse (who was also mayor), received sufficient authority from Napoleon III to carry out a program. When, in 1852, an imperial decree added the suburbs to Lyon, the political and spatial framework was set. Planning for Lyon was no slavish copy of planning for Paris on a smaller scale. Vaisse did not have an overall strategy to follow, as Haussmann had; nor were Vaisse's methods equivalent to Haussmann's, since both public and private funding were available in smaller proportions. Much of the money for Lyon was raised through the sale of bonds pledged by increased sales taxes. Haussmann borrowed one billion francs to finance two and a half billion francs' worth of public works; Vaisse's projects involved 120 million francs, of which 71 million francs were city obligations, and 50 million francs were grants and loans from the state. (Railroads spent some 80 million francs themselves in the 1850s on their Lyon infrastructure.)

Vaisse undertook to build public institutions such as hospitals, and public facilities such as quays, bridges, and parks; but his chief projects involved the creation of two streets running the length of the city's central peninsula to provide rapid communications, facilitate the movement of troops in case of insurrection (more common and alarming in Lyon in the 1830s and 1840s than in most other cities), and improve the standard of construction throughout the whole center city. Vaisse and the city devised a complex timetable and land-exchange schedules whereby the contractor, Poncet, had to make his profit from the rent of buildings he was to build alongside the new street that he was to construct. Estimates are that Poncet lost money on the roadway (as it cost him more in expropriations than he got back from the city for construction) but that he made a profit of just under 10 percent on the buildings he erected. (As speed and economy were very important to him, he called for iron beams of uniform strength to be used as reinforcements between the floors of these buildings. This produced some anomalies: some floors had more iron than they needed for the weight they had to bear, others not enough.)

In a decade-and-a-half, Vaisse modernized Lyon by adding major new streets and many new buildings, by modifying the outlying districts sufficiently to permit easy transport throughout the city, and by largely keeping urban development under the city's control separate from the railroads' projects.[33]

As Marseille's growth was much less directly dependent on the state, it contrasts effectively with Lyon and Paris.[34] Colonialism—in the form first of the conquest of Algeria in 1830, then of the construction of the Suez Canal (finished in 1859), and finally of late-century Asian and African conquest—certainly tied Marseille's port traffic to state politics. But the adaptation of both port and city to expansion were left largely in local hands. During the Revolution, both the port and the city's streets had been allowed to decay. Thus, as the city and its traffic grew in the 1820s and 1830s, it in fact differed physically very little from the city of the 1770s. Population in 1821 was 110,000; in 1831, 132,000; in 1841, 156,000; in 1846, 183,000; and in 1850, 195,000. The only major change made under public auspices to accommodate so many more people was the aqueduct bringing water from the Durance River. After eleven years of construction which involved the expenditure of 30 million francs, and the building of seventeen kilometers of underground channels and two massive aqueducts, the water arrived—in 1851.

Housing for newcomers was provided by large landowners and syndicates, proceeding first to construct streets, and then to erect houses; they also standardized the building type, improving upon a local model in a way that apparently pleased the populace. The city fathers retained control over the construction of housing only to set minimum standards for street widths; they did not impose a master plan on new growth.

However, they cared greatly about the port, in the traditional way in which Mediterranean oligarchies had for centuries. Decisions about the port were centralized in the municipal authority and in the corporate organization which managed the docks. From the 1840s on, multitudes of projects were proposed, and much land speculation can be linked to hopes for one or another of them. The city and port authorities opted for development toward the north. To the extent that the city then became involved in Haussmann-inspired projects for broad, straight streets (to facilitate circulation and to improve living conditions in depressed areas), it did so in the 1850s and after to integrate the port, the city, and industrial zones. But this kind of planning was less new in the context of Marseille's history than the visible evidence of particular streets or districts might indicate.

Haussmann-style methods of planning, building, and financing apparently could be lifted out of one context and applied to another. Haussmann used market mechanisms, respected the laws of private property, promoted profitable, private investment, and brought about badly needed and much appreciated improvements. But the kind of control over the environment that Haussmann wielded, only in a more democratic setting, eluded the midcentury generation. Capitalist paternalism in the one-company town and socialist management in visionary utopian communities were equally rigid and offered no real alternative; moreover, so great was their emphasis on permanent features (such as finished roadways, geometrically ordered street networks, and buildings), they actually petrified the city-building process in their efforts to build a workable city for the industrial age once and for all. Fascinating as both company towns and socialist utopias may be to study today, they offered little by way of example for the harassed city administrator, unimaginative legislator, and conservative investor.

By the time Britain and France industrialized, they had already passed through the political process of nation-state formation. Germany, on the other hand, industrialized, urbanized, and unified its territory within two generations, from around 1850 to 1920. In Germany, therefore, the political conditions relevant to the administration of urban affairs were sufficiently different from what they were in England and France to account for the creation of modern zoning techniques as instruments of urban control and planning.

German cities, on the eve of sudden industrial-urban growth, were largely unprepared to cope with the problems that growth would bring. Hamburg was the only large German city to be rebuilt midcentury, but that was after a fire in 1842 destroyed 4,000 buildings along seventy-one streets and left 20,000 homeless. Hamburg was rebuilt along new lines when William Lindley (1808–1900), a British-born engineer who had come to Hamburg to assist in railway construction and land drainage, carried out sweeping reforms; modern sewage systems, waterworks, and the like were set into place as a city commission succeeded where Londoners nearly two centuries before had failed in creating a new city differently organized than the older one destroyed by fire. Among its characteristics were new kinds of housing and street networks, and a marked separation of work and residence. Much of the result was judged aesthetically unappealing, though a few architectural critics such as Carl Reichardt thought otherwise. However, so marked was the isolation of German cities from each other that Reichardt's favorable appraisal—or any architectural critique, for that matter—received little attention elsewhere.[35]

In 1869, on the eve of unification, an industrial law was enacted that provided for a measure of zoning by separating factories from other parts of cities. With unification came the growth of the bureaucracy as a salaried, professional civil service, and the development of the universities as research centers. These factors interacted with large-scale urbanization in the 1870s and 1880s. Urban growth produced both overcrowding and suburban sprawl for speculative investment. The old regulatory structure of independent city government was transformed into bureaucratic control by engineers, imbued with a progressive, reformist concern for public health and welfare (the Association for the Preservation of Public Health was established in 1875). In 1875, a Prussian act regulated building depth and height, the ratio of building height to the width of the street, street layout, the location of factories, and master plans for districts. In 1876 Reinhard Baumeister (1833–1917), an engineer, architect, and planner, wrote what became the standard text for city engineers. Engineers shaped blocks according to rigid geometrical formulas that owed little to Platonic idealism and much to the kind of pragmatic efficiency that gave American cities a bad name at the same time. German engineers' obsession with public health and with ease of traffic movement made them discount the importance of the appearance of buildings in the cityscape; they copied the landscape of English public squares as singlemindedly as the repetitious facades of Parisian boulevards. Their approach to the city enabled German cities to add new housing, but it offered little protection for older city centers whose crowded, crooked streets seemed anachronistic. Moreover, this system could only have favored the ambitious, large-scale developer, who alone possessed the means to cope with bureaucratic regulations and with the lot and block size favored by the engineers.

Coping with city growth became a function of governmental structures, a situation that favored the provincial centers more than Berlin, where conflicts between national and local objectives and policies went unresolved. In Berlin, building regulations did not prevent the proliferation of speculative, high-density multistory structures (*mietskasernen*) around the older core; because builders had to pay for the costs of new streets, and because regulations made streets very wide, intensive use of building lots (many measuring 200m by 300m) was inevitable. Germans used regulatory techniques and planning schemes while denying themselves expropriation powers. In the nineteenth century Europeans could not get away from seeing expropriation as a limitation on the freedom to own property, which was itself seen in almost Lockean terms as the guarantor of an individual's political liberty and civil standing (true so long as property ownership was a test of voting rights). But unlike the British and the French, the Germans could accept the widespread adoption of municipal planning and regulation mechanisms when such efforts enhanced the traditional self-rule of cities; in France and England city-planning techniques were introduced in quite the opposite manner, as a response to greater centralization and accompanying a loss of municipal freedom.

This discussion could be continued at great length to touch upon Switzerland, Spain, Italy, Belgium, and the Netherlands; but interesting as each country would be to study and important as each may be in a comprehensive survey of European urban development, the examples would not, I believe, substantially modify the study of city building as told so far.[36] It scarcely need be said that cities evolved in each country somewhat differently according to historically conditioned factors. Italy and Germany created national governments at about the same time, yet Berlin and Rome are no more alike than

Hamburg and Genoa, Cologne and Milan, Nuremburg and Florence. Nevertheless, certain generalizations can be made about European urbanization and city building.

City planning may have affected city services, the selection of areas to develop, and the timing of development, but it did not affect the importance of economic criteria in city building or city building's conservative evolution. The differences between comprehensive or haphazard approaches did not matter much. At best, planning facilitated construction and improved transportation systems or public health facilities on a scale commensurate with a city's growth. As patterns of growth produced increasingly nucleated, specialized land uses, questions about urban growth were tied to questions about who would provide new services, and at what cost and profit.[37]

Of course, cleaner, quieter, healthier, safer cities appealed to many of those whose rights as property owners were necessarily affected by government policies, regulations, and investments in public works. Techniques to improve and control the environment gained acceptance with the support of social reformers, architects, engineers, philanthropists, big capitalists, and academics in political, social, and financial combinations which varied from country to country. What they had in common were appeals to social peace through a rationalization of the land market as a means to provide better housing for the poor, and to economic growth through a more efficient use of capital, technology, buildings, and space.[38] Social reforms and economic considerations coincided, as when public transport opened new areas to settlement and reduced travel times and costs, and the diffusion of primary and secondary educational systems shaped the labor force.[39] At this stage in the development of planning, government intervention was still conceived as an instrument to advance city building in the economic mode.

Planning, as utilized in the nineteenth century, not only had the effect of creating conditions propitious for investment and commerce; it also fueled private speculation, even when such speculation had been recognized to be a factor in the production of environmental conditions which planning of one sort or another was supposed to alleviate. Planning, as practiced in the nineteenth century, could not correct flaws latent in city building in the economic mode. The kind of planning which became common in the twentieth century was not the mature fruit of a patient, slow growth, or the final step of an incremental, cumulative process; but something different in scope, concept, and technique from nineteenth-century practice.

࿐ Adaptability and Intelligibility in the Nineteenth-Century City

Despite certain conspicuous differences, American patterns of urban development produced conditions which closely resembled what developed in Europe. At the beginning of the nineteenth century, many American cities already covered a vast expanse. Cincinnati, incorporated in 1802 with a population under 1,000, enclosed 8.3 square kilometers; Amsterdam had more than 200,000 people crowded into a slightly smaller area. Philadelphia, laid out in the 1680s, had main streets 30.5 meters wide two centuries before many European cities could boast the same. Detroit, rebuilt according to a new plan after a fire in 1805, was given streets 36.5 meters wide; New York's plan of 1807–11 included twelve north-south avenues 30.5 meters wide crossed by 155 streets running east-west 18.3 meters wide.[40]

In America, where wood was plentiful, simple structures were easily adapted to a variety of uses; the balloon frame in particular gave residential construction many of the advantages of simplicity and speed of prefabrication. Speculative investment based upon rising land values anticipated the need to rebuild and redevelop, and "ample lot sizes facilitated the enlargement or replacement of buildings."[41]

As rebuilding and expansion occurred, microdifferentiation of site use was replaced by macrodifferentiation of land use on a metropolitan scale to a greater degree than in Europe. "Separate types of production and consumption, diverse constructions, distinctive socio-economic classes and foreign-born contingents were becoming increasingly localized *relative* to proportions of such activities, structures or nationalities in the whole area or population of the city."[42] In the process of rebuilding, industrial and commercial structures such as railroad yards and warehouses were often relocated from the center to the periphery, with implications for housing and the conversion of older property. Rising land values at the center began a spiraling cycle which produced ever bigger buildings as profits were in proportion to the scale of investment. As new technologies in communication and transportation became available, the competitive position of some buildings and districts relative to other buildings and districts was affected.

Toward the end of the century there were noticeable signs of declining adaptability as a function of urban scale. Given the rate of growth and spatial differentiation, "a mounting *public* investment in facilities and services was necessary to keep [cities] productive and profitable for the essentially private interests which built and utilized them."[43] Yet, municipal indebtedness, which rose throughout the century and was considerably greater than the outstanding federal debt, limited the ability of municipalities to increase their intervention incrementally.

In America as in Europe, therefore, city building in the economic mode generated problems which existing environmental strategies could do little to alleviate. By the end of the nineteenth century, the destinies of European and American cities were converging. The process of urban development was inherently dynamic, and many short-term actions had far-reaching consequences which were not immediately apparent.

Despite the fact that construction remained labor-intensive because unskilled labor was cheap and plentiful, the capital cost of building increased; for as central-city land became scarce, demand for it pushed up land prices. Developers in desirable areas found that investing proportionally more in construction could yield higher rents; developers in areas not yet built up intensively speculated on the prospect of growth by failing to build well, thereby minimizing their risks until either the business cycle or the city's development produced the right opportunity. In the process of redevelopment, temporary, low-cost building was pushed out of the center city toward a peripheral zone where barrack camps, shacks, and tenements proliferated amidst factories too large and too foul to be accommodated in the city. The peripheral zone was itself a function of anticipated development: as it was absorbed into the city, a new peripheral zone took shape further out at the same time. This process created problems which, by the 1880s, became severe.

As the distance from the outskirts to the city center increased, problems of communication and transportation emerged which had not been present even in midcentury. Continued outward growth lacked any regulatory framework, such that cities could not control their future. As peripheral zones suceeded each other, they produced new areas of permanent, built-up city; but since each sucessive development phase affected the value of land that was relatively closer to the center and further from the periphery, the entire process provoked continual changes in economic and social land-use patterns throughout the urban area.[44] The cost and complexity of adapting city space increased. Beyond a certain point, such costs and technical problems meant that "a given quality of environment became increasingly expensive to secure relative to other goods and services."[45]

Fire protection was the principal and most visible example of a change in city-building practices which had the unintended consequence of reducing the latent adaptability of urban environments. As with so many other improvements, it increased the security of investments, thus taking some of the risk out of development even as the amount of capital at stake rose. In the absence of building standards designed to achieve a reduction in fire risks, the only incentives to replace temporary and flammable materials with more permanent and inflammable ones were economic (if the cost of the latter dropped or if a reduction in maintenance costs offset higher initial expense) and social (if brick and stone enhanced the reputation of commercial or residential occupants). Both economic and social incentives were strong in the eighteenth and nineteenth centuries, or else edicts and regulations imposing fire codes would have been difficult to enforce. Until cities were rebuilt or expanded in compliance with such codes, fires were frequent occurences.

The consequences of fires in early modern cities were not all bad; in the aftermath of a fire, resources were released for rebuilding and opportunities were created to improve properties and to engage in small-scale redevelopment. Of course, fires affected declining and growing towns differently. Over many decades, successive fires facilitated the removal of encroachments from streets, the replacement of shacks and temporary structures with more permanent ones, the widening of streets, and the standardization of house design. Rebuilding required little public intervention in the early modern period. No one has yet undertaken a systematic study of urban fires, but attempts have been made with England and Canada.

Discounting some 80 fires during the Civil Wars, there were 518 major fires in which at least ten houses were destroyed in provincial England between the sixteenth and the end of the nineteenth centuries, plus 57 fires in London between 1666 and 1839. As building improvements were made, the number of fires decreased. Rebuilding in brick and tile produced a ratchet effect, such that better-built blocks acted as fire breaks, lessening the severity of fires when they did break out. This effect may have been more important than increased water supply and fire-fighting improvements.[46] A fire gap emerged between the growing size of urban areas and the declining actual number of fire disasters. "Had fire retained its proportionate late seventeenth- and eighteenth-century significance the urbanisation of nineteenth-century England would have taken place under the equivalent of a rain of incendiary bombs."[47]

The breaking of the fire cycle implied an abrupt change in spatial dynamics and in the riskiness of urban investments. Highly destructive fires such as New York's in 1835 (which destroyed 674 buildings in the vicinity of Wall Street), Hamburg's in 1842, or Chicago's in 1871 (which consumed 18,000 buildings on 7.75 square kilometers and left 90,000 persons homeless) are examples of the scale and kind of disaster which might have affected more cities more severely had fire prevention not been achieved through city building. (In the twentieth century such a level of destruction can only be produced in war).

By default, fire prevention introduced a crude sort of zoning into cities whereby the spread of buildings in brick and stone correlated to certain kinds of social and commercial land uses. After a fire in 1877 in Saint John, Nova Scotia, which left 15,000 persons homeless and destroyed the business district, a fire code divided the city into three districts, of differing degrees of standards. One result—especially in the commercial district where standards were most severe—was to simplify building designs and to reduce the use of architectural ornamentation. In many Canadian cities, the conversion from a more flammable to a less flammable urban environment was taken only in the 1860s and 1870s, often after several fires in a given city had already occurred. Efforts were also made to raise building standards and widen and straighten streets to create fire breaks; but such efforts were often frustrated by conflicts over property rights as well as economic arguments based upon the inability of artisans, laborers, and small shopkeepers (not to mention the poor) to pay for better buildings.

The impetus for change was economic: pressures from insurance companies which discriminated in their rates against wooden buildings. As fires diminished in frequency and severity, and as more people took out fire insurance, the insurance companies had more money to invest in the economy (a factor urban historians have not yet begun to consider). The impact of fire prevention, when it came, involved the formation of fire departments with steam pumps, the spread of water mains, the development of telegraphic networks connecting buildings and districts to fire stations—the earliest example of the wired city—and the publication of fire insurance atlases which, along with the census, became the basic documents of nineteenth-century urbanization.[48]

The second elementary change in city-building practices involved the spread of sewer and water mains. In England, connections of all *new* houses to main sewers became compulsory in 1848, and of *all* houses in 1866. Edwin Chadwick's studies of sanitary conditions contributed greatly to the enactment of legislation; his plans combined the evacuation of waste water and sewerage in a common conduit, but kept the elimination of storm runoff in a separate conduit. Throughout the rest of the century, Americans and Europeans debated the merits of various combinations without understanding very clearly the implications of each system for public health and land issues over entire regions.

The relationship among the development of water sources, water purification, sewerage systems, flood control, and land reclamation still requires detailed historical analysis. It does seem that in the nineteenth century, the construction of water and sewer lines did not proceed synchronously; conflicts between engineers over construction techniques, between landowners and government over property rights, and between private syndicates and government over the financial organization of public utilities brought delays, such that systems spread slowly, long after the technological capability existed.[49]

Sometimes only a public health crisis created conditions favorable to action. A yellow fever epidemic in Memphis, Tennessee, in 1879–80 provided the occasion for a plan for a comprehensive reconstruction of the city. This included employment of a sanitation official; development of public water supplies; prohibitions on the use of wells, cisterns, and privies; drainage of bayous and redevelopment of shoreline into park; repaving of all streets; and abatement of all nuisances discovered in a systematic survey.[50] But even such comprehensive measures stopped short of planning in the modern sense. The rebuilding of Memphis was undertaken to safeguard public health; it was only intended to correct past abuses and mistakes, not to guide the city's future development or patterns of land use.

Laws, regulations, and technical and scientific knowledge still did not penetrate many urban districts. For instance, by the end of the nineteenth century, most of the streets of Bordeaux and Rouen were still without sewer lines; and 60 percent of the houses in Rennes, capital of Brittany, lacked sewer connections in 1905. Parallel streets in Manhattan often had radically different infrastructures. The owners of property in areas not served by modern facilities lacked an incentive to improve their buildings if people would not pay more to live there. As a result, reformers and officials began to think that the condemnation and wholesale redevelopment of certain urban districts would be necessary; simply bringing sanitary facilities to these overcrowded and poorly maintained buildings would not be enough.

The construction of water and sewer mains contributed to the transformation of the street. Pressures to pave and grade streets rose as the volume of traffic increased. Better drainage was necessary, not only to protect the street subsurface after paving but also to remove filth and manure from the surface itself. The number of horses in the United Kingdom not on farms trebled between 1851 and 1901, and the weight of their droppings must have reached 10 million tons per year. There were between 2 million and 5 million horses in American cities around 1900. Milwaukee, with 350,000 people, had 12,500 horses, producing 133 tons of manure daily. In fair weather, the manure dried into a powder that a wind could disperse; in wet weather, it formed cesspools in the street. Horses were also capricious and difficult to maneuver in a small space, factors which exacerbated traffic in cities. Moreover, many of them died in the street. In 1912, the city removed 12,000 dead horses from the streets of Chicago.[51]

Congestion and pollution on nineteenth-century city streets were all the more intolerable as the commercial and industrial sectors became the worst afflicted. Of the 8,000 kilometers of streets in eleven large American cities in 1880, 50.8 percent were unpaved; in the same cities, of 11,084 kilometers a decade later, 62.7 percent were unpaved; of 20,495 kilometers in 1902, 48.3 percent were unpaved.[52] Despite efforts to pave streets, the continued expansion of cities meant that as much remained to be done in 1902 as in 1880. Drainage, repaving, and even public transportation only seemed to facilitate access to the center, such that whatever improvements were made were only temporary palliatives. Beyond a certain point, improvements had no measurable effect on the conditions they were supposed to alleviate.

Congestion was as much a social and cultural as a physical phenomenon. People expressed their sense of being crowded through increased intolerance of noises, smells, and unsightly structures which they associated with urban life. The nature of the crowd was perhaps first explored by Charles Baudelaire, whose descriptions are still quoted sensitively by historians; in recent years, the analyses of Baudelaire and midnineteenth-century Paris by Walter Benjamin, dating from the 1920s, have received as much attention as Baudelaire's original work.[53] As Richard Sennett noted in *The Fall of Public Man*, urban society in the nineteenth century evolved cultural mechanisms which allowed people to be in a crowd but think themselves separate from it. In the process, the communitarian basis of public life and civic action that had been a part of urban experience since the Middle Ages was deformed, ultimately to be replaced by mass organizations and mass media.[54] At the same time, patterns of spatial segregation emerged which tended to confine the poor to their own neighborhoods or places of recreation, thus liberating the middle and upper classes to move throughout the rest of the city without risking unpleasant encounters. The rebuilding of museums, parks, and concert halls away from the promiscuous center of the city and nearer to socially exclusive residential districts was symptomatic of and contributed to this process.

Numerous new structures existed in the nineteenth-century city (such as the railroad station, the department store, sports stadia, and exhibition galleries) which had no parallel with older structures. These were either public buildings, access to which could reasonably be denied to some persons, or private buildings with a public function. Two issues emerged: controlling who may or may not enter, and regulating behavior within. As semiprivate, semipublic facilities evolved, they acquired many functions which until then had been associated with street life; the street, meanwhile, began to lose its public character and became a place in which social behavior and economic behavior could be regulated.[55]

The perception of urban space and the administration of streets which emphasized the mechanical functions of streets were in turn linked to and followed upon shifts in housing tastes, and clearly antedated the development of the automobile, with which such a transformation is popularly, but incorrectly, associated today.[56] (Surprising as it may seem, the automobile promised to reduce congestion, noise, and pollution when first introduced to a mass market.)

The regulation of the street involved such matters as the licensing of street peddlars and musicians, which in turn introduced the first modern attempts at abating noises for their social character as well as for their loudness. Precisely because the street was public, people were not free to do as they pleased in it.[57] As M. J. Daunton has pointed out, the regulation of street activities involved a change "from a cellular and promiscuous to an open and encapsulated residential style" which in turn was a function of the distribution of water and sewer mains and gas lines. The world of enclosed courts and alleys with shared space and common facilities, wherein each group of houses formed an enclave within the city, gave way to "an open layout where everything connected with everything else."[58]

The availability of gas, sewer connections, and running water to each dwelling made for a stricter separation between public and private spaces and functions. The gradual internal transformation of houses and apartments involving heating and ventilation, cooking facilities, bathing and lavatories, and lighting represented on the microscale what was happening to the city at large; within the house, as within the city, greater specialization of spatial uses depended upon the availability of certain common services.

This situation placed an enormous burden on the fine arts to create and communicate imaginatively new ways of perceiving and thinking about the city. Many artists and writers had no illusions about the social forces at work on urban forms and about the impact of urban growth on social values, but most were unable to treat city space on its own terms, without attributing to the environment a positive or negative moral influence, or without describing the environment as a metaphor for individual or collective conditions. The persistence of pastoral myths allowed city people to avoid any serious study of the city. As a result, "much that needed to be seen, in a complicated, often opaque, and generally divided society, could not, as a basis for common experience and response, be seen at all."[59]

Human actions in the city could be made intelligible more easily than the scale of the city and the pace of its growth. Because the urban scene was so often the source of shock, it is no wonder that artists and writers cared so little for images of it. Raymond Williams has claimed that Charles Dickens understood that the physical condition of the city dictated an altered literary consciousness if it was to be connected with man, as "of his making, his manufacture, his interpretation."[60] Dickens was able to describe the patterns of people moving along streets such that the apparent randomness of their paths appeared to form a larger design, and he transcribed the interaction of people in urban space into the very structure of his writing. The close connection between Dickens's inspiration and walking the streets has been pointed out. But even his achievement still suggested that the extension of city space lay beyond the comprehension of the individual or the control of organized, social institutions.

Emile Zola in *Bonheur des dames* came closer to explaining the process of physical change in the nineteenth-century city. Numerous and justly famous passages described the organization of the department store and its system of delivery, both within the great store and within the city at large, such that the application of organization and technology to the visual display and movement of commodities was linked to the social values and ideologies of Parisian groups. Zola even included passages in which individuals discussed how urban properties were assembled to provide land for larger buildings, and how the construction of new buildings launched speculative development in the city, thus exposing some of the mechanisms of urban spatial change. It is nevertheless to be wondered why other great writers of the century did not try to do more with the city than apply given motifs and repeat commonplace ideas.

The photograph was a quintessential medium of the age, but there is little evidence that the process of taking photographs stimulated a new kind of urban image before a few individuals composed photographs of the New York skyline in the 1880s and 1890s.[61] Scholars remain interested in examining the style and content of artistic and literary works from the nineteenth century because what artists and writers thought and felt is of interest for its own sake, but little effort has been made to follow Louis Chevalier's attempt to consider how literary and artistic works related to objective studies and statistical investigations during the nineteenth century.[62] In the absence of such studies, it is difficult to assess the extent to which urban perceptions and concepts formulated by intellectuals and creative people lagged behind the evolution of cities.

City building in the economic mode accompanied such an expansion in the size of cities that by the 1880s efforts to improve the urban environment through the elimination of certain dangers to property and life altered the relationships between different kinds of buildings and spaces. Some of the internal contradictions in city building in the economic mode were exposed in the process. Traditionally, people had not needed to provide for adaptability as a generalized feature; it had been an intrinsic quality of the environment, a byproduct of building patterns and construction techniques. But in the nineteenth century, the development of the city increased the amount of capital needed to build. Without more public intervention and investment, the climate for private development might deteriorate; yet, *some* government intervention and investment only appeared to lead to *more*, because environmental problems and conditions became more complex and intractable as private development accelerated. Growth and redevelopment produced new patterns of land use which in turn altered established uses elsewhere in a city; different areas of cities became more or less adaptable than others as sewers, fireproof buildings, paved and graded streets, and the like were spread unevenly. Eventually, the cost of urban redevelopment and expansion generated incentives to try a different approach.

A declining level of adaptability in urban environments must be accounted among the factors favoring the transition of city building from an economic to a regulatory mode. But the relative ease with which this transition was effected between the 1880s and the 1920s is nonetheless an indication that the urban environment around 1880, although less adaptable than in the 1820s or 1860s, could still be changed.

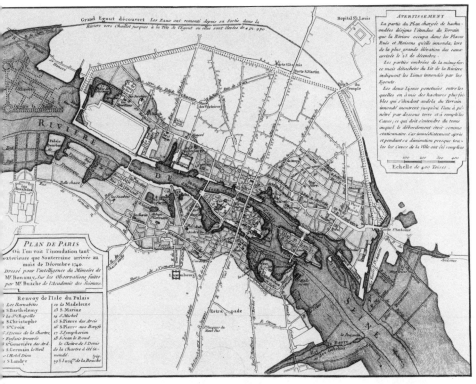

Map of Paris under flood, 1740. Philippe Buache designed the map to distinguish between areas flooded by the Seine overflowing its banks (darker shading) from areas flooded through basements and sewers (lighter shading). Note the encircling boulevards that replaced fortifications, and the open sewer beyond it, along the city's northern edge. The Hôpital St. Louis, in the upper right, next to the legend, was for contagious diseases.

BIBLIOTHÈQUE NATIONALE, PARIS, GE. F. CARTE 5640

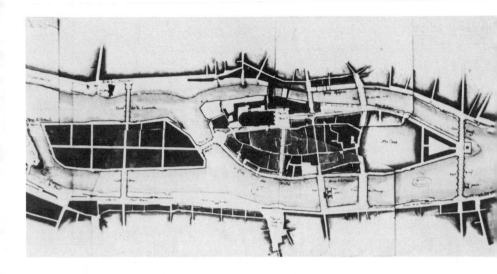

Maps for redevelopment of the Seine embankments. This was actually a single map with flaps. Version b, with flaps up, shows the actual condition of the river front; version a, with flaps down, shows plans for improvement. Suggestions included widening and straightening the quays, building new bridges, and building new streets and public squares on the Ile de la Cité.

ARCHIVES NATIONALE, PARIS, PARIS N III 568

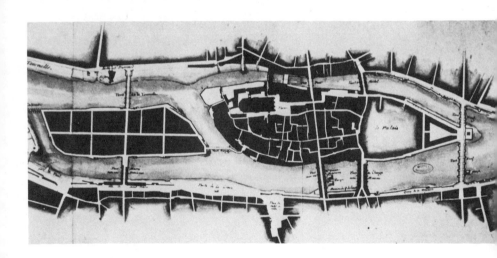

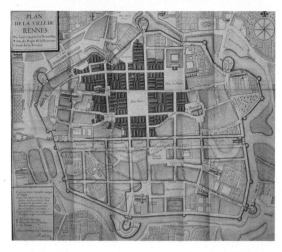

Rennes, showing the new district after the fire of 1720 and a new channel for the Vilaine River through straight embankments (the existing, more sinuous riverbed is also drawn on the map). Note how the new district is inserted into the existing urban fabric.

ARCHIVES NATIONALE, PARIS, N II ILLE ET VILAINE 4/3

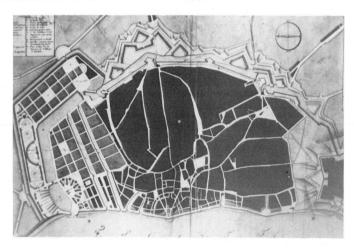

One of several Napoleonic plans for rebuilding Antwerp. This map shows a strong contrast between the existing city, with curving streets of ever-changing widths, and a planned district for expansion. The older city still has fortifications; the newer part does not. Notice also the semicircular shipyards in the newer part.

ARCHIVES NATIONALE, PARIS, F14 10212 = 17/4

Row Houses, New York, on West 133rd Street, c. 1877. This was urban development without prior infrastructure. The buildings were of fireproof material. Those that were built did not affect what developers could do on the unbuilt lots.

COURTESY OF THE NEW-YORK HISTORICAL SOCIETY, NEW YORK CITY

Juxtaposition of vernacular buildings in wood and stone, Torkel Knutssonsgatan, Stockholm 1896. Note the greater bulk of the stone building, as well as the greater use of glass. Utility wires, drainspouts, and gas lights testify to the presence of limited infrastructure services for the stone house alone. Only the paved street is available for all.

CITY MUSEUM OF STOCKHOLM

Congestion on Dearborn Street, 1909. Note the mixture of means of travel and the presence of utility lines.

COURTESY, CHICAGO HISTORICAL SOCIETY (ICHi–04191).

Victory Arch, Madison Square, New York. The Dewey Arch had been replaced by a different structure to commemorate the end of the World War in 1918. This picture was taken of the parade of the 27th Division on March 25, 1919. The backgrounds of this and the preceding photograph can be compared to show how rapidly New York was built up, literally, within a relatively stable spatial and architectonic matrix.

COURTESY OF THE NEW-YORK HISTORICAL SOCIETY, NEW YORK CITY

Dewey Triumphal Arch, Madison Square, Fifth Avenue looking north from 23rd Street, c. 1899. The streetcar line passes through the formal composition. Compare the hotel on the left with the building in the next picture that replaced it within twenty years.

Park Avenue at 50th Street, New York, 1922. This pedestrian mall was subsequently removed to permit more vehicular traffic on the avenue. St. Bartholomew's Church (right) has been the center of much controversy in recent years, because it is one of the few remaining low structures with open space around it left in midtown Manhattan.

Bremerhaven Container Terminal, c. 1980, is far removed from the city. With a total quay length of 3.2 kilometers and an overall area of 1.6 million square meters, this container facility is said to be the largest in Europe.

GERMAN INFORMATION CENTER, NEW YORK CITY

Frankfurt am Main, city center with the Roemer district, St. Paul's Church (right) and bank headquarters (background). The old structures in the picture are among the few that survived World War II; before the war, this area was full of medieval and early modern structures and streets. The approach to new high-rise construction in Frankfurt was to scatter the skyscrapers to avoid congestion. The result, however, is that the old Roemer district, once the center of Frankfurt life, is out of the main-stream. Moreover, given the distribution of office buildings, there is no obvious center to the city today. Plans are being drawn up for the second time since 1945 for the redevelopment of the Roemer district.

CHAPTER FIVE

The Regulatory Mode

❧ The Infrastructure

The word *infrastructure*, meaning the foundation of a building or engineering work, probably appeared in print for the first time in 1875, in French. It soon acquired additional meanings, referring to the permanent ground installations of a mobile operation for armies or airplanes, and to the basic framework of social and economic organizations and systems. Early English uses of the word have been found in the period between the two world wars; perhaps the English borrowed the word from the French during the 1914–18 war. Webster's *Second International Dictionary*, published in 1934 and revised in 1939, did not list the term, but it does appear in the *Supplement to the Oxford English Dictionary* (1976) and Webster's *Third International* (1961, revised 1981). Until recently, the word has been used in English by engineers and economists in reference to economic overhead capital in roads, power transmission systems, communications, banking, health and educational facilities, and governmental structures as these contribute to economic development. Debate among specialists has focused upon the timing of infrastructure development, the balance between public and private capital, the size of facilities, and pricing formulas, especially in terms of underdeveloped nations.[1]

Unlike public works, which it subsumes, the term *infrastructure* is at once a description of physical assests and of their economic, social, and political role. Used this way, the word became familiar to millions of Americans in the early 1980s as journalists called attention to collapsing bridges, crumbling highways, and decaying sewer and water mains; and as legislators considered proposals for spending on maintenance, rehabilitation, and expansion. Once a subject of interest to specialists alone, the urban infrastructure is receiving attention because its condition is approaching a state of crisis. Only now are we finding out how little we know about infrastructures, their development since the 1880s, and their relation to urban development.

Infrastructure elements, and associated tendencies toward increasing specialization of buildings and districts and toward increasing differentiation of public and private spaces and behavioral patterns, were already present in cities before the 1880s. But until the 1880s, infrastructure systems as varied as street paving and lighting, sewer and water mains, even fire-prevention codes were applied to limited areas; great contrasts existed between parallel streets or adjacent districts. As a result, much of the nineteenth-century city was characterized by the kind of visually unpretentious, easily modified, usually inexpensive utilitarian structures that had dominated the urban environment ever since the Middle Ages, that made few demands on urban resources, and that were easily adapted to frequent and unpredictable changes in conditions affecting urban life.

The difference between the development of infrastructure systems before and after the 1880s was a matter of extensibility, or coverage of an urbanized area. Infrastructure systems developed after the 1880s were applied to the entire urban environment. The potential of universal coverage was latent in modern infrastructures in their early forms, even though this potential was not often realized for years, even decades.

This interpretation of city building in the twentieth century emphasizes a fundamental continuity in the development of infrastructure systems since the 1880s. The obvious differences between spatial patterns (between 1880 and 1940) based on streetcars, apartment houses, and central business districts on the one hand, and (between 1940 and the present) patterns based on automobiles, suburbs, and decentralized economic activities on the other, should not stand in the way of an attempt to formulate generalizations about city-building methods that transcend the specific characteristics of cities in different decades.

Infrastructure systems are characterized by fixed useful-life spans, which can however be renewed and extended. For some systems, such as sewer mains, these can reach a century; for others, such as street pavements, these can be as short as twenty-five years. A historical perspective on modern city building should be based on a time frame that is long enough to observe the effects of infrastructure systems and to describe their temporal and spatial rhythms. Whether modern infrastructure systems have compromised the latent adaptability of urban environments is the central issue of chapters 5 and 6.

Elements of infrastructure systems developed before the 1880s were inserted into existing environments or were built into new districts without seriously affecting either street networks or the internal arrangement of buildings and property holdings. Their most pronounced effect on city building in the economic mode was to make certain streetfronts, buildings, or land parcels worth more than others. Although public services and amenities still have an impact on the values of land and real estate, infrastructure systems as they have developed since the 1880s have diminished the importance of purely economic criteria in city building.

Modern infrastructure systems have involved massive changes to street networks and major changes in the internal arrangement of buildings. Given the scale of modern infrastructure systems, bureaucratic organizations and regulatory frameworks have become the dominant actors in environmental design; and political and social strategies, the dominant criteria. Users and owners have much less control over property, which is now subordinated to social and political objectives that often have the force of law. The adoption of a permanent infrastructure as the spatial matrix for urban development, and the massive intervention of government in most matters relating to construction and land use which has accompanied the elaboration of infrastructure systems, have initiated a new phase in city building, based on political and social institutions and criteria far more than on economic factors.

Four factors encouraged the development of the infrastructure system in the first place. First, cities kept on growing. Natural increase, migration from the countryside, and international population movements supported claims that infrastructure investment was needed to accommodate population growth. Second, the existing urban fabric was still easily modified and replaced. Modest buildings of wood or stone looked unattractive compared with what could be built in their place. Furthermore, city and regional planning authorities did not yet exist in most cities to control the rapid conversion of urban space. Third, energy costs were declining in real terms, which meant that decentralization (which infrastructure systems fostered) substituted cheap energy for more costly labor and allowed cities to expand outward more economically. Fourth, rising standards of living and dissatisfaction with existing environmental conditions inspired visions of a better urban future, created demand for better services, and nurtured effective political coalitions in support of change.

The design and extension of infrastructure systems after the 1880s required different technologies and organizations than had been suitable until then. New forms of bureaucratic organization, new accounting procedures and office machines, increases in the numbers of engineers graduated from institutions of higher learning, and the successful application of mass-production techniques to materials as old as glass and as new as electrical equipment all contributed to the formation of infrastructures. Infrastructures also bore some of the capital cost of providing for water, power, waste removal, and communications that otherwise would have been more of a burden to industry and commerce.

In its early phase, therefore, the infrastructure system of city building was a component—perhaps a critical one—in the second industrial revolution, just as city building in the economic mode had been a part of the first one. To be comprehensive, this study should include accounts of glassmaking and steel-reinforced concrete, of modern forestry and of large construction machines, of efficiency studies and of professional management. As this is not possible without considerably enlarging the text, the example of electrification is presented as representative.

The growth of electric power systems illustrates the importance of both technological and organizational factors. Their growth occurred in stages. First came the direct-current systems such as Edison exhibited at the 1881 Paris Lighting Exposition; these had a limited and stable output, primarily suitable for lighting. By 1890, the Edison Electric Illuminating Company in New York had 1,698 customers operating 64,174 lamps. Then, from the 1890s to the 1920s, came the elaboration of urban systems connecting several generators and using alternating current. These systems stored and distributed power as demand for it fluctuated hourly and daily. The 1893 Columbian Exhibition in Chicago demonstrated the feasibility of a universal supply grid. Finally, networks on a regional scale emerged, especially after World War I.[2]

The critical transition came between the first and second stages. The power system in the first stage was too small to grow, and the power source had to be in the vicinity of the users. The switch from direct to alternating current permitted the generation of electricity in central supply stations and its transmission throughout an urban area. To achieve economies of scale appropriate to the cost of building large generators and transmission lines, managers had to learn to stimulate and satisfy demand; and to do that they needed to know instantly and continuously how the system as a whole was functioning. To operate successfully, the providers of electricity had to deal with financial, political, and social factors and organizations, as well as with a technology whose behavior and potential were as yet imperfectly understood. In system building, however, the nature and extent of the controls built into systems and imposed upon them from outside mattered as much or more than any purely technical factors.

The success of system builders is graphically illustrated by such facts as these: By 1915 there were 7,740 kilometers of transmission and distribution cables in Berlin; the capital demands on American electric utilities in the 1920s exceeded those on railroads in the decades of their most rapid expansion.[3] The greater availability of electricity encouraged the substitution of cleaner and more efficient power sources for dirtier and less efficient ones (principally coal and wood), but even less is known about energy consumption than about the utilities providing power.[4]

Electrification involved the elaboration of power systems. The system itself constituted an invention separate from that of any technical apparatus or procedure used within it.[5] It developed other characteristics typical of infrastructure systems. It brought a given service to every part of the city, providing universal access at a low initial cost. It placed great importance on managerial skills. It gave rise to a

permanent function for research as a part of normative operations, so
that critical problems standing in the way of the attainment of system objectives could be solved routinely. The compilation and analysis of information on system performance involved better record
keeping, generated a demand for information-processing services,
and depended heavily upon the telephone. Electrification also involved the development of national and international standards for
specific products and services. Finally, the evolution of a given system
in a given city, region, or nation was conditioned by political, social,
economic, geographic, and cultural factors, such that the organization and technology of a particular system, while having some characteristics common to all or most systems, also had a style and indi-
viduality of its own.[6]

Electrification had dramatic effects on city building on the macro
level of transportation and on the modification of internal environments within individual buildings. Together these effects had the
consequence in the decades before 1945 of permitting more people to
work in central business districts and reside further away from them,
but this particular configuration did not reflect the imperatives of
electrification; rather, electrification fitted into a spatial dynamic
composed of many variables and encouraged certain trends to dominate over others.

In matters of transportation, the key event was the electrification
of street railways. This began with an experiment in Richmond, Virginia, in 1888, the work of Frank Sprague, who had been impressed
with Edison's display at the 1881 Paris Exposition. Within two
years, 16 percent of America's street railways were electrified; by
1893, 60 percent; and by 1903, 98 percent. Electrification spread as
rapidly in Europe. It cut unit operating costs, thus allowing fares to
be lowered, speeds accelerated, and the size of cars enlarged, but it
also absorbed huge capital sums for the cars, for the extension of track
systems, and for the reconstruction of the track itself—to reduce the
friction of the bigger and faster cars.

In America, electrified street railways were little regulated at first,
but eventually widespread corruption and abuses antagonized the
public. In Europe, public criticism of the weighty apparatus of poles
and cables provoked municipal regulation such that European sys-

tems remained attractive to riders a generation later. In both Europe and America, street railway companies benefited at least as much by the rise in suburban land values that their systems promoted as by the direct operation of those systems.[7]

Trunk railroad lines were also electrified in dense urban areas, because the smoke of steam was a safety hazard as well as an obvious source of air pollution. The Gare d'Orsay in Paris, now being rebuilt as a museum devoted to the nineteenth century, was the first terminal ever built to be serviced exclusively by electric traction. The construction of a tunnel under the Hudson River and of Pennsylvania Station as well as the rebuilding of Grand Central Station and of the access tracks under Park Avenue are supreme examples of how railroad electrification altered the New York urban region and significant parts of Manhattan, producing in the process two stations which functioned magnificently yet also symbolized architecturally the style of metropolitan life.[8]

Electrification had equally dramatic effects on climate control in individual buildings. When the Pension Building in Washington, D.C., was constructed (1882–87), illumination came from windows, gas lights, and skylights over a central clerestory; when the Government Accounting Office was finished in the same city in 1951, it covered a square block and lacked either wings or courts to provide interior lighting, the sole source of which were fluorescent lights, a product of the 1930s. A workday of standardized duration the year long, the concentration of office functions in buildings of unprecedented height and of manufacturing in buildings of unprecedented length, and the proliferation of labor-saving machines of all kinds involved new problems (and their solutions) of lighting, noise and thermal insulation, heating, ventilation, and waste removal. Electrification has been the essential means of making power available to create livable, workable, interior environments in all seasons and climates, thereby contributing to the urbanization of the American sunbelt and of Scandinavia alike. This aspect of electrification may seem too obvious to need emphasis, but it is too easily overlooked. Unfortunately, the designers of macro systems covering metropolitan regions achieved stylistic maturity and created appropriate problem-solving strategies sooner than designers of individual buildings and their interiors, with results that are often unpleasant for people inside and outdoors alike.

Although architects may have been slow to consider the implications of electrification and environmental control for design, certain trends in architecture in the years after 1880 helped to create a visual experience appropriate to the metropolitan scale on which infrastructure builders worked. Between 1880 and 1914, increases in the size and complexity of individual buildings and in the sheer number of buildings were registered. Up to 1900, the reaction of architects as described by Barbara Miller Lane "was an effort to reduce the apparent size and mass of the individual building" by applying rich surfacing materials, polychromatic combinations, and detailed modeling of windows and balconies. The effect of such dematerialization of facades was a loss of a sense of the whole; the pedestrian, however, found the view from the sidewalk much more interesting. "Between 1900 and 1914 the opposite tendency can be observed in many buildings both 'historicist' and 'modern': an effort to increase the apparent mass of the individual building and at the same time to distinguish it sharply from its surroundings. Linked with this effort was a tendency to design larger subunits within the city itself . . . and thus to reduce urban complexity to a new order."[9] The tendency to cover a single block with a single building provided new opportunities to exploit sheets of plate glass for storefronts, which could be safely and economically illuminated after hours. But buildings on such a scale gave the pedestrian little or nothing to look at.

The relationship between infrastructure systems and individual buildings was expressed best and mattered most in the example of the skyscraper. Writers and photographers captured the visible impression skyscrapers made, but statistics are needed to grasp the scale of material resources which cities claimed as their daily tribute. New York was not typical, because its buildings and infrastructure systems were bigger than those of other cities; but people everywhere recognized New York as representative of a new urban era.

In 1939, *Fortune* magazine devoted its July issue to New York. At that time the fourth-highest building was at 40 Wall Street, and stood 927 feet and 70 stories high; originally it was to have been only 35 stories, but the cost of land did not justify that design. This building had 6,840 square meters of glass in 3,181 windows, 45 elevators powered by 165 motors and running on 72.8 kilometers of cable, 5,000 daily workers and 15,000 daily visitors, a permanent staff of 240, a 4-bed hospital, and enough lamps to take 20,000 fresh light bulbs a year. Such a building could not function if its needs for electricity, steam heat, water, waste removal, public transport, and the like overwhelmed the existing urban infrastructure. To some extent, such a building was a self-contained unit within the city, but for the most part it made demands on public and private utilities whose load capacity had been determined independently of the design of this particular building.

In 1939, New York City's subsurface infrastructure included 72,000 kilometers of pipes, conduits, mains, and ducts of all kinds; 1,250,000 manholes, basins, and service boxes; and thousands of tunnels and vaults. The whole was made of literally hundreds of thousands of tons of metal, pipe, and concrete. To service 1,651,000 telephones, the Bell System had installed 15,537 kilometers of cable which consumed 15,033,148 kilometers of copper wire. These service facilities were layered horizontally and vertically in patterns determined by the technical characteristics of each utility, such as 15.24 centimeters of cover for steam mains. Yet, no master map existed of these subsurface facilities; each utility and each municipal department had its own records. Covering this subsurface infrastructure were 5,600 kilometers of paved streets, on which were hauled 1,300,000 truckloads of garbage a year.[10] The problem of providing infrastructure services in the quantities needed at the appropriate place, when the demand was unpredictable and when the infrastructure itself encouraged spatial mobility, represents the city-planning dimension of the difficulty encountered by architects in considering the implications of infrastructures.

Infrastructure systems transformed cities by increasing the level of spatial and functional interconnectedness. Older ways of visualizing urban features, whether grounded in an artistic vision or in statistical concepts, were reassessed as creative people in the fine arts and in municipal administration alike tried to redefine the essential features of urban life. S. Hartmann, writing in *Camera Work* in 1920, dismissed the applicability of the "accepted laws of composition" to "the main thoroughfare of a large city at night, near the amusement center, with its bewildering illumination of electrical signs. . . . Scenes of traffic, or crowds in a street, in a public building, on the seashore, dock and canal, bridge and tunnel, steam engine and trolley, will throw up new problems."[11] Commuter patterns and transportation equipment inspired photographers; graphs, tables, and charts recorded the daily experiences of millions of people in visual forms of equally impressive clarity and conceptual sophistication. Implicit in much that appeared in the fine arts and in public documents was the assumption that ordinary people did not have an understanding of how entire urban societies functioned—indeed, could not have such an understanding, given the nature of the urban environment itself.

Jules Romains, a French novelist and dramatist, tried to make spatially diffuse, perceptually discrete patterns of urban development intelligible by transposing the problems of understanding urban form into problems of literary expression. This approach formed the background for his effort to show that the anonymity of city life could be transcended as individuals used the experience of city life to build a common identity and to discover a common humanity. In *Les Hommes de bonne volonté* (a twenty-seven–volume fictional series with hundreds of characters, written between 1932 and 1946 and describing events taking place between 1908 and 1933), Romains made the character and shape of the emerging metropolitan city into the organizing framework of the story.

The eighteenth chapter of the first volume, entitled "Introducing Paris at Five O'Clock in the Evening," contains some passages worth quoting. The chapter quickly focuses on the capacity of the city to stimulate and modify human behavior. This chapter, and its place in the novel, correspond to no conventional literary purpose of entertainment. One motif of the chapter was the density of the city; another, the location of its center.

> In the Metro stations travellers, with one ear cocked for the approaching rumble of a train, were studying the map, looking for a street. Others, when they saw them doing so, noticed the map and looked at it too. For the first time, perhaps, they realized what the shape of the city was like, and really thought about it. They were surprised to discover which way such-and-such a boulevard ran, how big such-and-such a district was.

Cab-drivers and taxi-drivers were picking up fares and listening to the names of streets hitherto unknown to them. Then Paris unfolded in their heads, in their whole consciousness—a tangible Paris, made up of lines that were alive, of distances which were something that you actually felt; a Paris soaked with movement like a sponge and distorted by the perpetual flux of things that approached and receded.[12]

And finally, as a summation which reordered everything preceding it in the chapter, these passages:

Where was the centre at that time? What were its limits? How was it to be recognized? Everybody believed that he knew it, and perhaps was in fact familiar with it, but still had only a vague idea about it.

To the north of the river, almost in the middle of the city, was a deep jungle of narrow, short streets, which were choked with men and vehicles from morning till night. But this characteristic of density, of fullness, or urban plethora, did not suffice to delimit the centre. It was to be found in too many places. It repeated itself, ramifying throughout the mass of Paris, along avenues, boulevards, former main streets, even as far as the approaches to the circumference, and forming nuclei of overcrowding, streaks of over-population, fountain-heads of animation, which were in themselves as warm, as swarming, as the heart of a town.

As a matter of fact, what marked the centre was its pulsation. What marked it was the way in which movement rained upon it in the morning; the points where this rain of movement fell, the places where it accumulated daily. What marked it was the way in which the suburbs, the circumference, shot more than a million people in practically converging directions at it, . . .

But in the evening this spongy mass disgorged the million people who had saturated it. It expelled them back to the circumference, to the inner and outer suburbs, in myriads whose movements were all uniform.

It was a pulsation which in no way resembled that of a human organism. It involved no dilation, no contraction. The city palpitated like a focus of radiation which turns back upon itself. To launch all this human material in alternating directions, the centre did not need to budge. If it had to bestir itself, it was not in the hard-working way that a living heart has to do—a heart that in turn, and without respite, distends and contracts, inhales and exhales, and for which no

operation is sufficient of itself. It was rather in the imperious fashion
of those physical organisms, apparently immobile and inert, which,
by their mere presence, modify a whole sphere of the world around
them, letting loose, and at the same time controlling forces, tendencies, radiations in it.[13]

The Paris of 1908 which Romains wrote about in 1932 was a city
in which cabs, automobiles, buses, bicycles, streetcars, and the
Metro subway coexisted, offering great choice. Although the streets
were congested, "a Parisian used to crowds, to traffic, and to choosing
his streets could still go for long walks at a steady pace and without
taking much care. . . . The idea of walking along reading a book
was not preposterous."[14] But when he wrote about the Paris of 1933
in the 1940s, Romains emphasized "the added density and complexity" in traffic patterns as suburban development redistributed land
uses and functions throughout the urban region. Even daily journeys
to and from work involved several stages and detailed calculation,
and "the sight of a gently hurrying pedestrian, reading his paper,"
has nearly become "a thing of the past."[15] Literary metaphors, visual
images, statistical tables and graphs tried to capture a sense of the
whole, but as writers, artists, and administrators struggled to comprehend the city, the city itself kept changing.

Frederick Law Olmsted, speaking at the Second National Conference on City Planning at Rochester, New York, in 1910, admitted
that he was "almost overwhelmed by 'the complex unity, the appalling breadth and ramification of real city planning.' He realized, not
for the first time, that he and his fellow practitioners were 'dealing
. . . with the play of enormously complex forces which no one clearly
understands and few pretend to.' . . . He hoped to master the complexities of the visible city 'through better knowledge of facts, clearer
definition of purpose, and through improvements of technique.' . . .
He did not mention that he himself was particularly perplexed by
the problem of interpreting facts and translating findings into sound
plans."[16]

Seventy years later we still confront the problems Olmsted posed.
His assumption, that with better and more complete information,
intelligent urban policy can be formulated, has yet to be proven.
Imperfect sampling techniques, statistical errors, inadequate storage

and retrieval systems, imprecise terms and incompatible units of measurement, time lags between collection and analysis of data, and uncertainty over which criteria in urban development are the most important have undercut the empirical basis of decision making; but policies are formulated that leave little margin for error and rarely provide for reassessment, and once set, are difficult to change even if the assumptions on which they are based no longer apply. As a result, specific phenomena can be known in reasonable detail; but a holistic, integrative, synthetic approach remains in the realm of speculation and theory.

This state of affairs only encourages city builders to consider each project, each system, in isolation, as if its impact on the larger urban region were irrelevant. In such circumstances, planning has become an effort at mediating conflict among city-building actors and organizations. Rarely does a city planning authority possess the resources and autonomy to deter other public and private agencies from making decisions which determine the shape of the urban environment. For the most part, infrastructure systems proliferated before the modern city planning movement developed. Each infrastructure system emerged according to its own logic. City leaders accepted the piecemeal growth of infrastructures because the capital for its development came either from the private sector or from the state. Typically, public officials did not give much thought to the effects of infrastructure systems on land use and urban policy in the future. They viewed with relief the decentralization which accompanied the spread of infrastructure systems, and they failed to anticipate how infrastructure systems would affect the entire urban environment.[17]

The impact of the automobile must be understood from this perspective. In America after World War I and in Europe after World War II, the triumph of the automobile caught planners and administrators by surprise. Given the polarization in theoretical analyses of city development between centralization and decentralization, the automobile aroused positive and negative reactions. For the most part, "planners were confronted with myriad challenges and distractions other than those directly involving urban transportation."[18] When the authorities finally considered designing infrastructure systems appropriate to automobiles, the projects they had in mind were of such a scale as to widen the difference that already existed between public works and ordinary buildings in new and existing cities. The distinctive urban features identified with the automobile age, such as strips and shopping centers which evolved largely in the private sector and the urban parkways of the New York area (all from the 1920s and 1930s), took shape on land which had been left underdeveloped until then. Of course, the automobile enhanced mobility and decentralization. But the fact that infrastructures appropriate to an automobile culture were more easily erected on the undeveloped fringes of older cities or in rapidly expanding but young urban centers than in already built-up environments is no less important for being obvious.

The extension of the urban infrastructure to cover building and space throughout the entire urbanized region has placed the city-building process in the hands of many different, autonomous professional groups. Each group operates in a narrow discretionary range which fragments responsibility. National government has been interested in employment, construction value, taxes, defense; labor, in employment and wages; insurers, in determining rates and keeping losses low; builders, in executing projects; realtors and developers, in the market for building and land; construction materials suppliers, in selling their products; bankers, in a profitable return on investment; city administrators, in enforcement of codes and zoning; architects, in the pursuit of style; engineers, in efficient and safe structures; and so on.

As Kevin Lynch has noted, "The leading agents . . . do not control city development in any directed, central fashion. Typically, they are single-purpose actors . . .[whose] purposes are usually remote from the city form that they shape."[19] Conflicts among these professional groups, which often reflect different approaches to urban problems, have not made the rational selection and implementation of a coherent urban strategy any easier. Although city and regional planners "asked that all relevant proposals be dovetailed into one interlocking program or master plan . . . authority over environmental change remained the province of numerous specialists who often worked in ignorance of one another." The plans which have had the most impact "have either treated limited geographic areas or addressed specialized functions within an urban territory."[20] Fragmentation of responsibility has depressed innovation by increasing the costs of risk taking, inhibited the assessment of construction methods and operating costs on a comparative basis, and left no one accountable for the multiple consequences of the city-building process on cities or people—or on the process itself.

Because city building has become so technical and complex, new professions have arisen which function to facilitate one aspect or another of city building. Ordinary citizens may have enough influence to modify or block a major project, but they have neither the knowledge nor the opportunity to participate in design or initiate projects. Political institutions and mechanisms which are supposed to give citizens some control over major city-building decisions operate through regulation; but bankers, developers, builders, corporations, and designers with the resources to carry out big projects have learned to manipulate the administrative mechanisms designed to regulate their behavior. These same mechanisms also allow some social groups to exploit local politics and regulatory rules to gain or protect advantages, often with self-serving arguments based upon public health and safety.

The critical quality of space has become controllability: who has jurisdiction over it and what people are allowed to do with it. Control, however, is less in the hands of users than under the power of legal, financial, and technological decision-making bodies, often without a constituency in the areas they administer. Space is allocated through political processes of decision making performing "a role analogous to that of economic mechanisms . . . though these two types of mechanisms differ in the criteria of allocation."[21] The difference that matters between one piece of land or building and another is how tightly or loosely it is controlled by public and private organizations and agencies. Change in the city therefore becomes a time-consuming, costly matter of bureaucratic and legal procedures, of financial and political manipulations, of public relations strategies. Such conditions seriously compromise the adaptability of cities to change and, hence, the process of adjustment to new patterns of urban life.

This situation has dysfunctional characteristics which have not been widely recognized. Many cities cannot afford to maintain or modify their infrastructure systems. In 1941, nearly a half-century after modern infrastructures were initiated, researchers for the United States government were startled to find out how poor were the accounting procedures of many municipalities. Noting that a corporation, while continuing to maintain a stable financial condition, manages to scrap old plants or machines, to rehabilitate others, and to introduce new operating methods, the government urged private and public actors in the city-building process to amortize "their enterprises within periods which . . . are adjustable to changing conditions and the need to have future land uses suited to new conditions."[22]

Yet, the synchronization of infrastructure developments with technological, social, and economic change remains as elusive as ever. The infrastructure system of city building with its regulatory framework has always been justified with arguments that the consequences of unregulated growth are harmful and preventable. My point is not that unregulated growth is benign, but rather that growth, with or without regulation, is inherently unpredictable. Unforeseen technological, economic, and political circumstances disrupt modern urban environments that were not designed to absorb change. The poor integration of buildings and cityscape that afflicts modern cities is one of the consequences.

A Critique of the Functionalist Paradigm in Design

The ways in which city-building professionals work within the infrastructure system have made any radical assessment difficult, even by architects and planners interested in developing such a critique. Planners and architects have been unable to cope with the city as a totality, except as a formal academic exercise. In this century many of the greatest designers have pursued the ideals of urbanism with passion and imagination, and their work—especially their texts and drawings of unexecuted projects—retains a protean, inspirational quality; some projects from the 1910s and 1920s still look revolutionary. But all too often the intellectual material of the designer has been placed in the service of institutions which are unresponsive to his ideals and vision.

At the turn of the century, leadership groups in cities were still committed to city living; as urban space has been extended to cover vast areas, the meaning of the city has contracted. With few exceptions, architecturally important buildings no longer depend upon their location in the city or their relationship to other buildings in their vicinity for their meaning. Planning, for its part, tends to determine land-use patterns with little regard for the appearance of buildings that are likely to be constructed. Ironically, in this highly urbanized age, many of the masterpieces of modern architecture and engineering are to be found in rural or semirural settings, or in countries such as Switzerland and Finland where the pattern of urbanization has been atypical. It would seem that society is less responsive than it once was to the optimistic vision of what life in cities can become.

The history of Marseille illustrates how difficult it has been to reconcile city planning, architecture, and urban growth to each other. In the center of Marseille, behind the Bourse, adjacent to the old port and to the Canebière and four other thoroughfares, once stood a dense mass of old housing penetrated by decrepit alleyways. Renovation of this district made sense to social reformers, traffic engineers, and building speculators, and was first proposed in 1850. Only in 1882 was renovation seriously considered by the city authorities, who thought of creating a new network of streets in that area. Similar projects with different designs were also considered and rejected in 1893 and 1896, always because costs looked excessive and the plans too simplistic.

In 1900, the bourse district once again received the authorities's attenton. The city proposed to undertake the design and financing because private companies and architects had been unable to produce a satisfactory plan; this proposal was a barely concealed attempt by the city's department of streets to seize control over the entire project and to obtain municipal financing. In 1906, the city, looking for new ideas, initiated a national competition. Over one hundred individuals submitted nearly 250 plans; among the prize winners was Tony Garnier, whose pioneering use of reinforced concrete in the design (exhibited in 1904) of an industrial city had been a milestone in the evolution of modern architecture.

Several things are striking about the long search for a plan to renovate the bourse district. The plans submitted (even Garnier's) lacked any conceptually original treatment of buildings and space (buildings were disposed in terms of a street network that had the primary function of structuring the entire district); financing plans had barely evolved beyond mid1850s practices; prices continued to rise, yet each successive plan was rejected as too costly; and, perhaps most important, changing conditions in the city were in no way reflected in the decision-making process about what to do with the city's center.

Five years lapsed until Marseille, in 1912, decided to go ahead with the first-prize plan; but the First World War made progress impossible. Buildings in the district were demolished in several phases, the last in 1927; the displaced residents probably found housing on the edge of the city. Only after the land was cleared was a street plan, by then twenty years old, traced out onto the land. The city, however, could do nothing more; as its financial resources prevented it from undertaking any large-scale building projects, the land remained barren. Meanwhile, Marseille's population and its role in the French economy had grown so large that the original purposes of renovation were ridiculously out of scale with the city's own growth. At no time had plans for the bourse district been related in any systematic way to the rest of the city and its needs. In 1906, the city's size was 517,478 inhabitants; in 1931, it was 803,228.

Marseille received its first metropolitan plan (by Jacques Gréber) in 1933, but this plan did not affect the bourse district because the Second World War interrupted its execution. By the 1950s, further changes were incorporated into the plan, and building commenced. In the 1960s, important discoveries of the original Greek port, nearly three thousand years old, were made under the land which had been cleared forty years earlier. Conflicts between the municipality and the national Ministry for Cultural Affairs froze all construction for several more years. Finally, in 1977, the last buildings projected for the bourse district's renovation were completed. The next year the city's first subway line was opened (the city's rock structure impeded construction earlier).

Few planners or architects who come to Marseille ever study the bourse district; they are attracted instead to the "unité d'habitation" by Le Corbusier, conceived in the mid1920s and constructed between

1945 and 1952. Le Corbusier designed a "single rectangular block
. . . containing apartments (mostly duplexes) and certain day-to-day
social services such as shops and [nurseries] subsumed within the
block." There are over three hundred apartments in this building,
but Le Corbusier's design minimized the potential of such scale to
overwhelm by "expressing the double height of the duplexes by a
single opening on the outside, and putting the whole thing up on
legs two storeys high (but looking only one [storey])." Originally
conceived before the war in terms of steel construction and intended
to occupy a whole suburb with a cluster of such blocks, the "unité
d'habitation" had to be redesigned to function by itself—and to be
built of concrete, as changing economic and political conditions produced "delays and reappraisals."

What emerged from the ground was perhaps the first truly great
monumental building of the postwar era. Le Corbusier allowed the
concrete to be poured in place, so that it retained the impress of the
wood in which it was cast, an effect that gave visible expression to
the plastic, aesthetic power of concrete. Concrete was poured into a
"fantastic collection of functional monoliths. . . . Seen against stun-
ning views of mountain, sea and sky, the powerful shapes of the ven-
tilators, lift-motor houses, play structures, platforms and stairs . . .
gave substance, triumphantly, to Le Corbusier's most famous definition of architecture—the cunning, correct and magnificent play of
volumes brought together in light."[23] As with other housing projects
by great and insignificant architects, the design of interior spaces was
considerably less successful and influential than the exterior.

But what one sees of the city from that roof shows how little the
builders who housed Marseille's growth borrowed from the master,
or followed the outlines of Jacques Gréber's interwar city plan. (Gréber developed plans for Lille, Ottawa, and Philadelphia as well.) Gréber's plans had included the construction of suburbs on the city periphery to be built by the city so that removal of older unsanitary
districts crowding the city center, depressing land values, and block-
ing expansion of surface transport, could begin. But the city, which
had not yet been able to complete the project for the bourse district,
was not about to execute a vastly more ambitious scheme.

When World War II brought about the destruction of much of the old popular neighborhoods in the city center, rectilinear blocks that owed more to imperial Berlin than to rationalist interwar design were erected as rapidly as possible to fill in the rubble, without any attempt at reallocating land use. As the city continued to grow in the postwar era, government-subsidized housing pushed apartment blocks of the most ordinary kind up against the base of mountains and along valley routes, without any regard for social or environmental consequences. It has been the fate of mass housing projects in the twentieth century to be executed in times of inflation, material shortages, and population pressure, forcing governments to accept every short cut. If the "unité d'habitation" itself could not withstand such pressures, how could it serve as a model for an alternative form of urban development?

Marseille is an example of several points of major significance. Projects and buildings often remain unexecuted or unfinished for a long enough period of time that their original purposes become outdated; many of the largest and most important cities (as well as many smaller ones) grow without the benefit of formal city planning until *after* other aspects of the infrastructure (utilities, highways and roads, housing projects) set the essential characteristics of the metropolitan city in place; formalized planning methods and progressive architectural styles often involve more resources than a city can commit quickly enough to realize the planners's and architects's objectives; a city can possess modern buildings of world renown without those buildings affecting normative growth and design; many of the important developments in architecture and city planning have been given general currency and applicability—often without regard to local conditions; the major episodes in urban development are punctuated by events outside the city's control (in the case of Marseille, two world wars, depression, the repatriation of French settlers from Africa, the closing and reopening of the Suez Canal, structural problems in local industries, etc.).

Doubtful about whether the benefits of modern cities satisfy the needs of man, we tend to dismiss optimism for modernity in the 1880–1920 period as naive; yet, this criticism is not really fair to people who had reason enough in their day to claim that their accomplishments justified confidence in the ability of modern man to meet the challenges of the future. The planners and builders of that period look heroic to us because they had so few doubts about what they were doing. The generation that produced the modern movement in both architecture and city planning believed that its efforts would allow urban civilization to emerge from the social prison of the tenement and ghetto, from the political jungle of self-serving, powerful factions, and from the cultural darkness of academic formulas and tradition. It welcomed alliances between social and political reformers to change laws, set standards, and accelerate the momentum of change. But a grave if excusable mistake was committed when city builders assumed that the spatial features of the evolving city would remain stable for many decades, thus justifying the enormous cost and scale of their undertakings. Much that we now seek to preserve and restore was built or planned sixty, eighty, or a hundred years ago. The fact that in many cities, office buildings, commercial structures, transportation facilities, and residential neighborhoods remain in use after fifty or a hundred years does not contradict this point, for their usefulness has been accomplished in most cases only by continual maintenance and modification, factors that their original designers often ignored.

Central to their self-confidence and dominating their legacy to this day was a belief in functionalism, that is, in the appropriateness of architectural and planning solutions to the problems of modern cities and their residents. The classic modern text of design functionalism, *Vers une architecture*, published in 1923 by Le Corbusier, is in Reyner Banham's view "almost the only piece of architectural writing that can be classed among the essential literature of the twentieth century." In his opinion, Le Corbusier's point is not "that an architecture that really matched up to modern technology would have to be radically different from any architecture that had gone before," but "that all the great styles of the past have been the equals of their own contemporary technologies, and that when our own architecture matches our own technology, then we shall have an architecture as good as the Parthenon."[24] Like Lewis Mumford, Le Corbusier found in the work of engineers, particularly in America, a model of the design process he wanted to apply to architecture and city planning.[25]

One example that particularly impressed Le Corbusier as the beautiful product of fundamental design was the steamship.

> In the painful gestation of this age as it forms itself, a need of harmony becomes evident. May our eyes be opened: this harmony already exists, the result of work governed by *economy* and conditioned by physical necessities. . . . If we forget for a moment that a steamship is a machine for transport and look at it with a fresh eye, we shall feel that we are facing an important manifestation of temerity, of discipline, of harmony, of a beauty that is calm, vital and strong. A seriously-minded architect . . . will prefer respect for the forces of nature to a lazy respect for tradition; to the narrowness of commonplace conceptions he will prefer the majesty of solutions which spring from a problem that has been clearly stated. . . . The steamship is the first stage in the realization of a world organized according to the new spirit.[26]

About the profile of the *Larmoricière*, a French Line ship, Le Corbusier commented: "new architectural forms; elements both vast and intimate but on man's scale"; about the promenade deck of the Canadian Pacific liner *Empress of France*: "an Architecture pure, neat, clear, clean and healthy."[27]

How many readers of *Vers une architecture* have realized that Le Corbusier's most cherished examples, directed to the point that a modern architecture which uses technology to meet our needs can be more functional and beautiful than designs which scorn the machine age, were really less functional than they looked? Le Corbusier probably never saw the interiors of the ships he praised, or studied their structural plans. What would he have made of work conditions in the engine rooms?

Until the late nineteenth century, whether at sea under sail or steam propulsion, travelers endured crowded, unventilated rooms, bad water and unpalatable food, strongly disagreeable odors, and upsetting motions. As the number of passengers and the size and speed of ships increased, shipping companies and shipbuilders quickly exploited the fears and prejudices of passengers by making the interior of ships more luxurious. In the process, ocean liners in the period 1870–1935 pointed the way of most building toward environmental control. The use of steel (perhaps earlier at sea than in buildings on land), the elimination of masts, and the adoption of twin screws and ventilation systems allowed engineers to erect a midship superstructure, high in the middle and low at the ends. Carved out as a traveling palace surrounded by open decks, the interior rooms, with glorious paneling and plush upholstery which resembled nothing so much as the houses and hotels the well-heeled traveler had left on land, isolated the passenger from his environment.

The *Oceanic* of 1870 had electric bells to summon the steward, but was still lit by candles. The *Adriatic* of 1872 had a gas light system fed from a gas plant on board ship. The *City of Berlin* sailed in 1878 with half-a-dozen electric light bulbs working. And in 1880, the *Columbia*, an American ship of 3,200 tons, sailed on its maiden cruise from the Gulf Coast to California around the Horn with 115 incandescent lamps; after two months at sea, the lamps had burned a total of 415 hours.[28]

Great ships such as the *Normandie* were once the largest structures ever erected on land. (The construction of the berth for the *Normandie* took longer than the twenty-one months required to erect her hull.) As in the eighteenth century, naval architecture bore a relationship to land construction that most historians of buildings have missed.

As owners and shipbuilders vied to outdo each other in the creation of such great liners as *Aquitania*, *Imperator*, *Olympic*, and, later, *Mauritania*, *Normandie*, *Rex*, and *Queen Mary*, they turned increasingly to the best interior designers of buildings on land. Instead of setting a model that landsmen might emulate, they minimized the differences between ships and buildings on land. Charles Mewès and Arthur Davis, creators of the Ritz hotels, designed the great HAPAG liners. In 1922, addressing the Royal Institute of British Architects, Davis said, "The people who use ships . . . want to forget when they are on a vessel that they are on a ship at all. . . . If we could get ships to look inside like ships, and get people to enjoy the sea, it would be a very good thing; but all we can do, as things are, is to give them gigantic floating hotels."[29] Of course, passengers in steerage could still experience the sea in a more elemental manner.

After the *Titanic* sank, Joseph Conrad lamented that even officers and seamen now thought of ships as floating tanks of steel, and lost a sense of the sea. An extreme case of an unseaworthy interior was that of the *Queen Mary*, whose designers had omitted railings from the corridors and dining tables on the assumption that such a large ship did not need any; they were added after 15,000 dishes were broken in a single season. Ship design began to change when the designers of the *Ile de France* (1927) embraced the avant-garde, when the *Orion* (1935), a P & O liner, made the sight of the sea accessible to the public rooms, and when the *Normandie* (1934) combined the most thoroughly researched hull before the *United States* with a deck design that emphasized the presence of the sea. (The decks, however, were the work of the Paris Beaux-arts architect Expert.)

Design was also influenced by the public's impression of what a ship *should* look like, though of course this had no necessary connection with what made a vessel seaworthy. The third funnel on the *Normandie* was a dummy, erected because the public expected three on a great ship; it contained a dog kennel. Designers numbered, shaped, spaced, and raked smokestacks with more than mere functionalism in mind; they treated sterns, bows, fulls, windows, and superstructures in the same way.[30]

One wonders if Le Corbusier ever visited an engine room or bridge, or looked at a deck plan closely; perhaps he formed his impressions of ships from photographs. (Of course, many engineering structures combine beauty, utility, and economy; but as David Billington has explained in a recent book, an appreciation of their aesthetic effects must be grounded in an analysis of the process of design.)[31]

Ship design is relevant to an understanding of modern city building, but not for the reason Le Corbusier had in mind. He misunderstood the relationship between technology and structure when he perceived the essence of the liner in its external characteristics. Le Corbusier thought that the hull and decks defined the liner's essential characteristics in reference to the maritime environment; he implied that the ship was better adapted to its environment than buildings in cities. But the external features of ships were merely a shell. The essence of the great liner was its machinery supplying motive power, and the environment which mattered was not the watery world outside but the cosseted atmosphere in which passengers traveled inside the ship.

The transformation of the interior of the ship in the 1880s and after gave rise to its outward appearance. Once established in the public mind, the superficial (literally and metaphorically) profile of liners were further refined for commercial purposes, to suggest how much more modern each new liner was than its predecessor. In the process, the fitness of ships for sailing was compromised. A functionalist critique should have called attention to aspects of the ocean liner which were strikingly relevant to the study of buildings: the poor relationship between a ship's interior and its exterior; the critical role of machine-power infrastructure systems for environmental control; the radically different visual and structural treatment given the ship's machinery and its passenger accommodations; the frailty of the ship if any one of its critical systems failed; and the spatially differentiated, hierarchical political, economic, and social order embracing both crews and passengers.

The liner carried its infrastructure systems within it, but the infrastructure systems on which individual buildings depend are spatially diffused and extended to such an extent that their patterns on the macro level appear to have little or no connection with the design of individual buildings. Architectural design and criticism operate on the scale of the individual building, which usually cannot take into account either the networks and systems which sustain a building in its larger urban setting, or the provision of heat, light, and sanitary services within a building.[32] When analyses of infrastructure systems and regulatory mechanisms are omitted from discussion of the quality of urban environments, many of the factors affecting the appearance of individual buildings and districts are overlooked. Such analyses do not hold up to close scrutiny any better than Le Corbusier's seemingly profound and prophetic treatment of ships.

Modern architecture should acknowledge both the extent to which cities are subject to continual economic, social, and technological change, and the extent to which infrastructure systems affect the adaptability of urban space to such forces of change. And planners and administrators should recognize the potential impact of their decisions on the context within which individual buildings and districts will be designed and will evolve.[33]

Le Corbusier and other pioneers of modern design conceived of modern structures as stabilized types, the perfect product of a rational process, rather than as potentially obsolete objects, subject to social, economic, and technological factors. Perhaps architects and planners prefer to ignore the impact of such factors which imply that formal aesthetic values and regularized planning methods are inadequate instruments to clarify and order the modern city. If this problem is to be confronted, then we must look at cities as Le Corbusier tried to look at ships, asking—only more critically—what the appropriate spatial patterns and architectonic forms are. We are scarcely closer now toward discovering how to maximize the opportunities for good design in modern cities than were the founders of the modern movement two generations ago.

ৡ❧ Cycles of Obsolescence and Renewal

The decades since 1880 have produced a variety of new urban structures and spaces, from paved streets and underground utility systems to skyscrapers and subdivisions at the end of the streetcar line or near the superhighway exit, all of which were treated as if the social, economic, and technological conditions to which they corresponded were permanent and so could be fixed into permanent form. Operating as if sudden and unforeseeable changes in the conditions affecting urban living were unlikely, city-building professionals responsible for design, construction, administration, and finance have produced buildings and spaces that are supposed to last a long time.

Yet, every decade of this century has brought substantial changes to the economic, social, political, and cultural activities and aspirations of city residents, changes that call existing urban spatial patterns into question. Building too much too well has produced cities with many prematurely obsolete structures and districts that conform to outdated patterns. Cities can and do change, but the evidence of new suburbs, urban renewal projects, and construction in central business districts only proves how difficult and costly—and frequently, how unsatisfactory—environmental change has become. The inequities and inefficiencies which are so obvious in modern cities arouse public dissatisfaction, but all too often remedial policies and ad hoc solutions have unintended consequences or bring little improvement because they treat only some of the effects of modern city building without altering the city-building process itself.

The problems New York City has confronted in recent years are an example of the extent to which the problem of obsolescence and renewal has been ignored. Writing in 1976, when serving as administrator of New York's Housing and Development Administration, Roger Starr urged New Yorkers to accept "the fact that the city's population is going to shrink" and that the city, to meet its fiscal crisis, must cut back on services. Large parts of the city were exposed to physical decay. "If the city is to survive with a smaller population," wrote Starr, "the population must be encouraged to concentrate itself in the sections that remain alive." In parts of the city which will be abandoned, "stretches of empty blocks may then be knocked down, subway stations closed, and the land left to lie fallow until a change in economic and demographic assumptions makes the land useful once again." New York was overbuilt, argued Starr, because like all modern cities it is burdened by a physical infrastructure that it must maintain and cannot modify easily, even after the assumptions prevalent at the time of its design and construction cease to be valid. New York's assumption was that growth would be constant, and would last forever.[34] Although New York's problems are far from typical, they are the product of city-building processes that are generalized throughout the western world.

The problem of obsolescence and renewal is not only a function of technological and social change, which reduces demand for certain kinds of buildings and locations and increases demand for others, but also of the cost and effort involved in modifying existing buildings and districts compared with the cost and effort of new construction.[35] It is obvious that infrastructure systems contribute to these conditions directly in transportation facilities; and indirectly in the degree to which regulation affects the cost and time of rehabilitation, and in the degree to which certain fixed services cannot be expanded or modified in a building or district to accommodate new uses. In America, the costs of renewal or rehabilitation already began to exceed the economic potential of modernized buildings by the 1930s. Urban development before modern infrastructures encouraged redevelopment and conversion to new uses, but infrastructures have provided people with attractive alternatives to redevelopment.[36]

In one sense, the problem of obsolescence and renewal is a problem of capitalism when the private sector no longer generates sufficient economic growth to make renewal and redevelopment profitable. Yet, public funds are not adequate, either. Around 1950, there were 163 square kilometers of blight in Detroit; yet, between 1937 and 1953, federal funds in the United States cleared only 20 square kilometers in eighty-six cities, or a total of 70,000 substandard living units. Even the major increase in public expenditures in the last twenty years has only made a dent in the problem.[37] Problems in European cities are different in their specific characteristics—for example, much of the blight in the Paris region is in the suburbs rather than the central city—but not in their root causes. Before solutions can be contemplated, there must first come a recognition that the creation of blighted areas which are difficult to renew and redevelop is not just the result of some social, economic, and political factors which converge in particular circumstances, but is instead intrinsic to and inherent in city building in the twentieth century. This is ironic, because modern city-building methods were promoted as a way of eliminating the environmental problems of nineteenth-century cities and of producing more liveable cities in the future. Of course, many buildings and districts built in the twentieth century have been maintained or adapted to new uses over long periods of time. The problem is that many are not.

There are few studies of this aspect of city building. One concept which relates city building to infrastructures is the transport-building cycle. In an article published in 1942, Walter Isard found that building cycles averaged seventeen to eighteen years, and could be related to "the irregular emergence of transport innovation and the jerky development of the transport network."[38] Such a pattern has significance for the problem of obsolescence and renewal after the development of infrastructure systems and building codes encouraged builders to erect buildings that would last much longer than the average cycle.

Another approach using business cycles was taken by George F. Warren and Frank A. Pearson. In a study published in 1937, they found that "skyscrapers are usually built late in building cycles."[39] As a result, buildings would become available "at a time when they cannot be filled," must be refinanced, and are "occupied during the upturn of the next building cycle."[40] The history of office construction in the United States in recent years would show that their analysis is still applicable. One reason offered by Warren and Pearson why the problem of obsolescence and renewal appears to many people to have particular, localized causes rather than generalized, systematic ones is that "the building cycle is so long that few people experience two complete cycles in their business life. Education, to be effective, must therefore be 'book knowledge' rather than experience."[41]

The most complete discussion of this problem to date has been provided by Larry Bourne in his study of Toronto, published in 1967. Bourne treated obsolescence and a failure to rebuild as a modern phenomenon related to the durability of buildings, to space-extensive technologies which reduce the demand for central-city locations, and to other social and economic factors which expand locational choices.[42] Part of the problem, Bourne wrote, is that the physical and economic life spans of buildings are not the same. "The result is that with the passing of time the character and distribution of the building stock of a city become increasingly out-of-phase with the demands of physical space. It is this *conflict between fixed real estate resources and highly mobile social and economic demands* which underlies many of the basic maladjustments in the spatial structure of modern cities."[43]

Arguing in favor of a structure-land-activity theory of urban change, Bourne found that redevelopment is highly selective, superimposes a new pattern on the old, and (at least in Toronto) magnifies differences between land use and density patterns that vary according to age.[44] He concluded that "there is also clearly insufficient knowledge relating to the relationship between social and physical space in the city and the degree to which changes in one are affected by and reflected in the other."[45] Although "concepts, such as concentric and sectoral variations in land use patterns, and invasion and succession as descriptions of expansion in socio-economic zones, are far too simplistic a view of a complex process,"[46] there seems little reason to believe that a more sophisticated model, if one could be constructed, would materially improve the planning process. As Peter Hall has pointed out, better forecasting may not matter as much as a self-critical attitude which includes both qualitative and quantitative analysis, and which treats the prospect of unpredictable changes in society as normal.[47]

Some businesses were quick to spot the hidden costs to themselves of poor adaptability in physical plant. John Stilgoe, finding evidence of systematic analysis of building sites from early phases of infrastructure formation in America, described the development of industrial zones at the edge of urban areas, where "lower real estate prices combined with pre-existing advantages like electric and railroad service to offer powerful inducements to locate," and where there was land for expansion.[48] Flexibility in the internal arrangement of space in industrial buildings is another matter of concern to business because it affects the ease with which a plant can be expanded and new equipment installed. Yet in commercial structures, as in houses, newer buildings are not necessarily more adaptable than older ones. Computers, for example, actually increase the amount of floor space per employee, the burden on ventilation systems, and the volume of space needed for cables. A first-class office building that is ten years old may be less easily adapted than an older property with roomier interiors. Costs for modification vary between $300 and $450 the square meter, depending on how extensive the structural change.[49]

The problem of adaptability and renewal ultimately affects infrastructure systems themselves; indeed, the difficulty of modifying fixed systems such as road networks and sewer and water mains contributes to the problem of obsolescence and renewal in smaller-scale districts and in individual buildings, and reinforces other constraints on adaptability, such as zoning.

The problem of obsolescence and renewal on the scale of infrastructure systems can be seen in modern port facilities. To understand this problem, we should consider changes in the structure of port districts since the eighteenth century, when distinctive waterside districts for shipyards and warehouses developed. The railroad made possible the growth and extension of such districts further away from the city center. No longer did people visit docks for pleasure. Instead, people who wanted to get near water took trains to seaside resorts, whose development was one of the spectacular innovations in nineteenth-century city building. The separation of port from city was functional to the extent that each could grow without getting in the way of the other. But at a certain point the lack of coordination between port development and urban planning can threaten their relationship.

Early in the twentieth century, most ships carried general cargo. Port cities offered shippers warehouses (some with environmental controls for certain commodities) as well as brokerage and factoring services. Time in port for a ship to turn around extended up to two weeks, thus giving sailors time for shore leave; certain waterside districts evolved to meet their various needs. A typical berth, together with warehouse and room for vehicular access, might have extended forty meters inland from the water. Increased traffic was accommodated by multiplying the number and length of wharves, warehouses, and railroad spurs, while electric motors on board ship and on dockside cranes aided stevedores. Warships and ocean liners imposed extraordinary demands, both by virtue of their size and because their time in port was necessarily brief.

Since World War II, a short turnaround has become possible for cargo vessels, too. As ship design changed, new ports had to be built because existing facilities could not be easily adapted. Modern ships require deeper channels and extensive dockside facilities. A typical berth today may be 200 meters long and as deep as the entire portside district of sixty or eighty years ago, and may handle four or five times as much tonnage per linear meter in a year as an older port. To be competitive in Europe, a port with basins and adjacent industrial zone has to be between 35 and 40 square kilometers.[50]

Container traffic also requires heavy volume to be competitive; few ports can generate sufficient volume. Tonnage in European ports from the North Sea to the Black Sea increased from 886 million tons in 1963 to 2 billion tons in the late 1970s. Some of the greatest ports today (Le Havre, Rotterdam) were of secondary importance a century ago; others then of great importance (London, Liverpool) have little trade left; some (Hamburg, Marseille) have maintained their rank. Faster turnaround for ships has also led to the disappearance of dockside districts, formerly characteristic of large ports. In modern big ports today, the port is often larger in area than the city near it, and necessarily is also isolated from it. The nature of modern ports is determined by the imperatives of shipping and ship design. It poses two problems: adapting older, obsolescent port districts; building ports as the demands of shipping change.

In many port cities, older dockside areas are being actively redeveloped or converted to new recreational, residential, and commercial uses. This is happening along riverfronts and coastal seaports in both Europe and America wherever older port developments have left behind facilities such as brick warehouses which can be converted to new uses, and where older ports were located relatively near the city center. (The cost of redevelopment for London's docklands has been estimated at £2 billion.) Obsolete port districts built up before 1945 will be more easily redeveloped by virtue of their structural and locational characteristics than port districts which have been constructed since. In other words, the ports we are building today may be the urban renewal problems of tomorrow.

What is needed is a planning approach which relates decaying waterfronts, protected areas, economic port development, and the rest of the urbanized region to each other. This issue, however, is largely ignored because the spatial organization of port cities has kept port and city planners and administrators from having much to do with each other.[51] The situation in the United States is typical; more than forty federal organizations deal with port development, often duplicating each other, often working at cross purposes. Critical choices over land uses in coastal regions are all too often made on the basis of insufficient knowledge, misapplied information, and irrelevant criteria. To adjudicate between competing claims on coastal space, governments require technology and environmental assessment studies; these are themselves costly, commonly produce inflationary delays in projects, and encourage different groups claiming a need for waterfront space to inflate their demands and attempt to manipulate the regulatory process.

At the same time as the redevelopment of older, functionally obsolete port districts advances, current port facilities must be expanded. Given the scale of modern ports, their development frequently is a matter of years, perhaps (like airports) a decade. In the meantime, trade patterns and shipping techniques can change so much as to compromise the initial design. If in the next ten years ocean trade doubles, there is barely enough time, using present methods, to plan and build the port facilities that will be needed. A major exporting port can cost upwards of $1 billion. In the early 1980s, demand from overseas for American coal exceeded the ability of ports to meet the burden of shipping. Many new port projects were launched, to be completed only years later; if all had been completed, the supply of port facilities might well have exceeded demand. Yet, within two years, the volume of coal exports dropped, encouraging many developers to cancel projects which may one day be needed. As Hoyle and Pinder conclude from a recent world survey:

> The cityports of the future must therefore respond to technological, demographic and socio-economic evolution, and their response must be conditioned by efficient and integrated planning mechanisms designed to reflect not only the interdependence of ports and cities but also the intricacies of the global economy. . . . But improvements in one part of a 'problem complex' can easily make matters worse unless the planning mechanisms involved are sensitive to unexpected, as well as anticipated, results of development strategies. The recent rapid expansion of maritime commerce and port-industrial growth has not produced any radical rethinking of the ways in which cityports should be built, but the creation of new types of cityport and the further development of existing growth centres are as important for those involved in maritime trade as they are for urban and regional authorities.[52]

Perhaps this is unlikely to occur. Those involved in the city-building process no doubt find it easier to adjust their objectives and methods to the infrastructure system, with its patterns of fragmented authority and with its effects on the adaptability of city space, than to criticize the status quo. Along with many professionals, the public may well think that the system can be improved but not replaced. The status quo appears so pervasive that we easily confuse its concrete features with abstract values, such that to question the status quo is to threaten our quality of life.

Yet, the values we cherish took shape in societies that built cities very differently from the way we build them now. As Pierre Dansereau has commented, "There is little sense in arguing these points with many people . . . whose cultural fixation is of the nature of moral certainty and sociopolitical commitment."[53] Yet, a profound reassessment of infrastructure systems, with consequences for people's attitudes, values, and political behavior, may well be inevitable as the infrastructure itself poses ultimate questions of obsolescence and renewal.

Whether from lack of maintenance or from social, economic, and technological obsolescence, many aspects of infrastructure systems will have to be changed, rebuilt, or abandoned in the years to come. Several systems, all at the same time, are approaching the end of their useful life cycles and now require attention: superhighways built twenty-five years ago, sewer and water mains built a half-century ago, bridges built a hundred years ago. The costs involved are seemingly astronomical. Rebuilding one kilometer of central city sewer in England costs £800,000; in northwest England alone, over 1,900 kilometers need replacing. The total bill is so great that public authorities can only undertake needed work piecemeal; but by stretching the work over many years, the total bill will be considerably higher. In New York City, at the current rate, it will take 180 years to repave the city's streets and nearly 300 years to replace its water and sewer mains. Yet, New York should invest over $40 billion in the 1980s to repair, service, and rebuild 1,000 bridges, nearly 10,000 kilometers of paved streets and of water lines, and 4,500 buses.

In many cities, adequate maps of infrastructure systems do not exist, and there are no standardized replacement/repair analyses. "Only the most limited information exists about various techniques to extend the life of present facilities, or about conservation and cost-cutting mechanisms."[54] We know in general that almost half the bridges in the United States must be rebuilt or abandoned, that nearly 320,000 kilometers of highway need some level of capital investment in the 1980s, and that one-half of the nation's communities have wastewater treatment systems that cannot support further economic expansion. The cost of maintaining existing levels of service in America has been put at between $2.5 and $3 trillion, but at current expenditure levels less than a third of the funds will be available.

Rebuilding the urban infrastructure will be vastly more difficult than its original construction because the conditions that favored its construction have altered. First, few cities are growing rapidly; many of the largest, where the infrastructure has deteriorated most severely,

are stable or declining in size. Second, the costs of urban development have risen enormously, a reflection in part of larger scale and
technological complexity. The regulatory framework, very modest
eighty years ago, now imposes additional social costs, retards construction, and politicizes many decisions. Third, energy costs are
likely to rise in real terms. Other resource-related factors may affect
rebuilding. "The losses of obsolescence cannot simply be reckoned as
the costs of rebuilding. . . . They may also include the exhaustion of
resources which cannot be replaced."[55] Finally, public attitudes on
such matters as historical preservation and environmental safety affect
judgments about what should be preserved and what should be rebuilt.

Public recognition of the infrastructure problem has been slow in
coming. As a result, the problems may get much worse before action
is taken. The cost of rebuilding the infrastructure is so high that it
will not be met. Inevitably, some parts will be rebuilt, others abandoned, others modified substantially. Yet, this process of change need
not reduce the quality of life. On the contrary; in the final analysis,
city builders will have to think about how the environment might
be reshaped for the better. Harvey S. Perloff had something important
to say about this:

> [Planning agencies] have become significantly involved with the
> problems of maintaining, improving and building public assets.
> Only if the assumption that urban planning in the latter part of the
> 20th century must focus on the need to bring about major transfor-
> mations in urban life and functions is accepted, and that this, in
> turn, involves detailed attention to the changing urban infrastructure
> and other capital assets, can a new relationship of planning agencies
> to capital programming and budgeting be expected.[56]

But can bureaucratic and regulatory structures that tend to perpetu-
ate the status quo find ways of encouraging flexibility and innovation?

As one commentator wrote recently, "The combination of highly
permanent construction and lack of realism in its conception is one
of the worst legacies our time is leaving to posterity."[57] Admittedly,
evidence that cities have problems because modern city-building

methods interfere with their adjustment to rapid social and technological change is scarcely liable to empirical testing. More research
on specific aspects of the infrastructure and the politics of regulation
must be accomplished; but even if an agenda for research could be
drawn up, twenty years would pass before enough evidence could be
accumulated and analyzed. And even in the unlikely event that specialists could agree on the nature of urban problems and on appropriate remedies, political leaders might be reluctant to act. Change,
when it comes, will likely be sudden, not gradual, in response to an
overwhelming set of problems. By then, knowledge about urban development during the twentieth century may have little prescriptive
value. No one is suggesting that changes in city-building methods
will remedy the ills of the modern city; we are suggesting, rather,
that the changes in city-building methods which occurred since the
1880s are neglected in analyses of modern problems, that older city-
building processes allowed for a greater measure of adaptability, and
that changes in contemporary practices ought not to be put off out of
a belief that modern city-building methods work well enough.

CHAPTER SIX

Total War and Infrastructures

THE EVENTS OF TWO WORLD WARS illuminate normative city-building processes in ways that the study of cities at peace alone cannot. In particular, war has highlighted the importance of adaptability in city building: how people change environments, and how environmental features interfere with or facilitate that process.[1] The relationship between peacetime and wartime city building can only be grasped if urban conditions in both Europe and America in both world wars are discussed together. The history of cities and war in the twentieth century should be the subject of a book by itself, but for the moment attention will be drawn only to the conspicuous role of infrastructures in cities at war. Whatever the implications for contemporary strategic policy of the history of cities and war might be, it seems to me that the proper focus of such a study includes something else: the relevance of urban developments in world war to contemporary urban affairs.

Infrastructure systems have made some cities particularly vulnerable to natural disasters such as floods, earthquakes, tornadoes, and hurricanes. These are cities which have grown in areas of climatic extremes, or where natural conditions are otherwise unsuitable for modern living. Such cities are viable only because of their infrastructure systems. Many people who live in areas where natural disasters are more likely to occur adjust psychologically to such risks, and even discount them altogether. William James, who was in San Francisco at the time of the earthquake, observed that because everyone there had camping skills and had already participated in the creation of a city, the survivors were neither helpless nor hopeless.[2] But today many people who live in vulnerable areas have neither lived through a life-threatening catastrophe nor possess the outlook and skills of pioneers. Little is known in general about which risks people consider acceptable, or about what people learn from disasters, or, as the case may be, why they fail to learn anything.

In America, planners who try to anticipate mass emergencies must cope with a seemingly impossible situation; many natural disasters cannot be predicted with reasonable accuracy until it is too late to manage a mass evacuation. Evacuation of a coastal region from the path of a hurricane may take three days and cost $60,000 a kilometer (on the East Coast of the United States), but the path of a hurricane cannot be predicted three days in advance. In 1980, 950,000 people from Galveston, Texas, were evacuated from Hurricane Allen at a cost of $41 million, but the hurricane did not hit. Evacuation costs, however, are modest compared with the cost of a storm; in August 1983, Hurricane Alicia brought damages of $1 billion in the Houston area and left 200,000 or more people without essential services for days. Forecasting uncertainties are not likely to be resolved in the near future, and, in any case, some natural disasters will come without warning altogether. Moreover, disasters "produce the paradox that the need for information rises at precisely the moment when the normal channels of communication may be destroyed."[3]

People who live with the risk of a natural disaster may not take seriously the extent to which their land-use patterns or building techniques can affect the degree of damage sustained during a disaster, but vulnerable cities nevertheless try to protect themselves through planning, public education, and changes in spatial layout and building codes which promise to reduce loss of life and property. As Michael Barkun has observed, historically people may have grasped the possibility of understanding and controlling the causes and effects of disasters before the operational means of control were available.[4]

From this perspective, it would seem that society has made more progress in limiting the risks associated with natural disasters than with man-made catastrophes, of which war remains the supreme example. The severity of a disaster is affected by the degree to which people are prepared to cope with its effects and associated stresses, by the latent adaptability of the environment and the degree to which resources can be recovered or replaced with substitutes, and by the extent to which people comprehend the reasons for the disaster. Homeostatic disasters do not interrupt the development of a society; a return to the status quo ante is not a problem. A return to equilibrium is difficult after a metastatic disaster, that is, an artificial catastrophe with unclear spatial and temporal boundaries such as conventional war; and is impossible after a hyperstatic disaster, which obliterates discernible spatial and temporal boundaries and destroys systems on a continental or global scale.[5]

The following discussion of cities and world war has been organized around four propositions.

1. The strains of war affected cities far from the front as well as those in the line of fire. These strains were partly a function of infrastructures, which could not be adjusted rapidly to meet new conditions. A combination of government intervention and private initiative alleviated many strains, but professional city builders and their constituencies, concerned about the postwar implications of wartime measures, restricted government actions.

In its impact on cities as in so much else, World War I had not conformed to expectations. The rapid field movements of the early battles damaged numerous medieval and Renaissance sites, but the scale of damage was comparable to what had been sustained in previous wars. Ypres, Arras, Reims, and Lille witnessed something newer and more sinister: battles lasting nearly as long as the war itself, occupation by the invader, and a civilian population left increasingly to its own devices, finding shelter in caves, cellars, attics, and shacks. These cities would have to be rebuilt because damage had been indiscriminate and widespread. Along the static front, the war utterly transformed city and countryside, and subsequently brought into being a new man-made landscape which included cemeteries, monuments, and memorials.

A realization that World War I was unlike other wars was slow in coming. Not until the war was well underway did states begin to modify economic, social, and political structures to sustain total war or begin to prepare for the reconstruction of war-damaged areas. In most combatant countries, estimates of needed supplies and of production goals were constantly rewritten, tens of millions of workers were relocated, and goods and services reallocated; yet, with the exception of Russia, the productive capacity of national economies never reached their maximum limits, so great and rapid was their expansion, so enormous was their potential.

The economic, social, and political conditions of world war affected cities far from the front as much as cities in the battle zone. The spectacular effects of aerial bombardment in World War II have blinded us to the more subtle but no less important changes which accompanied population migration, wartime inflation, industrial development, and the introduction of new bureaucratic mechanisms in cities everywhere during both world wars.

Cities in France between 1914 and 1918 provide excellent examples.[6] In Bourges, an influx of refugees, workers, and eventually of Americans swelled the population from 46,000 to over 110,000. The reconstruction of the city's sewer and water infrastructure, incomplete in 1914, was hastened, but a shortage of maintenance personnel and of funds as well as a massive increase in heavy traffic meant that the condition of the city's streets remained bad.

The increase of industrial workers was greatest in Paris, more than doubling between January 1915 and April 1916; city and suburbs grew by 300,000 people during the war. Their needs stimulated a demand for new kinds of public welfare services, such as medical clinics, child-care facilities at factories, cooperative restaurants, and public housing. Inflation (390 percent above the 1914 base by 1919) forced the government to provide 162 outlets where people could buy subsidized food. The modern welfare state grew faster during war and acquired new dimensions. The city took on an explicitly military character as capital of the Allied cause. Soldiers and administrators from many nations enhanced its cosmopolitan tone; the renaming of streets (rue Guynemer, l'avenue Galliéni, l'avenue Georges V, etc.) interwove Paris's wartime role into its urban fabric; and the burial of the unknown soldier under the Arc de Triomphe on 28 January 1921 transformed its most important monument and spatial axis into a national symbol of sacrifice and victory. Posters, announcements, charity drives, even museum shows introduced war into the media and into high and low culture.

In the port of Rouen, a British center because the rail lines toward its sector (many of which were newly built for the purpose) terminated there, tonnage increased from 1,500,000 tons in 1914 to 4,215,000 tons in 1918, and the length of railway tracks in the port area more than doubled, from 47 to 113 kilometers. As many as 30,000 British troops passed through Rouen each day, and the city's population increased altogether by 30 percent.

War accentuated Paris's role as an industrial center at the expense of other cities, but it increased competition among ports. Marseille had experienced congestion before the war and already had a complicated plan for expansion underway. During the war half of the storage area in Marseille was requisitioned. To expand France's maritime trading facilities, the French and Americans channeled funds to Marseille's competitors, such as Bordeaux. There, new port facilities were constructed by 8,000 blacks working in three eight-hour shifts for five months with supplies imported from America. Between March and August 1918, nearly 100,000 American soldiers landed in Bordeaux and after the war, 50,000 officers and 36,000 men returned to the States from there.

In America in World War I, the United States government planned to build and own sixty-seven housing projects for 300,000 persons in forty-seven cities affected by housing shortages; but only twenty-seven projects for some 6,000 families were completed, and none earlier than January 1919. The program cost the government $52 million, but income from the sales of these projects netted only $27 million. The failure to coordinate housing needs and war production in the United States reinforced negative attitudes toward the role of the federal government in housing.[7] In America, most of the housing projects had been laid out without the basic infrastructure of civilian life.

In England, government housing for workers in munitions factories involved provision of a high fixed-cost infrastructure.[8] (But the English also were willing to use temporary expedients, as when a rail-ferry terminal was developed at Richeborough near Sandwich; twenty-two million officers and men passed through Richeborough during the war without Richeborough acquiring the means to grow into a new city in peace.)

In America in World War II, 53 percent of wartime civilian housing needs was satisfied by more efficient use of existing structures, 5 percent by private conversion, 1 percent by public conversion, 21 percent by new construction, 15 percent by publicly financed temporary housing, and 5 percent by new, publicly funded permanent construction.[9] Government programs often became effective too late in the war to matter very much. The expedient solutions of emergency building cut profoundly against everything planners, administrators, private builders, and architects believed to be sound practice; such solutions also were opposed by local realtors and homeowners, and upset townspeople. Many workers lived as best they could: in trailers, parks, barns, boarding houses, even alternating occupancy of the same dwelling by doubling up with another family.[10] Poor living conditions in the vicinity of the Willow Run, Michigan, bomber factories were associated with a high turnover in the labor force, low morale, and high absenteeism. Production at the factories increased only by cutting the number of man-hours to make a plane, by lengthening the workday, and by increasing the size of the work force.

Massive population shifts related to the war raised conflicts over the degree to which national government should be held financially responsible for ameliorating local (and perhaps temporary) conditions. Many communities were less concerned about appalling social and economic conditions affecting workers—in the hope that workers would move once the war was over—than they were about the impact government programs to alleviate such conditions might have on postwar development. There was a widespread tendency in combatant countries to minimize war-related changes in the belief that war would be short, and in the hope that there would be quick return to prewar normality. While some degree of strain was no doubt inevitable, living conditions in many communities were probably much worse than they need have been.

The strains of total war affected cities in several ways. The inelasticity of the housing supply affected the siting of new factories and the expansion of existing ones. War-induced inflation stimulated a demand for rent control and housing subsidies. The long hours required of factory workers and the great distances many of them had to travel meant that normal patterns of daily life were impossible.

New railroad lines and port facilities had to be built which threatened to alter the comparative advantages of some cities after the restoration of peace. Wartime experience therefore impressed upon the public and the government how complex and interrelated are the variables in modern industrial-urban systems.

Infrastructure systems affected military production by causing or exacerbating delays and shortages, and by complicating the daily lives of workers. Such issues meant that housing and other urban services were as critical to the war effort as the production of steel or rubber. But whereas governments attempted to coordinate planning of industrial production, they frequently lacked the political energy to tackle less glamorous aspects of city life. War gave government the opportunity to extend its administrative and regulatory jurisdiction over more aspects of urban life, and to intervene directly in the construction of housing. Such actions on the part of government were often rationalized as necessary for the duration of the emergency. Political speeches resounded with good intentions, but the postwar implications of wartime changes in such matters as housing and transportation created bureaucratic, ideological, and political conflicts that defined the limits to which local communities would make sacrifices for the national cause.

2. Military builders succeeded far better than their civilian counterparts in meeting the demands of war, but their methods lacked heuristic value in the eyes of civilian city builders.

War led to conspicuous examples of the effectiveness of improvisation and decentralized decision making. Nowhere was this more evident than in the provision of military camps. In contrast to the dismal record of the United States government in providing housing for workers stands its record in building camps for soldiers. At the start of each world war the government was unprepared for mobilization. Collaboration between civilian experts and military officers produced streamlined administrative and design procedures. Ironically, it seemed that in this case the government used its enhanced war powers to delegate great authority and decentralize decision making.

Army camps in the United States during World War I were built by over 200,000 workmen using 300,000 linear kilometers of lumber, 7,360 square kilometers of roofing paper, and similarly huge quantities of other materials. The largest camp housed 45,500 men; a total of 1.7 million men passed through thirty-two camps, four ports of embarkation, and other centers. In addition, the government provided 276 square kilometers of industrial storage, a slightly larger amount of munitions storage, and 3,900 meters of docks. All this was done in a matter of months because design and construction proceeded simultaneously, a process which deviated not only from civilian practice but from peacetime military practice as well. Such methods apparently worked better during war than normative procedures during peace. There was, however, no incentive to institutionalize this achievement either in the peacetime military or in the civilian sector.

The scale of military building in World War II exceeded that of the previous conflict.[11] Military architecture was continuously adaptive to rapid changes in the availability of labor and materials, and responsive to environmental conditions from the arctic to the tropics and to such diverse requirements as standardization, salvageability, and indestructability. In World War I, the Canadians had designed the Nissen hut, a shelter which weighed one ton and could be erected in four hours by four men; 20,000 of these structures served a half million people by 1918. The American quonset hut in World War II was based on the Nissen hut; adaptable to forty-eight different uses, over 150,000 were built. At the other extreme of durability was the Atlantic Wall, a composite military line of 9,300 fortified works; four of the largest casemates needed 14,400 cubic meters of concrete, yet even these were completed in ten weeks. Huge labor forces and prefabrication were critical to the completion of many projects, some of which, like the English army and navy coastal forts, were unprecedented. Military architecture was good utilitarian building, accommodating people and their collective purposes, and coordinated to and sustaining the concentrated, precise application of both manpower and material to sometimes specific, sometimes unpredictable objectives.

Camps for millions of soldiers were built by compressing design and construction into incredibly short periods. The Farragut Training

Station for 45,000 sailors in the U.S. Navy was representative.[12] The contract was let in July 1942. Construction involved moving 982,000 cubic meters of earth, and building 63.6 kilometers of road, 20.8 kilometers of railroad track, 41.6 kilometers of water mains, and 32 kilometers of electricity transmission lines. The entire project was completed in early March 1943. The U.S. Navy alone spent over $9 billion on public works programs between 1941 and 1945, usually on contracts which eliminated competition on the basis of cost, placed the burden of risk on the government, and permitted construction to commence before the design phase of a project had been completed. The useful life-span planned for most military buildings was for the duration of the war, estimated at five years. As a result, little maintenance was planned once construction stopped. The U.S. Army acquired 32,000 square kilometers of land during World War II, and constructed over 3,000 projects which contained nearly 93 million square meters of buildings, 100,224 kilometers of roads, 36,160 kilometers of electricity cables, 20,000 kilometers of sewer lines, 6,828 kilometers of railroad lines, 3,576 kilometers of gas lines, and 2,444 kilometers of steam lines. The U.S. Army was also directly responsible for the construction of industrial plants worth $3 billion and covering a larger surface area than the combined areas of New York, Chicago, Philadelphia, and Detroit. Yet, when the drive for mobilization had begun in 1940, the government had been unprepared to design, supervise, and construct on this scale.

Some designers such as Albert Kahn, who had created factories that were truly modern in the extent to which they enhanced the manufacturing process, understood the potential contribution of civilian building to the war effort. Kahn designed factories as a totally integrated architectonic complex which had to be as adaptable to change as the manufacturing process is to innovation. Although he built some 2,000 factories in his career, including the great River Rouge complex of Ford, the war brought Kahn his greatest challenge.

In 1939, the Glenn L. Martin Company asked Kahn to design an aircraft assembly plant north of Baltimore that could accommodate a ninety-meter wingspan—at a time when no building with a flat roof ninety meters wide had ever been built. Kahn managed the task, and the factory assembled the aircraft with the largest wingspan in the war. On 5 February 1939, Martin requested an additional building to be ready for use by 1 May. Relying on unprecedented measures, Kahn planned some parts of the factory to be completed before plans for other parts were ready. The building was finished on 23 April, and production commenced four days later.

The Chrysler Tank Arsenal in Warren, Michigan, was designed by Kahn with maximum flexibility because the design of the tank to be assembled in it was not yet complete, but the first tank was constructed there five months ahead of schedule, even before the plant was finished; eventually the factory produced 25,059 units, and the extra five months production gained may have made the difference in the defeat of the Germans in North Africa. From December 1939 until December 1942, Kahn's firm designed over $200 million worth of construction.[13]

Neither the contribution of wartime factory design to the massive increase in output, which no one in 1939 had thought possible, nor its effect upon postwar economic development need further elaboration. What must be emphasized, however, is how little was learned about housing and infrastructures by example from the construction of military camps and factories.

The critical difference between military and civilian city building in war began outside the factory and camp. Infrastructure systems of transportation and communications had too many break points at which merchandise and information had to be handled and manipulated in order to be expedited, and the systems themselves did not connect with each other efficiently. Supplies needed to modify urban and interurban infrastructures were often needed immediately as war material. Strategies to organize these systems better during the war only revealed how little managers of different systems knew about how each system interacted with and affected other systems. Somehow people learned to manipulate these systems in ways they were not designed to be used, but little was learned from the experience about the value of adaptability and improvisation.

   3. The dependence of cities upon infrastructure systems and regulatory frameworks made them appear vulnerable to physical destruction. Strategic bombing assumed a breakdown in morale or in mili-

tary operations would follow from the destruction of vital infrastructures. But the effects of bombing were rarely severe. Military planners, however, discounted evidence of the ineffectiveness of bombing.

The ability of cities to function despite their handicaps should have brought observers of the urban scene to realize that people can improvise successfully with little help from the professionals of the city-building world. Instead, military strategists and statesmen, acting on the assumption that modern cities cannot function if their infrastructure systems are destroyed, ordered the bombing of cities (from Rotterdam to Nagasaki) from 1940 to 1945. From this perspective, the modern city appears destined to tragedy. Its very characteristics—those features that distinguish it from cities in earlier periods—have made the modern city more vulnerable to destruction in war.

The birth of aviation gave rise to attempts to outlaw aerial bombardment. In 1907, the United States, Norway, Great Britain, Switzerland, and the Low Countries declared their rejection of aerial bombardment; but their statements at the Hague Conference did not amount to a legal prohibition. The Hague War Land Regulations of 1907, however, did prohibit "attack or bombardment, by any means whatever, of towns, villages, habitations, or buildings which are not defended." This statement was later refined to include places which, though not defended, "had within them military works, military or naval establishments, depots of arms or war material," or even just factories of military utility.[14] Jurists tried hard to distinguish between civilians and combatants, but strategists knew that in total war such a distinction was specious. The precedent had already been set in World War I by naval blockade and submarine warfare based on assumptions of the inseparability of home front and battle front.

The overriding objectives of bombardment for Germany, Britain, and the United States had been to avoid costly losses of soldiers in an invasion—a German invasion of Britain, a British invasion of Germany, or an American invasion of Japan. In an attempt to defeat an enemy, governments became willing to make civilians suffer as much as public opinion would allow, in the hope that they would put pressure on their leaders. The civilian was presumed to lack fortitude and resourcefulness, a view which may have been reinforced in the military mind by the social and physical problems of many potential conscripts from large industrial centers. The line of reasoning which consciously or unconsciously led to large, deliberate air raids against cities assumed that civilians were heavily dependent upon numerous services. Assuming further that the complex fabric of housing, transportation, food supply, and communications and power systems could be easily disrupted, and that once damaged could not be repaired quickly, it followed that bombing could break civilian morale, and hence the will of the enemy to fight. The enemy would be forced to choose between maintaining his fighting capacity or diverting supplies and manpower to the home front. The few bombing incidents of World War I gave rise to expectations of social and economic collapse if bombing were heavy. But the bombing scenario was flawed in one critical respect. Bombing, however sudden or unexpected in World War II, came to cities whose social, economic, and political fabric had already been disrupted by months or years of war. People were better prepared to endure and adapt than military planners expected.

Although military planning was affected by such considerations as the range of bombers, the quality of bombsights, and the probable effectiveness of ground and air defenses, from the beginning of bombing—that is, from World War I and the interwar years—a fundamental choice existed between area bombing and precision bombing. Area bombing was rationalized on the assumption that the city constituted a single, functioning entity. It therefore did not matter whether production was interrupted by destroying the workers's housing, factories, or critical infrastructure systems such as railroad facilities and power generators. Precision bombing operated on the premise that certain factories produce goods which are more critical to a war effort than others, and that certain transportation facilities play a critical role in the organization of supply in a given region.

Although the Royal Naval Air Service had engaged in limited precision bombing in 1916, the development of this approach was largely the work of instructors at the U.S. Army Air Service Tactical School in Langley, Virginia, in the 1930s. Their efforts matured into the Air War Plans Division in 1941; and eventually into the United

States Strategic Bombing Survey, to evaluate the effectiveness of precision bombing and the selection of targets (with the possibility that such analysis might affect the planning of industrial establishments and even cities in the future).[15]

Precision bombing even took into account the need to avoid destroying monuments of importance. Lists of buildings of artistic or historic importance in each European country were made at Harvard University in early 1943, and large-scale maps were prepared of selected areas and cities showing their locations. Using aerial photographs, information was prepared for the use of flight commanders, but with results on the ground that were less than completely successful.

In theory the distinction between precision and area bombing appears significant, and it certainly had major implications for the technical and strategic organization of an air force; but it should not be drawn too sharply. The presence of so many industries and bases in or near heavily urbanized areas made discrimination between purely civilian and purely military aspects of urban order difficult if not impossible. Both precision and area bombing focused upon urban infrastructure systems, and even the USSBS shifted its attention from a narrow analysis of physical damage to a broader investigation into social and pyschological matters, or the constituents of morale.

The effects of bombing were not as great as air strategists thought they would be. After the Blitz, an index of activity in British towns was compiled to evaluate psychological and physical damage. This study showed how limited were the consequences of bombing. The great German raids on Coventry—a city where housing and factories were truly intermingled—dropped one ton of bombs per 800 inhabitants. Overnight, economic activity in Coventry fell 63 percent but recovered in thirty-five days. From this the British deduced that successive attacks over a period of months at one-month intervals would be necessary to reduce activity to zero. Morale did not collapse in Britain, even though prewar planning exercises had indicated to the government that aerial bombardment of British cities would be devastating.[16] Casualties were much more modest than planners had estimated, and the loss of production did not strain the British economy to the breaking point. The damage caused by bombs, therefore, only raised the level of stress, but both before and after bombing that level was a manageable one.

In the City of Westminster, one of London's central districts, 1,047 high-explosive bombs, a smaller number of miscellaneous bombs, and thousands of small incendiary bombs killed 786 persons and seriously injured 1,338. From the rubble of destroyed buildings and the refuse of daily life, needed supplies were salvaged: over 3,000 tons of iron, 1,230,000 bricks, 13,113 tons of waste paper, and enough processed food recycled from kitchen waste (throughout the war) to feed 31,000 pigs. Total debris carted away weighed 332,340 tons.

Much of the worst physical damage occurred to the street surface and its subterranean utilities. A representative of the city engineer controlled the many tasks that had to be performed at each site of damage. First, the site had to be cleared of debris and mud, and the extent of lateral damage to underground utilities determined. Priorities were fixed, but usually began at the bottom—often six meters down—and advanced upward from the sewer mains to the electricity and telephone cables and the gas and water mains, until the road surface itself could be refinished. Complications were frequent, though interruptions of service did not last long. One bomb that fell near Piccadilly in April 1941 damaged two 46-centimeter, one 18-centimeter, two 15-centimeter, and three 10-centimeter water mains; one 51-centimeter, one 46-centimeter, one 31-centimeter, two 15-centimeter, and two 10-centimeter gas mains; various electricity cables, duct lines, and telephone cables; 31.5 meters of 1.65-meter sewer, 4.5 meters of 31-centimeter sewer, and three street drains. Repairs were not fully complete until September.[17]

The British did learn that incendiary bombs were worse than explosive bombs and that more man-hours of production were lost from destruction of gas, electricity, and water supplies than from the physical destruction of factories. (Much engineering data about the strength of building materials of great value for the postwar era were gathered from the results of bombing.) Yet the British never reevaluated their assumptions about the probable effects of bombing German cities in light of the limited consequences of German air attacks against British cities.

British bombing of German cities was supported by such arguments as the need to help Russia and a desire to retaliate after German raids against England. It was also justified with arguments that the German economy was different from the British in ways that would magnify the effects of bombing. The British assumed that the German economy was operating at full capacity or, in other words, was stretched to the point that damage from bombing would seriously disrupt it. Further, the British assumed that the German population was already suffering alienation from the Nazi regime and could be provoked into a crisis of morale by bombing. The percentage of houses destroyed in German cities over 100,000 inhabitants ranged from 3 to 60 percent.

Arguably the worst raid was on Hamburg in late July 1943. The firestorm that erupted there at 1:20 A.M. on 28 July destroyed an area of 10.32 square kilometers and 16,000 dwellings; 56 percent of the city's housing was destroyed, 900,000 persons became homeless, and 44,600 civilians died (nine out of ten deaths were in the firestorm). Yet, there was no starvation, no rebellion. Within days, communications between Hamburg and other large German cities had been restored.[18] Electricity supply exceeded demand in Hamburg by the ninth day after the bombing.

Had Britain been able to destroy simultaneously several German cities on such a scale, perhaps the awful consequences promised by the advocates of strategic bombing might have resulted. Even the American bombing of Tokyo on 9–10 March 1945, which achieved a level of destruction greater than the atomic bombs dropped on Hiroshima and Nagasaki, did not produce terror and break morale. (In Tokyo, 20.76 square kilometers of built-up area were destroyed; this included 63 percent of the commercial area. Over one million people were left homeless, 84,000 dead, and 41,000 wounded.) British bombing of German cities was based on flawed assumptions about economic and social conditions in Germany.

Fred Iklé's book, *The Social Impact of Bomb Destruction* (1950), written with the possible consequences of nuclear war in mind, drew upon extensive analyses of the effects of bombing in World War II. His book explains why the effects of bombing on morale and production were much less than anticipated. The ratio of consumers to resources is very elastic; the greater the elasticity, the better destruction losses can be cushioned. But repeated attacks leave an ever smaller amount of resources to cushion the impact.[19]

In World War II, the level of physical destruction as a percentage of building stock was much greater than the level of casualties as a percentage of the population. In German cities, 25 percent of the housing stock had to be destroyed before heavy civilian casualties occurred; in Japanese cities, the threshold was lower, at only 10 percent of the housing stock, a difference attributable to differences in building materials and structure. Manpower loss was not equivalent to housing destruction, as strategists thought it would be, because survivors were reaccommodated within the remaining housing supply, albeit at higher densities. In other words, housing was more elastic than other resources, and hence its destruction was less disruptive. Even the destruction of infrastructure systems which strategists thought were highly vulnerable and indispensable, such as water supply systems, did not produce epidemics.

Wartime assumptions about the consequences of bombing on cities were flawed because they were grounded in distorted perceptions of how cities function. Statesmen and soldiers alike operated on the assumption that the interconnections between social, economic, and political activities in modern cities are rigid, inflexible, and heavily dependent upon fixed, physical service systems that are difficult and costly to repair. Yet, the record of the war itself showed that people in cities were much more resourceful and adaptive than the advocates of either area or precision bombing assumed they would be.

> 4. War increased the scope for government regulation and planning in the postwar era, but the high hopes that planning on a larger scale would solve urban problems were frustrated after the war.

Some wanted to think of the war as an interruption in the development of society and the state; yet, the political rhetoric of war aims also encouraged others to hope that the war would bring about permanent social and political change. Already in the years preceding World War I, the planning movement had reached a peak of activity. In 1906, the New York Bureau of Municipal Research was incorporated; in 1908, the Berlin-Charlottenburg Seminar on City Planning opened; and that same year in Paris, 4,000 people attended a meeting on planning for the French capital. In 1909, the first National Conference on City Planning and the Problems of Congestion was convened in Washington; the British Parliament approved a limited town planning act; the University of Liverpool established the world's first academic department of city planning; Harvard University pioneered an American course in city planning principles; and Burnham and Bennett published their great *Plan of Chicago*.

The return to pre-1914 norms of city building was in fact impossible because even before the war those norms were changing. The war in most countries left social and economic conditions which compelled government to intervene and regulate the cost and provision of housing, public services, and major infrastructure systems. To redeem wartime political promises and to regularize their powers of intervention and control, governments embraced city planning. Planning laws were passed around the end of the war, not just for areas where the level of physical destruction compelled reconstruction but for all cities above a certain (modest) size. These laws made municipalities responsible for the provision of a comprehensive plan.

Because the planning laws did not provide for systematic land policy, there was unregulated suburban development by speculative builders. The case of Paris is perhaps typical but spectacular; a competition for a plan to use the land around Paris where the fortifications stood was announced in 1919, but the fortifications were not fully demolished until 1932. Each of the plans submitted called for costly, large-scale projects and assumed the land would remain vacant during construction. In the meantime, parcels of land from Paris's edge were developed piecemeal for institutional use and housing, eventually supporting 15,000 houses and nearly 900 factories.[20]

According to plans from competitions staged in the 1920s and 1930s, the Rond Point de la Defense and the Porte Maillot, along the splendid western axis of the Arc de Triomphe, were supposed to have been planned as an ensemble; they were built up after the 1950s with skyscrapers and a convention center respectively, with little concern for their impact on that spatial axis.[21] More research is at last being done on cities and villages that were reconstructed after the war, and about decisions to retain or alter parts of the prewar city.[22]

A new kind of citizen met the challenge of city life disrupted by war. In cities attacked from the air, people developed their own strategies for coping with the numerous petty but critical disruptions in daily life. From Belfast to Bucharest, people managed somehow to maintain an extraordinary degree of normality. Yet beneath the outward appearance of daily life, a more profound change occurred that may have sustained the civilian in his city. By necessity, the civilian became more involved in maintaining his city and in supplying for himself many services he had previously received with little or no effort on his part. Whether in civil defense work in Hamburg or London, or as part of a resistance network in Copenhagen or Lyon, or as part of a labor force in Seattle or Glasgow, people acquired and exploited a more intimate knowledge of a city's social and technological complexities. In England, the poet Stephen Spender glimpsed an awakening of civic consciousness as people learned to act effectively on their own and in groups, and acquired pride along with responsibility. He hoped that the attitudes and values of civilian life in the war might be retained after the restoration of the peace.[23] In America, under Eleanor Roosevelt's leadership, civil defense was similarly considered to be the nucleus of a movement to revitalize community life after the war.[24]

Unfortunately, with few exceptions, the return to peace and the tasks of reconstruction, rehabilitation, and redevelopment also restored familiar political incentives, financial methods, and planning concepts. If anything, World War II had a ratchet effect upon prewar trends toward greater governmental and regulatory control and toward more reliance upon infrastructure systems. During the war, some administrators, planners, and architects glimpsed the implications of wartime improvisation for peacetime city building; but after the war, conditions were highly unfavorable to innovative building methods and planning approaches. The peace of 1945, even more than the peace of 1918, gave government the opportunity to set stronger planning mechanisms in place. But frequently the kind of planning that was enshrined in law was far less radical and ambitious than what visionary reformers contemplated in time of war.

In America, for example, the work of the National Resource Planning Board as leader of postwar urban redevelopment and neighborhood conservation was short-lived. Conservatives and liberals disagreed over the extent to which urban planning should be limited to the provision of low-income public housing and over jurisdictional issues in the American federal system.[25] Eleven states had enacted redevelopment laws by 1945, but only two had appropriated funds. The kind of planning that emerged after the war gave far more emphasis to the provision of physical services and far less to social, economic, and political conditions than planners with a holistic vision of their profession hoped would be the case. The reasons why this happened may be primarily political, but if so it would appear that the isolation of planners from national politics and popular culture contributed to their defeat.

In Europe, at least initially, the prospects for a radical break in city-building methods looked better. The effect of aerial bombardment had been to clear away vast tracts of land all at once; normal peacetime city-building methods were too restrictive to exploit such opportunities. The areas destroyed included many structures that should have been preserved in any redevelopment scheme, but also included thousands of slum dwellings and technologically obsolescent industrial and commercial structures which should have been removed in any case. The level of destruction was of course awesome: 1,500,000 dwellings and 91,000 factories in France, for example.

Rebuilding could not be postponed while designs were created and revised. It began, therefore, at a time when the economic, technological, and social characteristics of the postwar era were difficult to perceive, and when the availability of trained labor and quality materials was low. By working fast, builders and planners inevitably built cities that more closely resembled prewar conditions than might otherwise have been the case. Yet because they built structurally sound buildings, postwar cities could not be easily modified once their limitations became apparent and the means to improve them became available.[26]

The housing supply in Europe and America grew more rapidly after 1945 than after 1918 because capital funds were more plentiful, not because building methods or designs had changed in any fundamental way. Governments saw the need to rebuild cities as an opportunity to extend their control over cities, but tended to limit their direct responsibilities to the provision of buildings. Urban policy since 1945 has been shaped by other policies involving labor, education, the environment, health, and social security which have had unintended consequences for cities, far more than by any deliberate, coherent program.

Resistance to innovation has been a conspicuous feature of modern city building. Each world war loosened old habits; provided ample evidence that peacetime city-building practices were unable to adjust urban environments to rapid social, technological, and political change; and aroused expectations of higher living standards for the future. Yet, the return to peace frustrated hopes that the war would make better city building possible. The poor quality of postwar design in Europe is understandable on its own terms as a reflection of that period, but it defined environmental values and conditions that have been easier to criticize than to improve.

Much of the stress in cities related to war can be attributed to relative inelasticity and inadaptability in city-building patterns. City planners and administrators did not realize that the conditions of war produced strains which were in many ways equivalent to the pressures of social, economic, and technological change in times of peace. Precisely because the war was an emergency, wartime measures, taken as expediency dictated, lacked heuristic or model value in the eyes of city-building professionals, who did not realize that the failure of normative city-building methods during war was not a function of the war but of the fundamental inability of infrastructure systems to respond efficiently to forces of change that may be as strong in peace as in war.

The potential for changing the permanent infrastructure system and for moderating its effects on city space and urban activities has yet to be determined. When significant technological innovations produced the infrastructure system of city building in the first place, cities at the end of the nineteenth century still possessed a high latent capacity to absorb physical change at low cost. The evidence of two world wars substantiates our view that modern urban environments have become less adaptable, and that modern city building places great—and perhaps exaggerated—importance upon the provision and regulation of fixed, physical facilities.

The infrastructure system has narrowed the quality of life to a matter of counting the number of parking spaces or toilets per capita, but at least it has succeeded at making parking spaces and toilets widely available. It has also made the challenge of innovation more difficult and costly. The risks of not meeting that challenge are manifest in the mounting social, financial, and environmental burdens of declining and expanding cities alike. Attempts to slow the rate of change through government regulation are increasingly perceived to be inflationary, to give unwarranted power to well-organized special-interest groups, and to reduce the growth of productivity without significantly improving the effectiveness of urban policies. People are coming to realize what they should have learned by 1945, that the rapid rate and unpredictable course of modern civilization is of vital significance to the city-building arts.

CHAPTER SEVEN

Toward the Future

NOTHING MAY LOOK LESS LIKELY to change in a radical way than the status quo in city building, but nothing else may be more likely. The nineteenth century corresponded to the First Industrial Age of iron, steam, and coal; the twentieth, so far, to the Second Industrial Age of glass, petroleum, and electricity. What the Third Industrial Age will be like remains to be seen; given the discontinuous, intermittent pattern in the evolution of basic technological innovations, most of the innovations to be produced in the second half of the twentieth century may only appear in the 1980s and 1990s.[1] It will be surprising if the transition from the Second to the Third Industrial Age does not bring with it a mutation in city building as significant as the one that occurred nearly a century ago. No one can predict what city building will be like in thirty years, just as no one in the 1870s could have predicted conditions prevailing at the end of the nineteenth century.

The alternative futures of city building and technology have been characterized as the choice between "hard" and "soft" approaches. City building in the twentieth century has provided "hard" solutions which emphasize fixed, physical structures, regulatory frameworks, and technology as machinery. The pursuit of "hard" solutions has located power over the environment in government agencies and private-sector corporations, and has minimized the extent to which users can provide for their own needs. "Soft" solutions would favor individual initiative, social innovation, improvisation, institutional flexibility, and designs for alternative futures.[2]

It is tempting to depict "soft" solutions not only as the antithesis of current city-building practices but also as the expression of an antitechnological ideology. But technological innovation might itself favor "soft" solutions if some of the forecasts of how microcomputers could alter work roles and patterns are accurate. Technology will be important whether "hard" or "soft" solutions are pursued. The difference between them is in the kinds of technologies and skills that become indispensable. "Hard" solutions may continue to dominate city building, but if history has anything to teach us it is that we must be careful about extrapolating current trends into the future.

If a new phase of city building commences it will begin with a period of transition during which several approaches and directions may well compete for dominance. Such a period of transition will place a premium on improvisation and imagination. Whether or not the next phase of city building enhances the latent adaptability of environments, the transition to this phase will require major readjustments in existing environments.

Because contemporary city-building practices have made change more difficult and time-consuming, the first thing we must do is acknowledge how ill-prepared we are for a period of major environmental change. As Lewis Mumford wrote fifty years ago, "Renewability in architecture does not mean designing buildings that must collapse in fifteen years: still less does it mean making pre-fabricated houses whose superficial shape will undergo as many ephemeral and foolish style-changes as the motor-car. . . . Renewability means the design of buildings in such materials, and by such technical methods, that they may be easily made over, section by section, structure by structure, even neighborhood by neighborhood."[3] The historic preservation movement has taught us to pay attention to those features of older buildings that facilitate their conversion to new uses, yet we do not tend to incorporate that knowledge into buildings we are erecting today. On the contrary, much that has been built more recently will prove difficult to renew and modify. Adaptability in the past was a by-product of normative practices, but now it must be provided deliberately.

Kevin Lynch has advised us to study cities in the past; to see what historical conditions have allowed subsequent change to occur more easily; to design flexibility into our most important, costly, and large-scale infrastructure systems; and to try to identify those elements of our cities that are most likely to change in the future.[4] Because adaptation is a process, the ideas, values, and organizational structures of decision-making agencies may matter more than the physical characteristics of the buildings or districts being adapted. "Reducing the lead time between challenge and response, establishing rapid and effective monitoring and control, contingency planning, decentralized decision to the points of best information, experimenting, and developing testable alternatives" may all help.[5] The qualities of an urban environment inherently adaptable and open to change have been discussed thoroughly by Amos Rapoport; he advocates open-ended design, which determines certain parts of the city while allowing change to occur spontaneously elsewhere once we find out "what is the least that needs to be planned, designed and fixed."[6] Although Mumford, Lynch, Rapoport, and other critics of contemporary city building have written visionary descriptions of what city-building processes that emphasize adaptability might be like in the future, no one knows how to get from the present to the future.

It may well be that an energy crisis will provoke a more systematic reevaluation of city-building processes, even though uncertainties about energy costs and supplies—factors that should indicate the need for a more flexible approach to city building—only seem to discourage people today from taking the energy issues seriously. Richard Stein has written most eloquently about how conventional design methods have contributed to the energy crisis by making changes in energy use difficult to accomplish both on the scale of the individual structure and on the scale of the larger urban region, but he has posed the question of transition in city building darkly:

> Architecture and building are grounded not only in social relationships of a political character in a free society, but also in political structures, as the state regulates both building standards and the property market. Can change take place without state intervention? If the state does intervene to produce these changes, what will that mean for the variety, freedom and creativity of our society? Yet if the state does not intervene, can the society working freely reorient itself to new priorities and methods, to a new vision of things and nature?[7]

Infrastructure systems pose issues for democratic societies which have not yet been confronted. Ironically, concern for the environment was an obligation of residents in communities which were not democratic; mass democracies have yet to develop ways for people to participate in environmental design and care.

The problem of contemporary city building is not just that it produces so many unattractive buildings and districts, because throughout history much that has been built in cities has been unattractive. It is commendable that so many people want to improve the quality of design and enhance the appearance of urban environments; but piecemeal efforts, ameliorating isolated aspects of the environment, are unlikely to effect a fundamental change in city building. Such a change in city-building methods may be less likely to come from a direct attempt at improving the environment than indirectly as a function of other changes in our social, political, cultural, and economic affairs.

The obstacles to innovation inherent in contemporary city building are no secret. Regulations, building codes, commercial practices, and the like vary so much from place to place that a lack of uniformity impedes institutionalized cooperation among owners, architects, engineers, builders, manufacturers, and lenders. Information about building design and performance is inadequate, and the means for gathering and disseminating such information are still primitive. And the attitudes of professionals frequently discourage the introduction of radically new approaches, if only because the financial risks of change are great.[8] Kevin Lynch had this to say about the difficulty to reforming the current city-building mode:

> Our lack of achievement in environmental design is not inevitable, but it is not due to some easily exorcised cause, such as a lack of money, public apathy, errors in administrative structure, or political intrigue. One root difficulty is the divorce of the users of a place from control over its shape and management, which leads to inappropriate form and the imposition of alien purposes. Another is our inability to control real estate development, due above all to the chaos of local government and to the private exploitation of land. . . . A further difficulty is our lack of understanding of the direct effects of the environment on human beings and of how to control those effects to suit

our rather vague, and certainly complex, purposes. We are inexperi-
enced and burdened with outworn attitudes.[9]

Here we encounter one of the paradoxes of modern city building. On
the one hand, city builders, in Anne Spirn's phrase, "rarely appreciate
the cumulative impact of their incremental actions. Design and planning professionals normally concern themselves with a single scale,
that of an individual building project or that of planning for metropolitan services." Many decisions which affect the city as a whole or
which affect other aspects of city building are made without regard
to such consequences. As a result, "uncoordinated attempts to solve
narrowly defined problems" often create new problems.[10] On the
other hand, more regulation, more levels of planning, and more centralization of control may only exacerbate and do little to correct this
condition. "It is important to remember that the effects of actions
taken within the complex urban ecosystem," Spirn advises, "are often
counterintuitive."[11]

Yet, there are also positive signs that some designers, investors,
planners, and administrators are aware that the range of needs in the
population requires a wider variety of solutions and approaches. The
Campaign for Urban Renaissance in Europe and other programs of
the Council of Europe have nurtured a spirit of civic mindedness and
helped to reverse a long historical trend in the flow of power from
local communities toward central governments. Partners for Livable
Places in the United States has brought city government, private
enterprise, and the arts communities together out of a recognition
that urban amenities and economic development are compatible, mu-
tually reinforcing strategies for growth and change. Guidebooks on
cities have proliferated in recent years, making it easier for people to
explore and enjoy cities. These and other recent trends in urban culture will multiply the centers of innovation, thus creating an even
greater demand than already exists for the dissemination of information and the exchange of views.[12]

In 1968, a report of the National Commission on Urban Problems
entitled "Building the American City" contained an idea which
should not be left forgotten, as is the fate of so many reports. The
authors of the report recognized the need for new approaches in city

building that reestablish urbanity as an environmental quality.[13] "What we need most of all is working capital for *ideas*; that is, for *design*. . . . 'Design' as used here does not just mean building design. It means social, legal, and financial design. It means creative thinking in all fields. Money must be made available for all these functions. . . . A start might be made by establishing a *design development bank*. There are development banks of all kinds for international development. It seems sound to apply this principle to design."[14] The idea of an institution to assume some of the financial risk of innovation may have many inherent problems, but it might be worth considering again.

To enlarge the variety of approaches to city building and the number of people participating in city building involves risk. Are we willing to make mistakes, to experiment, to enjoy the open conflict between competing ideas, to accept the implications of change? Or will we prefer to choose from a narrower range of options?[15] Our ability to initiate and sustain new relationships, activities, and investments; our capacity to admit error; our potential for self-renewal and community development are all affected by how we play—first as children and then as adults.

Significantly, the environmental conditions of the industrial city that gave rise to the infrastructure system also promoted attitudes toward outdoor recreation, sports, and cultural activities which, like the infrastructure system itself, survive long after the original stimulus passed. As city building evolves, so will our leisure habits. It is equally true that the way we play—how we travel, entertain, enjoy music, encounter new ideas and sensations—in turn affects our attitudes toward our environment, and our ability to generate and sustain change. Indeed, skills and attitudes suggestive of new approaches to city building and urban living often emerge first, with disarming spontaneity and innocence, in cultural and recreational settings. Is it a coincidence that in the nineteenth century many of the best aspects of urban design were related to landscape architecture? We know from studies of children that they like to manipulate their environments, but playgrounds designed for children offer them very limited opportunities at best. If we can learn to introduce recreational opportunities for adults and children throughout the city,

then we will be on the way to learning how to design environments
capable of sustaining many activities and supporting many groups
simultaneously. By reconsidering the recreational needs of people of
all ages and backgrounds, we may come to a better understanding of
modern city building.

In fact, environmental design can be a form of play itself, taking
the meaning of recreation literally. There is an exhilaration in solving
a problem in design which combines structural integrity with technical innovation, and relates what is new to what is old.[16] The integration of the new with the old, of innovation in form with structural
integrity, of art and science, of respect for nature and the social and
material needs of men, represent great challenges to creative people.
These challenges can only be met if people are free to test the limits
of their abilities and of the materials with which they work. But
there is concern that we do not encourage experimentation. As Jacob
Bronowski warned a quarter of a century ago:

> Our populations have begun to fear science instead of learning it; if
> this goes on, we are doomed. For societies are not bound to go for-
> ward, from freedom to greater freedom. . . . In the intellectual revo-
> lutions of the past, architecture has been the point of fusion: the most
> sensitive point at which new ideas in science and a new conception of
> the arts have crossed and influenced one another. . . . [Great design-
> ers] assume responsibility for making science as well as art visible and
> familiar, and for having each influence and enter into the other.[17]

Can architecture perform this function if science and art are increasingly the preserve of the wealthiest and most powerful institutions
and agencies in our societies, and if well-educated people lack even
an elementary knowledge of art and science? There is a critical role
for architecture and planning to play, though the frequently arrogant
and arcane debates about designers shed little light on what it should
be. Architecture is not a license to be as different or as innovative as
possible; its legitimacy lies in the hope that with good design we
might gain greater control over ourselves, deepen our sensibilities,
and utilize our resources more wisely than without it. Its symbolic
and inspirational properties are as intrinsically important as its functional purposes. Good design should therefore expose our routines

and assumptions to reassessment and provide us with options. The test of design ought to be its influence on our way of life. It is, therefore, an inconclusive art: It accomplishes a little so that we can accomplish more; it helps us prepare for and accept the process of change itself.

After all, vital cities are never finished. The utopian dream of a problem-free city fosters unrealistic expectations and unreasonable demands. Perfection in matters of urban design is unattainable, but the human spirit is not defeated by failure. We live in uncertainty, not in despair, knowing that our problems are generated as much by success as by failure. City building is not for defeatists. Long before cities were a source of great wealth, city people formed an image of human dignity, nurtured a sense of values, and projected ideals. The sea is vast and indifferent, yet we do not stay close to shore, for there ships are in the greatest danger; instead, we venture toward a point beyond the horizon, steering our course by the stars we cannot reach. Our cities are still instruments of our dreams; that is why we care so deeply about their condition.

The hope that urban history can contribute to the formation of public policy has yet to be realized; perhaps it never will be.[18] Those who are concerned about the present and the future of cities confront problems which will not wait; and what urban historians know about the factors which have made possible the presence of cities in the western world for the past millennium cannot be reduced to a formula. The city, however slowly or rapidly it evolves, has survived for so long by adapting to the changes which its very presence has precipitated and diffused. In the past, urban history has contributed very little to an understanding of this process of change and of the role of city building in it, but the study of history may well become important if the challenge of making urban growth and change economically feasible, socially tolerable, and culturally desirable is to remain a protean force in western civilization.

Notes
Bibliography
Index

Notes

᠄᠍᠍᠍᠍᠍᠍ *Introduction*

1. James E. Vance, Jr., *This Scene of Man: The Role and Structure of the City in the Geography of Western Civilization* (New York: Harper and Row, 1977).

2. Kevin Lynch, *A Theory of Good City Form* (Cambridge, Mass.: MIT Press, 1981), 184.

3. Kevin Lynch, *What Time Is This Place?* (Cambridge, Mass.: MIT Press, 1972; reprint 1980), 110.

4. Ibid., 194.

5. Ibid., 205.

6. Lynch, *Theory*, 171–72.

7. John R. Stilgoe, *Common Landscape of America, 1580 to 1845* (New Haven: Yale University Press, 1982), ix. Discussing common or vernacular building in terms of an unself-conscious design process, Philip Steadman wrote that it did work, "if not universally, at least in many and widespread instances. It was capable of producing artefacts which are undoubtedly extremely ingenious in their design, which exploit physical effects or properties of materials which scientific analysis is only just coming to appreciate; and all this done without the unselfconscious designer having recourse to theoretical principle or understanding. . . . The second point is that the products of unselfconscious design have been achieved within very severe limitations of material and manufacturing technique, much more restricted than those available to the selfconscious designer." *The Evolution of Designs: Biological Analogy in Architecture and the Applied Arts* (Cambridge: Cambridge University Press, 1977), 171–72.

8. George R. and Christiane C. Collins, "Camillo Sitte Reappraised," in *Planning for Conservation*, ed. Roger J. P. Kain (New York: St. Martin's Press, 1981), 64.

9. The environment takes shape within "a system of consistent choices
. . . based on the application of certain criteria which may be explicit, but
are commonly implicit and unstated, so that many alternatives are never
considered at all being, as it were, eliminated through major cultural constraints. . . . The question then becomes how, and for what reasons, choices
are made, and criteria based." Amos Rapoport, *Human Aspects of Urban Form:
Towards a Man-Environment Approach to Urban Form and Design* (Oxford: Pergamon, 1977), 16–17.

10. Lewis Mumford, *The City in History: Its Origins, Its Transformations,
and Its Prospects* (New York: Harcourt Brace and World, 1961).

11. Roy Lubove, "The Urbanization Process: An Approach to Historical
Research," *Journal of the American Institute of Planners* 33 (1967), 33.

৯ঌ *1. The Middle Ages*

1. On Roman urbanization, *see*: Ferdinando Castagnoli, *Orthogonal Town
Planning in Antiquity* (Cambridge, Mass.: MIT Press, 1971); E. A. Gutkind, *Urban Development in Southern Europe: Italy and Greece*, vol. 4, *Interna-
tional History of City Development* (New York: Free Press, 1969); Mason Hammond, assisted by Lester J. Bartson, *The City in the Ancient World*
(Cambridge, Mass.: Harvard University Press, 1972); J. B. Ward-Perkins,
Cities in Ancient Greece and Italy: Planning in Classical Antiquity (New York:
George Braziller, 1974); idem, "From Republic to Empire: Reflections on
the Early Provincial Architecture of the Roman West," *Journal of Roman
Studies* 60 (1970); Norman J. G. Pounds, *An Historical Geography of Europe,
450 B.C.–A.D. 1330* (Cambridge: Cambridge University Press, 1973);
M. W. Barley, ed., *European Towns: Their Archaeology and Early History*,
Council for British Archaeology (London and New York: Academic Press,
1977). The unmaking of an ancient city is particularly well described by
Richard Krautheimer in *Rome: Profile of a City, 312–1308* (Princeton:
Princeton University Press, 1980). *From Classical Antiquity to the Middle
Ages: Public Building in Northern and Central Italy, 300–850* by Bryan Ward-
Perkins (New York: Oxford University Press, 1984) appeared after my man-
uscript was finished.

2. On urban developments in southern France after the collapse of Rome,
see: Georges Duby, "Les villes du Sud-Est de la Gaule du VIIIe au XIe siè-
cle," in *Hommes et structures du moyen-âge: recueil d'articles* (Paris and The
Hague: Mouton, 1973), 111–31; on Paris, *see* Anne Lombard-Jourdan,
Paris, Genèse de la 'ville': la rive droite de la Seine des origines à 1223 (Paris:
Editions du CNRS, 1976), and Bernard Rouleau, *Le tracé des rues de Paris:*

formation, typologie, fonctions (Paris: Editions du CNRS, 1967); for other regions, *see* Josiah Cox Russell, *Medieval Regions and their Cities* (London: Newton Abbot, David and Charles, 1972).

3. Lynn White, Jr.,*Medieval Technology and Social Change* (London: Oxford University Press, 1962); Robert S. Lopez, *Naissance de l'Europe* (Paris: Armand Colin, 1962); H. van Werveke, "The Rise of the Towns," chap. 1, *Economic Organization and Policies in the Middle Ages*, ed. M. M. Postan, E. E. Rich, and Edward Muller, vol. 3, *Cambridge Economic History of Europe* (Cambridge: Cambridge University Press, 1963), 3–41.

4. Susan Reynolds, *An Introduction to the History of English Medieval Towns* (Oxford: Clarendon Press, 1977), 34; Georges Duby, *The Early Growth of the European Economy; Warriors and Peasants from the Seventh to the Twelfth century*, trans. Howard B. Clarke (London: Weidenfeld and Nicolson, 1974), 66–67.

5. Spiro Kostof, "The Architect in the Middle Ages, East and West," in *The Architect: Chapters in the History of the Profession*, ed. Spiro S. Kostof (New York: Oxford University Press, 1977), 73; Walter Horn and Ernest Born, *The Plan of St. Gall*, 3 vols. (Berkeley and Los Angeles: University of California Press, 1979).

6. Rosamond McKitterick, "Town and Monastery in the Carolingian Period," in *The Church in Town and Countryside*, ed. Derek Baker, Studies in Church History, vol. 16 (Oxford: Basil Blackwell for the Ecclesiastical History Society, 1979), 93–102; Michael Richter, "Urbanitas-Rusticitas: Linguistic Aspects of a Medieval Dichotomy," ibid., 149–57. For a different view, that urban life did not idealize Christianity and that the revival of cities did not depend upon Christian institutions, however greatly these had been urbanized in the late Roman Empire, *see* Bernd Moeller, "The Town in History: The Reformation in Germany," ibid., 257–68. Vance suggests that monasteries were urban models; *Scene of Man*, 117. Along with monks, Jews played a part in the rapid diffusion of knowledge about cities; *see* Irving A. Agus, *Urban Civilization in Pre-Crusade Europe*, 2 vols. (New York: Yeshiva University Press, 1965), 1:ix, 4, 7–8. On the development of the Mendicant Order in an urban context, *see* Jacques LeGoff, "Ordres mendiants et urbanisation dans la France médiévale: état de l'enquête," *Annales E.S.C.* 25 (1970).

7. "For the decisive change that creates the city is not just an increase in numbers but a transformation of its institutions and the creation of a new pattern of city life. The city is an emergent. . . . In an emergence, the introduction of a new factor produces an overall change, not a mere addition, but a change such as we see in the passage of relatively unorganized

matter into crystalline form. . . . On the new plane, all the old components
. . . have qualities and potentialities that they did not possess in their original states." Lewis Mumford, "Concluding Address," in *City Invincible* ed.
Carl H. Kraeling and Robert M. Adams (Chicago: University of Chicago
Press, 1960), 232.

8. Pierre Lavedan and Jeanne Hugueney, *L'Urbanisme au moyen âge* (Paris:
Arts et métiers graphiques; Geneva: Droz, 1974); David M. Nichols,
"Medieval Urban Origins in Northern Continental Europe: State of Re-
search and Some Tentative Conclusions," *Studies in Medieval and Renaissance
History* 6 (1969): 53–114.

9. Archibald R. Lewis, "Northern European Sea Power and the Straits of
Gibraltar, 1031–1350 A.D.," in *Order and Innovation in the Middle Ages: Es-
says in Honor of Joseph R. Strayer*, ed. William C. Jordan, Bruce McNab, and
Teofilo F. Ruiz (Princeton: Princeton University Press, 1976), 139–64.

10. Pounds, *Historical Geography*, 310; Maurice Beresford, *New Towns of
the Middle Ages: Town Plantation in England, Wales, and Gascony* (New York:
Praeger, 1967); Philippe Dollinger, *La Hanse* (Paris: Aubier, 1964).

11. Vance, *Scene of Man*, 186; on medieval new towns in general, 174–
99.

12. A. B. Hibbert, "The Origins of the Medieval Town Patriciate," *Past
and Present*, no. 3 (1954); Jacques Lestocquoy, *Aux origines de la bourgeoisie:
les villes de Flandre et d'Italie sous le gouvernement des patriciens, XIe–XVe siècles*
(Paris: Presses universitaires de France, 1952).

13. Diane Gwen Hughes, "Urban Growth and Family Structure in
Medieval Genoa," *Past and Present*, no. 66 (1975). On the political implications of two urban networks in the same territorial state, one commercial
and the other agrarian, *see* Edward Whiting Fox, *History in Geographic Perspective* (New York: W. W. Norton, 1971).

14. Robert Bautier, *The Economic Development of Medieval Europe* trans.
Heather Karolyi (London: Thames and Hudson, 1971); C. Lis and H. Soly,
Poverty and Capitalism in Pre-Industrial Europe (Atlantic Highlands, N.J.:
Humanities Press, 1979), 8–52; David M. Nichols, "Town and "Country-
side: Social and Economic Tensions in Fourteenth-Century Flanders," *Com-
parative Studies in Society and History* 10 (1968).

15. A. B. Hibbert, "The Economic Policies of Towns," chap. 4, *Economic
Organization and Policies in the Middle Ages*, vol. 3, *Cambridge Economic History
of Europe*, 157–129.

16. Kevin Lynch, *The Image of the City* (Cambridge, Mass.: MIT Press,
1960).

17. R. Murray Schafer, *The Tuning of the World* (New York: Alfred A.
Knopf, 1977), 43, 53–67.

18. Lynch, *Theory*, 131.

19. Ibid., 126.

20. Rapoport, *Human Aspects of Urban Form*, 185–201.

21. Pounds, *Historical Geography*, 348–50.

22. Vance, *Scene of Man*, 120.

23. LeRoy Dresbeck, "Winter Climate and Society in the Northern Middle Ages: The Technological Impact," in *On Pre-Modern Technology and Science: A Volume of Studies in Honor of Lynn White, Jr.*, ed. Bert S. Hall and Delno C. West for The Center for Medieval and Renaissance Studies, University of California, Los Angeles (Malibu, Calif.: Undema, 1976); White, *Medieval Technology*; more general than its title suggests (because it relates population growth, the exploitation of forests, and the rise of the coal trade) is the article by William H. TeBrake, "Air Pollution and Fuel Crisis in Preindustrial London, 1250–1650," *Technology and Culture* 16 (1975).

24. Jean-Pierre Sosson, *Les travaux publics de la ville de Bruges, 14e–15e siècles: les matériaux, les hommes*, Collection Histoire Pro-Civitate, no. 48 (Brussels: Crédit Communal de Belgique, 1977); J. A. van Houtte, "The Rise and Decline of the Market of Bruges," *Economic History Review*, 2d ser., 19 (1966); M. D. Lobel and E. M. Carus-Wilson, "Bristol," in *The Atlas of Historic Towns*, vol. 2, ed. M. D. Lobel (London: Scholar Press, 1975), 1–27; Nikolaus Pevsner, *North Somerset and Bristol* (Harmondsworth: Penguin Books, 1958).

25. Sosson, *Les travaux publics de Bruges*.

26. Richard A. Goldthwaite, *The Building of Renaissance Florence: An Economic and Social History* (Baltimore: Johns Hopkins University Press, 1980), 172–79; Johanna Hollestelle, *De Steenbakkerij in de Nederlanden tot omstreeks 1560* (Assen: Van Gorkum, [1961]). By comparison, in the period 1817–25, when half of the houses added to England's stock between 1810 and 1830 were built (possibly 350,000–400,000 units), British builders used 10,280 million bricks. J. Parry Lewis, *Building Cycles and Britain's Growth* (London: Macmillan; New York: St. Martin's Press, 1965), 37.

27. Ir. R. Meischke, *Het Nederlandse Woonhuis van 1300–1800; vijftig jaar vereniging 'Hendrik de Keyser'* (Haarlem: H. D. Tjeenk Willink & Zoon, 1969).

28. Carlo M. Cipolla, *Clocks and Culture, 1300–1700* (New York: W. W. Norton, 1977); Jacques LeGoff, "Au moyen-âge: temps de l'église et temps du marchand," *Annales E.S.C.* 15 (1960); David S. Landes, *Revolution in Time: Clocks and the Making of the Modern World* (Cambridge, Mass.: Harvard University Press, Belknap Press, 1983), which is built upon but supersedes previous writing on the subject.

29. Marjorie Nice Boyer, *Medieval French Bridges: A History*, publication

no. 84, (Cambridge, Mass.: Medieval Academy of America, 1976), 159.

30. Ibid., 166.

31. Philippe Wolff, "Pouvoir et investissements urbains en Europe occidentale et centrale du treizième au dix-septième siècle," *Revue historique*, no. 254 (1977); *Les constructions civiles d'intérêt public dans les villes d'Europe au moyen-âge et sous l'ancien régime et leur financement* Colloque internationale, Spa 1968, Collection Histoire Pro-Civitate no. 26 (Brussels: Crédit Communal de Belgique, 1971). The cost of a wall can be grasped by the example cited by Bernard Chevalier: A very small enclosure of two kilometers with four handsome gates and about thirty towers, together with a moat or ditch, cost £80,000 at a time when a town of such a size might have had an annual revenue of no more than £2,000. *Les Bonnes villes de France du XIVe au XVIe siècle* (Paris: Aubier Montaigne, 1982), 117. On the subject of possible overcrowding in a walled city and a decline in public sanitation, see Philippe Contamine, "Les Fortifications urbaines en France à la fin du Moyen-Age, aspects financiers et économiques," *Revue historique* 102 (1978); 44–45.

32. Goldthwaite, *Building of Renaissance Florence*, 367; on conservative trends, such that medieval buildings can be studied from sixteenth- or seventeenth-century practices, *see* Reynolds, *Introduction to English Towns*, 188–96, and Krautheimer, *Rome*, 289. Michael Laithwaite has some perceptive comments about the impact of urban growth and decline in the preindustrial period on the stability of major buildings and vernacular construction, and about the need to see urban buildings in the context of rural construction. "The Buildings of Burford: A Cotswold Town in the Fourteenth to Nineteenth Centuries," in *Perspectives in English Urban History*, ed. Alan Everitt (London: Macmillan, 1973), 60–90.

33. Peter Burke, *Popular Culture in Early Modern Europe* (New York: Harper and Row, 1978).

34. Robert Mark, *Experiments in Gothic Structure* (Cambridge, Mass.: MIT Press, 1982).

35. John Harvey, *The Master Builders: Architecture in the Middle Ages* (New York: McGraw-Hill, 1971), 22. *See also* idem, *The Medieval Architect* (London: Wayland Publishers, 1972); Robert Branner, *St. Louis and the Court Style in Gothic Architecture* (London: A. Zwemmer, 1965); Lon R. Shelby, "The 'Secret' of the Medieval Mason," in *On Pre-Modern Technology and Science*, ed. Hall and West, 201–19.

36. Robert S. Lopez, "Economie et architecture médiévales: celà aurait-il tué ceci?," *Annales E.S.C.* 7 (1952). A debate on the economic dimensions of cathedral building can be followed in H. Thomas Johnson, "Cathedral Building and the Medieval Economy," *Explorations in Entrepreneurial History*

4 (1967); B.W.E. Alford and M. Q. Smith, "The Economic Effects of Cathedral and Church Building in Medieval England: A Reply," ibid., 6 (1969); H. Thomas Johnson, "The Economic Effects of Cathedral and Church Building in Medieval England: A Rejoinder," ibid., 6 (1969).

37. E. A. Gutkind, *The Netherlands and Great Britain*, vol. 6, *International History of City Development* (New York: Free Press, 1970), 188. *See also* Lewis Mumford, *City in History*, 311–12; Karl Gruber, *Die Gestalt der deutschen Stadt* (Munich: Callwey, 1952; reprint, 1977).

38. Elias Canetti, *Crowds and Power*, trans. Carol Stewart (New York: Seabury Press, 1978; reprint, New York: Continuum Press, 1981).

39. Michel Mollat and Phlippe Wolff, *Ongles bleus, Jacques et Ciompi: les révolutions populaires en Europe aux XIVe et XVe siècles* (Paris: Calmann-Levy, 1970), 294. On delinquency and insurrection, *see* Chevalier, *Les Bonnes villes*, 287–308.

40. Natalie Zemon Davis, "The Sacred and the Body Social in Sixteenth-Century Lyon," *Past and Present*, no. 90 (1981): 42. *See also* the comments by Bernd Moeller on the tensions between urban and institutions and culture and between ecclesiastical institutions and culture; these Reformation factors call attention to cities as centers of education and printing, to the Protestant concept of a priesthood of all believers that undermined the clergy's privileged position, to an emphasis on preaching over ritual, and to an appeal to the spiritual responsibility of the individual Christian; "The Town in History." A. L. Bier relates urban living conditions to deviant behavior in "Social Problems in Elizabethan London," *Journal of Interdisciplinary History* 9 (1978).

41. Davis, "Sacred and Social in Lyon," 57.

42. Ibid., 57.

43. Ibid., 58.

44. Nora Temple, "The Control and Exploitation of French Towns during the Ancien Regime," *History: The Journal of the Historical Association* 51 (1966); Josef W. Konvitz, "Grandeur in French City Planning under Louis XIV: Rochefort and Marseille," *Journal of Urban History* 2 (1975). The parallel example of Paris is described by Leon Bernard in *The Emerging City* (Durham, N.C.: Duke University Press, 1970). Christopher Friedrichs is at work on a longer study of the peak and decline in urban riots in Germany, a topic he has broached in "German Town Revolts and the Seventeenth-Century Crisis," *Renaissance and Modern Studies* 16 (1982). Currency values are given in the monetary unit and period relevant to the text.

45. Richard Mowrey Andrews, "Paris of the Great Revolutions: 1789–1796," in *People and Communities in the Western World*, ed. Gene Brucker, vol.

2 (Homewood, Ill.: Dorsey Press, 1979); Richard Cobb, *The Police and the People: French Popular Protest 1789–1820* (Oxford: Clarendon Press, 1970); idem, *Paris and its Provinces 1792–1802* (London: Oxford University Press, 1975); Mona Ozouf, "Le Cortège et la ville: les itinéraires parisiens des fêtes révolutionnaires," *Annales E.S.C.* 26 (1971); George Rudé, "The Growth of Cities and Popular Revolt, 1750–1850, with Particular Reference to Paris," in *French Government and Society 1500–1871: Essays in Memory of Alfred Cobban*, ed. John Bosher (London: Athlone Press, 1973), 166–90.

46. Andrews, "Paris of Revolutions," 88.

47. Ibid., 81, 89.

48. Charles Tilly and R. A. Schweitzer, "How London and its Conflicts Changed Shape," *Historical Methods* 15 (1982), 67.

49. Andrews, "Paris of Revolutions," 85.

50. James Billington, *Fire in the Minds of Men* (New York: Basic Books, 1980), 28.

51. Tilly and Schweitzer, "London and its Conflicts," 70.

ஓ 2. Architecture and Urban Growth

1. Samuel Y. Edgerton, Jr., *The Renaissance Rediscovery of Linear Perspective* (New York: Harper and Row, 1975). Additional sources on the early Renaissance city include: Giovanni Fanelli, *Firenze, architettura e città*, 2 vols. (Florence: Vallechi, 1973); Eugenio Garin, "La cité idéale de la Renaissance," in *Les Utopies à la Renaissance*, (Brussels: Presses universitaires de Bruxelles; Paris: Presses universitaires de France, 1963), 11–37; Pierre Francastel, "Imagination et réalité dans l'architecture civile du Quattrocento," in *Hommage à Lucien Febvre: éventail de l'histoire vivante* (Paris: Armand Colin, 1953), 2:195–206; Wolfgang Lotz, *Studies in Italian Renaissance Architecture* (Cambridge, Mass.: MIT Press, 1977); Leopold D. Ettlinger, "The Emergence of the Italian Architect during the Fifteenth Century," in *The Architect: Chapters in the History of the Profession*, ed. Spiro Kostof (New York: Oxford University Press, 1977), 96–123; Catherine Wilkinson, "The New Professionalism in the Renaissance," Ibid., 124–60.

2. Pierre Lavedan and Jeanne Hugueney, *La Représentation des villes dans l'art du moyen-âge* (Paris: Vanoest, 1954); John A. Pinto, "Origins and Development of the Ichnographic City Plan," *Journal of the Society of Architectural Historians* 35 (1976), and P. D. A. Harvey, *The History of Topographical Maps: Symbols, Pictures and Survey* (London: Thames and Hudson, 1980), 66–84.

3. Goldthwaite, *Building of Renaissance Florence*, 2.

4. Ibid., 4.

5. Ibid., 68; idem, "The Florentine Palace as Domestic Architecture," *American Historical Review* 77 (1972).

6. Idem, *Building of Renaissance Florence*, 15–16.

7. Ibid., 384, 392.

8. Giulio C. Argan, *The Renaissance City* (New York: George Braziller, 1969), 25–26.

9. Goldthwaite, *Building of Renaissance Florence*, 424–25.

10. Carroll William Westfall, *In This Most Perfect Paradise: Alberti, Nicholas V, and the Invention of Conscious Urban Planning in Rome, 1447–1555* (University Park, Pa.: Pennsylvania State University Press, 1974); Joan Gadol, *Leon Battista Alberti: Universal Man of the Early Renaissance* (Chicago: University of Chicago Press, 1969). Krautheimer describes overcrowded medieval Rome as a "labyrinth of houses large and small, tiny piazze, open or enclosed, courtyards with or without walls, narrow and dark passages. . . ." *Rome: Profile of a City*, 283.

11. Literary communication and artistic architectural representation are discussed by Rudolph Wittkower in *Architectural Principles in an Age of Humanism* (London: A. Tiranti, 1952) and *Studies in the Italian Baroque* (London: Thomas and Hudson, 1975). *See also* Denis Cosgrove, "The Myth and Stones of Venice: An Historical Geography of a Symbolic Landscape," *Journal of Historical Geography* 8 (1982).

12. Jean Delumeau, *Rome au 16e siècle* (Paris: Hachette, 1975); Paolo Portoghesi, *Rome of the Renaissance*, trans. Pearl Sanders (London: Phaidon, 1972).

13. On attitudes toward the use of artificial city boundaries in space and culture to diminish anxiety about social and economic change, *see* William J. Bouwsma, "Anxiety and the Formation of Early Modern Culture," in *After the Reformation: Essays in Honor of J. H. Hexter*, ed. Barbara C. Malament (Philadelphia: University of Pennsylvania Press, 1980), 215–46.

14. René Descartes, *Discours de la méthode*, ed. E. Gilson (Paris: Vrin, 1964), 59–60; translation is this author's.

15. Horst de la Croix, *Military Considerations in City Planning: Fortifications* (New York: George Braziller, 1972), 39–55; Idem, "Military Architecture and the Radial City Plan in Sixteenth-Century Italy," *Art Bulletin* 42 (1960).

16. On the military revolution: *See* Michael Roberts, "The Military Revolution," in *Essays in Swedish History* (London: Weidenfeld and Nicolson, 1967), 195–225; Geoffrey Parker, "The Military Revolution: 1560–1660— A Myth?" *Journal of Modern History* 48 (1976).

17. P. Parent, *L'Architecture civile à Lille au 17e siècle* (Lille: Raost, 1925).

18. Line Teisseyre-Sallmann, "Urbanisme et société: l'exemple de Nîmes aux XVIIe et XVIIIe siècles," *Annales E.S.C.* 35 (1980); Anne Blanchard, *Les Ingénieurs du 'Roy' de Louis XIV à Louis XV: étude des corps des fortifications*, Collection du Centre d'histoire militaire et d'études de défense nationale de Montpellier, no. 9 (Montpellier: Université Paul-Valéry, 1980), 436–51.

19. Anthony Blunt, *Neapolitan Baroque and Rococo Architecture* (London: A Zwemmer, 1975), describes the rise and fall of a local tradition. On the social function of architectural style and on the substitution of classicism for the vernacular, *see* Peter Borsay, "Culture, Status and the English Landscape," *History* 67 (1982).

20. "Thus the eighteenth century has no coherent stylistic physiognomy; it is pre-eminently a century of stylistic revivals and even to a certain extent of stylistic chaos." Rudolph Wittkower, *Palladio and Palladianism* (New York: George Braziller, 1974), 177.

21. Helen Rosenau, *Social Purpose in Architecture* (London: Studio Vista, 1970); Allan Braham, *The Architecture of the French Enlightenment* (London: Thames and Hudson, 1980); Thomas Cassirer, "Awareness of the City in the 'Encyclopédie'," *Journal of the History of Ideas* 24 (1963); Joseph Rykwert, *The First Moderns: The Architects of the Eighteenth Century* (Cambridge, Mass.: MIT Press, 1980); Thomas A. Markus, "Buildings for the Sad, the Bad and the Mad in Urban Scotland 1780–1830," in *Order and Space in Society: Architectural Form and its Context in the Scottish Englightenment*, ed. Thomas A. Markus (Edinburgh: Mainstream, 1982), 25–114.

22. Jean-Louis Harouel, "Les Fonctions de l'alignement dans l'organisme urbain," and Richard Eitlin, "L'Air dans l'urbanisme des lumières," *Dix-huitième siècle* 9 (1977); Pierre Francastel, "L'Esthétique des lumières," in *Utopie et institutions au 18e siècle, le pragmatisme des lumières*, ed. Pierre Francastel (Paris and The Hague: Mouton, 1973), 331–57. For a fascinating example of use of color to blend assymetric, dissimilar structures into a seemingly organic whole, *see* Giovanni Brino and Franco Rosso, *Colore e Città, il piano del colore di Torino 1800–1850* (Milan: Idea Editions, 1980).

23. Peter Collins, *Changing Ideals in Modern Architecture, 1750–1950* (London: Faber and Faber, 1965), 185–97.

24. As quoted in David Daiches and John Flower, *Literary Landscapes of the British Isles, A Narrative Atlas* (New York and London: Paddington Press, 1979), 40.

25. Arthur Young, *Travels in France During the Years 1787, 1788, and 1789*, ed. Constantia Maxwell (Cambridge: Cambridge University Press, 1950), 22

26. Ibid., 171–72.

27. Ibid., 115–16.
28. Ibid., 59.

3. The Development of the Economic Mode

1. Josef W. Konvitz, *Cities and the Sea: Port City Planning in Early Modern Europe* (Baltimore: Johns Hopkins University Press, 1978), 20–24, 34–65; Hugo Soly, *Urbanisme en Kapitalisme te Antwerpen in de 16de Eeuw*, Collection Histoire Pro-Civitate no. 47 (Brussels: Crédit Communal de Belgique, 1977); Goldthwaite, *Building of Renaissance Florence*, 152–55. Van Schoonbeke developed twenty-four new streets measuring 2750 meters long, or 31 percent of all new streets in Antwerp in his era; he also developed between twenty-three and twenty-five hectares in the new parts of Antwerp, constructed three markets and 29,000 cubic meters of city wall, and built two of the city's seven important civic monuments.

2. Josef W. Konvitz, "Spatial Perspectives on Port City Development, c. 1780–1980," *Urbanism Past and Present* (1982); the original paintings by Joseph Vernet are in the Musée de la Marine, Paris.

3. D. Swann, "The Pace and Progress of Port Investment in England 1660–1830," *Yorkshire Bulletin of Economic and Social Research* 12 (1960); idem, "The Engineers of English Port Improvements 1660–1830," *Transport History* 1 (1968); T. S. Willan, *River Navigation in England 1600–1750* (London: Frank Cass, 1964); Jacob Price, "Economic Function and the Growth of American Port Towns in the Eighteenth Century," *Perspectives in American History* 7 (1974). *See also* Ted Ruddock, *Arch Bridges and Their Builders, 1735–1835* (Cambridge: Cambridge University Press, 1979).

4. John F. Riddell, *Clyde Navigation: A History of the Development and Deepening of the River Clyde* (Edinburgh: John Donald, 1979). An equally valid example is Bristol: *See* W. E. Minchinton, "Bristol—Metropolis of the West in the Eighteenth Century," *Transactions of the Royal Historical Society*, 5th ser., 4 (1954); Alan F. Williams, "Bristol Port Plans and Improvement Schemes of the 18th Century," *Transactions of the Bristol and Gloucestershire Archeological Society* 81 (1962); Patrick McGrath, ed., *Bristol in the Eighteenth Century* (London: David and Charles, Newton Abbott, 1972).

5. Patrick Colquhoun, in his *A Treatise on the Commerce and Police of the River Thames* (1800), estimated theft in the port in 1797 at half a million pounds. His study and prescriptions revolutionized port administration; *see also* John Pudney, *London's Docks* (London: Thames and Hudson, 1975), which covers the period from the eighteenth century to the present.

6. Alain Demangeon and Bruno Fortier, *Les Vaisseaux et les villes, l'arsenal*

de Cherbourg (Brussels: Pierre Mardaga, 1978); Charles C. Gillispie, *Science and Polity in France at the End of the Old Regime* (Princeton: Princeton University Press, 1980), 337–44, on Duhamel de Montceau and the scientific evaluation of shipbuilding.

7. Eugene S. Ferguson, "Mr. Jefferson's Dry Docks," *The American Neptune* 11 (1951).

8. Bruno Fortier and Bruno Vayssière, "L'Architecture des villes: espaces, cartes et territoires," *URBI*, no. 3 (1980); Alain Demangeon and Bruno Fortier, "La Politique de l'espace urbain, la ville des années 1800," *Architectural Design* 48 (1978); Giorgio Morachiello and Georges Geyssot, "State Town: Colonization of the Territory during the First Empire," *Lotus* 24 (1980).

9. Jean-Claude Perrot, *Genèse d'une ville moderne, Caen au XVIIIe siècle*, 2 vols. (Paris and The Hague: Mouton, 1975).

10. Alan Everitt, "The English Urban Inn 1560–1760," in *Perspectives in English Urban History*, ed. Alan Everitt (London: Macmillan, 1973), 91–137; idem, "Country, County and Town: Patterns of Regional Evolution in England," *Transactions of the Royal Historical Society*, 5th ser., 29 (1979); Peter Borsay, "The English Urban Renaissance and the Development of Provincial Urban Culture, c. 1680–1760," *Social History* 2 (1977).

11. Eric L. Jones and M. E. Falkus, "Urban Improvement and the English Economy in the Seventeenth and Eighteenth Centuries," *Research in Economic History* 4 (1979). In a comment which links the economic changes in vernacular building in the eighteenth century to the substitution of cosmopolitan for local building styles, R. Machin has written: "We require a theory of building history which will explain (with regional variations in timing) the medieval preference for impermanent building, the emergence of permanent vernacular building in the fifteenth century, its extension and the successive rebuildings of vernacular houses from the late sixteenth to the early eighteenth century, and the replacement of vernacular by 'polite' or 'pattern book' architecture from the mid-eighteenth century." "The Great Rebuilding: A Reassessment," *Past and Present*, no. 77 (1977), 55. Equally illustrative of the transformation of an older city in wood into a newer one of stone as part of the transformation of city building from a cultural to an economic mode is the example of Stockholm. Marianne Råberg, "The Development of Stockholm since the Seventeenth Century," in *Growth and Transformation of the Modern City*, ed. Ingrid Hammarström and Thomas Hall (Stockholm: Swedish Council for Building Research, 1979), 13–26.

12. Neil McKendrick, John Brewer, and J. H. Plumb, *The Birth of a Consumer Society: The Commercialization of Eighteenth-Century England* (Bloomington: Indiana University Press, 1982); on the proliferation of crafts and the urban consumer economy, see Everitt, "Country, County and Town,", 98–105.

13. Jones and Falkus, "Urban Improvement," 226. Peter Burke warned against confusing differences between large cities and small towns with differences between preindustrial and industrial ones in "Some Reflections on the Pre-Industrial City," *Urban History Yearbook 1975* (Leicester: Leicester University Press, 1975), 19–20.

14. Everitt, "Country, County and Town," 105.

15. E. A. Wrigley, "A Simple Model of London's Importance in Changing English Society and Economy 1650–1750," *Past and Present*, no. 37 (1967).

16. Ibid., 65–67.

17. Norman Brett-James, *The Growth of Stuart London* (London: Allen and Unwin, 1935); Valerie Pearl, "Change and Stability in Seventeenth-Century London," *London Journal* 5 (1979); Lawrence Stone, "The Residential Development of the West End of London in the Seventeenth Century," in *After the Reformation*, ed. Barbara C. Malament (Philadelphia: University of Pennsylvania Press, 1980) 167–212.

18. T. F. Reddaway, *The Rebuilding of London after the Great Fire* (London: Jonathan Cape, 1940).

19. The plans by Evelyn, Hooke, Wren, and others ought not to be taken any more seriously by historians than they were by the authorities in 1666. Illustrations of several of these plans, together with some perceptive comments, appear in: A. E. J. Morris, *History of Urban Form: Prehistory to the Renaissance* (London: George Godwin, 1972), 190–94.

20. F. M. L. Thompson, *Chartered Surveyors, The Growth of a Profession* (London: Routledge and Kegan Paul, 1968), 66–67.

21. The coal duty taxes were collected at the port and inland, wherever any route came within a certain number of miles of London. Coal revenues eventually paid off the City's debts in 1834. Thereafter, revenues were applied to improvements in roads, embankments, and sewers until the tax was rescinded in 1889.

22. Sir John Summerson, *Georgian London*, rev. ed. (London: Barrie and Jenkins, 1962, reprint 1970), 45. In London, financiers speculated in land and houses, craftsmen in houses only. Craftsmen often worked in groups, "each trade making its appropriate contribution, so virtually no capital was required" (p. 45).

23. M. J. Power, "East London Housing in the Seventeenth Century," in *Crisis and Order in English Towns 1500–1700*, ed. Peter Clark and Paul Slack (London: Routledge and Kegan Paul, 1972), 237–62.

24. Dan Cruickshank and Peter Wyld, *London: The Art of Georgian Building* (London: Architectural Press, 1975), 199–200.

25. Donald J. Olsen, *Town Planning in London: The Eighteenth and Nineteenth Centuries* (New Haven: Yale University Press, 1964).

26. C. W. Chalklin, *The Provincial Towns of Georgian England: A Study of the Building Process 1740–1820* (London: Edward Arnold, 1974). *See also* the model study by M. J. Wise, "Evolution of Jewellery and Gun Quarters in Birmingham," *Transactions of the Institute of British Geographers* 15 (1949).

27. A. J. Younger, *The Making of Classical Edinburgh 1750–1840* (Edinburgh: Edinburgh University Press, 1966), 104, 110.

28. The material on urban cartography in France is from a larger study on cartography in France, the research for which was facilitated by a Fellowship for Independent Study from the National Endowment for the Humanities and a Grant-in-Aid from the American Council of Learned Societies. For background information on cartography, *see*: Howard Carter, "The Map in Urban History," *Urban History Yearbook* (Leicester: Leicester University Press, 1979), 11–31; J. Schulz, "Jacopo de Barbari's View of Venice: Map Making, City Views and Moralized Geography before the Year 1500," *Art Bulletin* 60 (1978); Pinto, "Origins and Development of the Ichnographic City Plan." A study to be compared with French evidence is Griseri Andreina, "Urbanistica, cartografica e antico regime nel Piemonte Sabaudo," *Storia della Città*, nos. 12/13 (1979). Two map-oriented studies of Parisian urban development are Olivier Zunz, "Etude d'un processus d'urbanisation: le quartier du Gros-Caillou à Paris," *Annales E.S.C.* 25 (1970), and Françoise Boudon and Hélène Couzy, "Châteaux de cartes: l'histoire de l'architecture et la cartographie," *Storia della Città*, nos. 12/13 (1979).

29. "Dénombrement . . . de Valenciennes," Département des Manuscrits, Bibliothèque nationale, Paris, Fonds français ms 8526.

30. Jeanne Pronteau, "Le Travail des limites de la ville et faubourgs de Paris, 1724–1729: législation et application des textes," *Annuaire de l'Ecole pratique des hautes études*, 4th section, 110 (1977–78; pub. 1979), 707–45.

31. De La Grive, "Neuvième plan de Paris . . . avec les bornes et limites qui y ont été posées en conséquence des déclarations du Roy" (1728), engraved.

32. The last panoramic survey map of Paris was executed by Louis Bretez, who showed every building to scale; it is usually called the "Plan de Turgot," after the official who patronized Bretez.

33. Pierre Patte, *Monumens érigés en France à la gloire de Louis XV* (Paris, 1765), 221.

34. Bullet and Blondel manuscript map of Paris (1676) is in the Département des cartes et plans, Bibliothèque nationale, Paris, Ge. A. 53. See also Bernard, *The Emerging City*, 284–85. Bernard Jaillot, "Nouveau plan de la Ville et Faubourgs de Paris . . . très exactement levé et mesuré sur les lieux, augmenté de tous les nouveaux batiments et nouvelles rues qui y ont été faites jusqu'en 1713," engraved.

35. Philippe Buache, "Cartes muettes de Paris," 47 sheets, Département des cartes et plans, Bibliothèque nationale, Paris, Ge. DD. 2738.

36. The Bibliothèque de l'Institut in Paris has a triangulation table by Jeaurat, ms 2462; other documents relating to Jeaurat's work are in the Centre de documentation, Ecole nationale des Ponts et Chaussées, ms 2395.

37. Jeanne Pronteau, "L'Oeuvre architecturale d'Edme Verniquet," *Annuaire de l'Ecole pratique des hautes études*, 4th section, 108 (1975–76; pub. 1976), 641–49.

38. "Plan général de la nouvelle enceinte de Paris, divisé en dix-huit cartes," Archives nationales, Paris, N IV Seine 66.

39. H. Monin, "Les travaux d'Edme Verniquet, et, en particulier, le plan de Paris dit 'Plan des Artistes'," *Bulletin de la Bibliothèque des travaux historiques* 3 (1908).

40. Archives nationales, letter of Guichard to Robinet, 6 September 1785, $Q^1 1102^2$.

41. Archives nationales, Verniquet, "Mémoire sur l'utilité des plans de la Ville de Paris," $O^1 1693$.

42. Sylvie Buisson, "Le Plan des Artistes, 1794–1797," *La Vie urbaine*, no. 55 and no. 57 (1950).

43. E. Coyecque, "Les plans cadastraux de la ville de Paris aux Archives nationales, d'après un rapport de la direction générale des contributions directes," *Bulletin de la société de l'histoire de Paris* 35 (1908).

44. Bruno Fortier, "La Maitrise de l'eau," *Dix-huitième Siècle* 9 (1977).

45. N. de Fer, "Plan de la conduite des eaues des fontaines de la ville de Paris."

46. De La Grive, "Plan des fontaines de la ville et des faubourgs de Paris."

47. Pierre Patte, *Mémoire sur les objets les plus importants de l'Architecture* (Paris, 1769).

48. Moreau-Desproux, "Plan général des différents projets d'embellissements les plus utiles et les plus convenables à la commodité des citoyens et à la décoration de la ville de Paris" (1769), Département des Estampes, Bibliothèque nationale, Paris, Ve 36 pet. fol. For a general survey of design

trends, see André Chastel, "Problèmes d'urbanisme à Paris au XVIIIe siècle," in *Sensibilità e Razionalità del Settecento*, ed. Vittore Brana (Venice: Sansoni, 1967), vol. 2, 617–28.

49. Jean Bouchary, *L'Eau à Paris à la fin du XVIIIe siècle; la compagnie des
eaux de Paris et l'entreprise de l'Yvette* (Paris: Rivière, 1946).

50. Bonamy, "Mémoire sur l'inondation de la Seine à Paris, au mois de
décembre 1740, comparées aux inondations précédentes, avec des remarques
sur l'élévation du sol de cette ville," *Mémoires de litteratures, tirés des registres
de l'Académie royale des Inscriptions et Belles-Lettres* 17 (1741–43; pub. 1751).

51. Philippe Buache, "Plans et coups du sol de Paris et de ses souterrains,
par rapport aux débordements de la Seine" and "Exposé d'un plan hydro-
graphique de la ville de Paris," *Mémoires de l'Académie royale des Sciences*
(1742). *See also* Bralle, *Précis des faits et observations relatifs à l'inondation de
Paris* (Paris, 1803), and Gustave Bord, *Les Inondations du bassin de la Seine,
1658–1910* (Paris, 1910).

52. Buache's maps of the Seine and related materials are in the Département des Cartes et plans, Bibliothèque nationale, Paris, Ge. DD. 2334,
5525, 5527, and 5533, and Ge. AA. 1374; *see also* his "Carte générale du
cours de la Seine de Paris à Rouen" (1766), Archives nationales, Paris,
F[14]10078[I]2.

53. Pierre-Simon Girard, *Recherches sur les eaux publiques de Paris, les distributions successives qui en ont été faites, et les divers projets qui ont été proposés pour
en augmenter le volume* (Paris: Imprimerie nationale, 1812).

54. *See* the series of maps in Archives nationales, Paris, F[14]10125[II, III].

55. I have benefited greatly from conversations with Barrie Ratcliffe,
whose research on canal and railway schemes has paralleled my own on
cartography.

56. Maire, *La Topographie ou plan détaillée de la ville de Paris et de ses faubourgs* (Paris, 1808); idem, *Atlas administratif de la ville de Paris* (Paris,
1821).

57. Claude Nières, *La reconstruction d'une ville au XVIIIe siècle; Rennes,
1720–60* (Rennes: Université de Haute-Bretagne, Institut amoricain de recherches historiques de Rennes, 1972); François Loyer, "Rennes et ses deux
places: unité ou hiérarchie?" *Monuments historiques*, no. 120 (1982). Both
contain complete references to and illustrations of the Forestier and Robelin
maps. *See also* Roger J. P. Kain, "The Rebuilding of Rennes," *The Connoisseur*
190 (1975).

58. Jörg Garms, "Le Plan d'urbanisme de Strasbourg dressé par Jacques-
François Blondel en 1764–69," *Cahiers alsaciens d'archéologie, d'art et d'histoire*
21 (1978); *see* notes 1 and 2 on p. 122 for complete references to the maps
and registers in the Strasbourg municipal archives.

59. I am indebted to James K. Pringle for sending me a copy of his paper "Land Use and Political Culture in Late Eighteenth Century Marseille," presented to the Western Society of French History at its 1982 meeting in Winnipeg.

60. Fourcroy, "Mémoire et projet général pour procurer au Havre un aggrandissement du Port et de la Ville proportionnée à l'acroissement de son commerce et de sa population," Bibliothèque de Génie, Paris, ms in-40 91.

61. François de Dainville, "Grandeur et population des villes au XVIIIe siècle," *Population* 13 (1958); Jean Meyer, *Généralités—France*. vol. 1, *Etudes sur les villes en Europe occidentale: milieu du XVIIIe siècle à la veille de la Révolution française*, (Paris: Société d'édition d'enseignement supérieur, 1983), on the enlargement of cities and spatial density, 135–62, and on extensions between newer and older parts, 163–75.

62. "Résultats du travail fait au Bureau de Cadastre pour connoitre la superficie et la population du territoire français," Centre de documentation, Ecole nationale des Ponts et Chaussées, ms 2149.

63. José-Augusto França, *Une Ville des lumières: la Lisbonne de Pombal* (Paris: SEVPEN, 1965).

64. G. B. G. Bull, "Thomas Milne's Land Utilization Map of the London Area in 1800," *Geographical Journal* 122 (1956).

65. Ida Darlington and James Howgego, *Printed Maps of London, circa 1553–1850* (London: G. Philip, 1964); Ida Darlington, "Edwin Chadwick and the First Large-Scale Ordnance Survey of London," *Transactions of the London & Middlesex Archeological Society* 22 (1969); H. J. Dyos, "A Guide to the Streets of Victorian London," in *Exploring the Urban Past: Essays in Urban History by H. J. Dyos*, ed. David Cannadine and David Reeder (Cambridge, Cambridge University Press, 1982), 190–201.

66. Olsen, *Town Planning in London*, 205–6.

67. Saul Jarcho, "Yellow Fever, Cholera, and the Beginnings of Medical Cartography," *Journal of the History of Medicine and Allied Sciences* 25 (1970).

68. Frank Arneil Walker, "The Glasgow Grid," in *Order and Space in Society*, ed. Thomas A. Markus, 155–99. On the hybrid treatment of Washington, D.C., combining utilitarian and monumental street planning, and the problems of mapping, *see*: Ralph E. Erenberg, "Mapping the Nation's Capital: The Surveyor's Office, 1791–1818," *Quarterly Journal of the Library of Congress* 36 (1979).

69. James A. Leith, "Space and Revolution: Architecture and Urban Planning during the French Revolution," *Proceedings of the Consortium on Revolutionary Europe*, 2 vols. (Durham, N.C.: Duke University Press, 1980), 2:24–53; idem, "Desacralization, Resacralization, and Architectural Planning during the French Revolution," *Eighteenth-Century Life*, 7 (1982).

70. Jeanne Pronteau, *Les Numérotages des maisons de Paris du XVe siècle à nos jours*, Ville de Paris, Commission des travaux historiques, sous-commission de recherches d'histoire contemporaine, no. 8 (1966).

৪৶ 4. *The Nineteenth Century*

1. Asa Briggs, *Victorian Cities* (1963; reprint, Harmondsworth, Pelican Books, 1968), 96.

2. Ibid., 91; François Vigier, *Change and Apathy, Liverpool and Manchester during the Industrial Revolution* (Cambridge, Mass.: MIT Press, 1970), 137–139.

3. Nikolaus Pevsner, *A History of Building Types*, Bollingen Ser. no. 35 (Princeton: Princeton University Press, 1976), 214, 225–26, 277.

4. When Karl Friedrich Schinkel, the architect-planner charged with the redesign of aristocratic Berlin, visited Manchester in July 1826, he wrote that the factories were nothing but "monstrous masses of red brick, built by a foreman, without any trace of architecture and for the sole purpose of crude necessity, making a most frightening impression." Schinkel recognized nonetheless that their shape and construction, reordered according to aesthetic principles, could enhance a design for a warehouse complex in Berlin. Herman G. Pundt, *Schinkel's Berlin: A Study in Environmental Planning* (Cambridge, Mass.: Harvard University Press, 1972), 166.

5. Briggs, *Victorian Cities*, 125–26.

6. Steven Marcus, *Engels, Manchester, and the Working Class* (New York: Random House, 1974), 65.

7. Ibid., 61.

8. Ibid., 66.

9. Briggs, *Victorian Cities*, 108ff.

10. Marcus, *Engels*, 178.

11. H. J. Dyos, "The Speculative Buildings and Developers in Victorian London," in *Exploring the Urban Past: Essays in Urban History by H. J. Dyos*, ed. David Cannadine and David Reeder (Cambridge: Cambridge University Press, 1982), 157.

12. Eric E. Lampard, "The Urbanization of the United States: The Capitalization and Decapitalization of Place," in *Villes en mutation XIXe–XXe siècles*, Collection Histoire Pro-Civitate, no. 64 (Brussels: Crédit Communal de Belgique, 1982), 147–200; Lampard wrote of the nineteenth-century city that it was "built by everyone in general and nobody in particular," 179.

13. Dyos, "Speculative Buildings," 164.

14. David Cannadine, ed. *Patricians, Power, and Politics in Nineteenth-Century Towns* (Leicester: Leicester University Press, 1982); idem, *Lords and Landlords: The Aristocracy and the Towns, 1774–1967* (Leicester: Leicester University Press, 1980).

15. Eric E. Lampard, "The Nature of Urbanization," in *The Pursuit of Urban History*, ed. Derek Fraser and Anthony Sutcliffe (London: Edward Arnold, 1983), 40–41.

16. Ibid., 38–39.

17. Andrew Lees, "Perceptions of Cities in Britain and Germany, 1820–1914," in *The Pursuit of Urban History*, ed. Derek Fraser and Anthony Sutcliffe (London: Edward Arnold, 1983), 157–66.

18. C. K. Yearley, "The 'Provincial Party' and the Megalopolises: London, Paris, and New York, 1850–1910," *Comparative Studies in Society and History* 15 (1973); E. P. Hennock, "Central/Local Government Relations in England: An Outline 1800–1950," *Urban History Yearbook 1982* (Leicester: Leicester University Press, 1982), 38–49, mentions suspicion of central government, belief "that what was done locally was a local matter and did not significantly affect the lives of others," and the assumption "that those who belonged to a locality knew better than anyone else what that locality needed" (39). See also Anthony Sutcliffe, "Environmental Control and Planning in European Capitals, 1850–1914: London, Paris and Berlin," in *Growth and Transformation of the Modern City*, ed. Ingrid Hammarström and Thomas Hall, 71–88.

19. John R. Kellett, *The Impact of Railways on Victorian Cities* (London: Routledge and Kegan Paul, 1969), 125ff.

20. John Summerson, *The London Building World of the Eighteen-Sixties* (London: Thames and Hudson, 1973), 7.

21. Kellett, *Impact of Railways*, 19, 291.

22. Ibid., 422–23.

23. Anthony S. Wohl, *The Eternal Slum: Housing and Social Policy in Victorian London* (London: Edward Arnold, 1977); Anthony Sutcliffe, ed., *Multi-Storey Living: The British Working-Class Experience* (London: Croon Helm, 1974); John Nelson Tarn, *Five Per Cent Philanthropy: An Account of Housing in Urban Areas Between 1840 and 1914* (Cambridge: Cambridge University Press, 1973); Enid Gauldie, *Cruel Habitations: A History of Working-Class Housing 1780–1918* (London: Allen and Unwin, 1974); J. A. Yelling, "The Selection of Sites for Slum Clearance in London, 1875–1888," *Journal of Historical Geography* 7 (1981); H. J. Dyos and Michael Wolff, eds. *The Victorian City, Images and Realities*, 2 vols. (London: Routledge and Kegan Paul, 1973).

Most of the remaining courtyard dwellings in Liverpool were destroyed in World War II or thereafter, but similar structures, complete with stone privies, have survived in Roubaix, France, where they will be preserved as part of a unique social-environmental museum.

24. Peter Aspinall, "The Internal Structure of the Housebuilding Industry in Nineteenth-Century Cities," in *The Structure of Nineteenth-Century Cities*, ed. James H. Johnson and Colin G. Pooley (New York: St. Martin's Press, and London: Croom Helm, 1982), 75–106; Richard Rodger, "The Growth and Transformation of Scottish Towns: The Role of the Building Cycle, 1860–1914," in *Growth and Transformation of the Modern City* ed. Thomas Hall and Ingrid Hammarström, 115–24. On the absence of fundamental changes in building techniques, *see* C. G. Powell, *An Economic History of the British Building Industry, 1815–1979* (London: Architectural Press, 1980). On the relation between incomes and spending patterns on the one hand and the quantity and quality of housing on the other, *see* Anthony Sutcliffe, "In Search of the Urban Variable: Britain in the Later Nineteenth Century," in *Pursuit of Urban History*, ed. Derek Fraser and Anthony Sutcliffe, 234–63; and Ingrid Hammarström, "Urban Growth and Building Fluctuations: Stockholm 1860–1920," in *Growth and Transformation of the Modern City*, ed. Ingrid Hammarström and Thomas Hall, 29–47.

25. Pevsner, *Building Types*, 244.

26. Gilbert Herbert, *Pioneers of Prefabrication: The British Contribution in the Nineteenth Century* (Baltimore: Johns Hopkins University Press, 1978).

27. Sutcliffe, "Environmental Control and Planning," 78–79.

28. Jeanne Hugueney, "Les Halles Centrales de Paris au XIXe siècle," *La Vie urbaine* 66 (1968).

29. David Pinckney, *Napoleon III and the Rebuilding of Paris* (Princeton: Princeton University Press, 1958); Louis Chevalier, *Classes laborieuses et classes dangereuses à Paris pendant la première moitié du XIXe siècle* (Paris: Plon, 1958); Jeanne Gaillard, *Paris la ville, 1852–1870* (Paris: Plon, 1977); Anthony Vidler, "Paris under the Academy: City and Ideology," *Oppositions* 8 (1977), 95–115; Adeline Daumard, "Quelques remarques sur le logement des Parisiens au XIXe siècle," *Annales de démographie historiques* (1975), 49–64; Anthony Sutcliffe, *The Autumn of Central Paris: The Defeat of Town Planning 1850–1970* (London: Edward Arnold, 1970); idem, "Architecture and Civic Design in Nineteenth-Century Paris," in *Growth and Transformation of the Modern City*, ed. Ingrid Hammerström and Thomas Hall, 89–114; idem, *Towards the Planned City: Germany, Britain, the United States and France, 1780–1914* (New York: St. Martin's Press, 1981); Norma Evenson, *Paris: A Century of Change, 1878–1978* (New Haven: Yale University Press, 1979);

Gérard Jacquement, "Belleville aux XIXe et XXe siècles: une méthode d'analyse de la croissance urbaine à Paris," *Annales E.S.C.* 30 (1975); Maurice Daumas, "La géographie industrielle de Paris au XIXe siècle," in *Villes en mutation XIXe–XXe siècles,* 91–145; Ann-Louise Shapiro, "Housing Reform in Paris: Social Space and Social Control," *French Historical Studies* 12 (1982).

30. Françoise Boudon, André Chastel, Hélène Couzy, and Françoise Hamon, *Système de l'architecture urbaine: le quartier des halles à Paris,* 2 vols. (Paris: CNRS, 1977); Françoise Boudon, "La 'Haussmannisation' du centre de Paris: le nouveau parcellaire," *Storia della Città,* no. 5 (1977).

31. "Whatever the qualities of the Haussmannic aesthetic as creator of a unified townscape, it seriously limited the freedom of the Parisian architect and tended to reduce him to the role of lackey of the property speculator." Sutcliffe, "Architecture and Civic Design," 89. *See also Le Parisien chez lui au XIXe siècle, 1814–1914* (Paris: Archives nationales, 1976).

32. Adeline Daumard, "L'Avenue de l'Opéra de ses origines à la guerre de 1914," *Bulletin de la société de l'histoire de Paris* (1967–68).

33. Charlene Marie Leonard, *Lyon Transformed: Public Works of the Second Empire, 1853–1864.* vol. 67, University of California Publications in History (Berkeley and Los Angeles: University of California Press, 1961). Other examples are given by Marcel Roncayolo, "La Production de la ville," in *La Ville de l'âge industriel, le cycle haussmannien (1840–1950),* ed. Maurice Agulhon, vol. 4, *Histoire de la France urbaine,* ed. Georges Duby (Paris: Editions du Seuil, 1983), 77–155; also Michel Lacave, "Stratégies d' expropriation et Haussmannisation: l'exemple de Montpellier," *Annales E.S.C.* 35 (1980).

34. Gaston Rambert, *Marseille, la formation d'une grande cité moderne* (Marseille: S. A. du Semaphore de Marseille, 1934).

35. Background information can be found in Collins, *Camillo Sitte and Modern City Planning.* Andrew Lees, "Perception of Cities in Britain and Germany," provides many valuable references. *See also* his articles, "Debates about the Big City in Germany, 1890–1914," *Societas* 5 (1975), and "Critics of Urban Society in Germany, 1854–1914," *Journal of the History of Ideas* 40 (1979). On Berlin, *see* Sutcliffe, "Environmental Planning in European Capitals," and Ingrid Thienel, "Verstädterung, Stadtische Infrastruktur und Stadtplannung: Berlin zwischen 1850 und 1914," *Zeitschrift fur Stadtgeschichte, Stadtsociologie und Denkmalpflege* (now *Die Alte Stadt*), no. 4 (1977).

36. On Belgium, *see* Yvon Leblicq, "L'Urbanisation de Bruxelles au XIXe et XXe siècles (1830–1952)", in *Villes en mutation, XIXe–XXe siècles,* 335–94, which is especially good on the conflict between Haussmann-style development and the more circumspect approach of Buls later in the century,

and focuses upon plans for a rail link between the North and South stations through the center; and Wilfried Krings, "Perception et aménagement du centre historique des villes; contributions belges, 1870–1914," Ibid., 395–425; on Italy, *see* Alberto Mioni, "Industrialisation, urbanisation et changements du paysage urbain en Italie entre 1861 et 1921," Ibid., 277–325; reference has already been made in other notes to articles on Scandinavia in *Growth and Transformation of the Modern City*.

37. Sutcliffe, *Towards the Planned City*, 203.

38. Ibid., 208.

39. David C. Hammack, *Power and Society: Greater New York at the Turn of the Century* (New York: Russell Sage Foundation, 1982), 56.

40. Lampard, "Urbanization of the United States," 153–57; David Cannadine, "Urban Development in England and America in the Nineteenth Century: Some Comparisons and Contrasts," *Economic History Review*, 2d ser., 33 (1980); Michael J. Doucet, "Urban Land Development in Nineteenth-Century North America: Themes in the Literature," *Journal of Urban History* 8 (1982).

41. Lampard, "Urbanization in the United States," 158.

42. Ibid., 170.

43. Ibid., 180.

44. Lampard, "The Nature of Urbanization," in *The Pursuit of Urban History*, ed. Derek Fraser and Anthony Sutcliffe, 39.

45. Anthony Sutcliffe, "The Growth of Public Intervention in the British Urban Environment during the Nineteenth Century: A Structural Approach," in *The Structure of Nineteenth-Century Cities*, ed. James H. Johnson and Colin G. Pooley, 114.

46. Eric L. Jones, S. Porter, and M. Turner, "A Gazeteer of English Urban Fire Disasters, 1500–1900," Historical Geography Research Series, forthcoming 1984. I am grateful to Professor Jones for sending me a copy of this paper prior to its publication.

47. Ibid.

48. John C. Weaver and Peter de Lottinville, "The Conflagration and the City: Disaster and Progress in British North America during the Nineteenth Century," *Histoire sociale/Social History* 13 (1980). Sven-Erik Åström, "Town Planning in Imperial Helsingfors, 1810–1910," in *Growth and Transformation of the Modern City*, ed. Ingrid Hammarström and Thomas Hall, 59–67, contains maps of building zones for 1825, 1859, and 1875 showing areas where all houses were of stone or brick, where houses were only faced in these materials on the street side, and where houses of wood were allowed, as well as the locations of industries using wood or open fires.

49. Blake Nelson, *Water for the Cities: A History of the Urban Water Supply Problem in the United States* (Syracuse: Syracuse University Press, 1956); Eugene P. Moehring, *Public Works and the Patterns of Real Estate Growth in Manhattan, 1835-1894* (New York: Arno Press, 1981).

50. Jon A. Peterson, "The Impact of Sanitary Reform upon American Urban Planning, 1840-1890," *Journal of Social History* 13 (1979); Joel A. Tarr, "The Separate vs. Combined Sewer Problem: A Case Study in Urban Technology Design Choice," *Journal of Urban History* 5 (1979); Louis P. Cain, "An Economic History of Urban Location and Sanitation," *Research in Economic History* 2 (1977); Stanley K. Schultz and Clay McShane, "To Engineer the Metropolis: Sewers, Sanitation and City Planning in Late Nineteenth-Century America," *Journal of American History* 65 (1978); Martin V. Melosi, ed., *Pollution and Reform in American Cities, 1870-1930* (Austin: University of Texas Press, 1980), and idem, *Garbage in the Cities: Refuse, Reform, and the Environment, 1880-1980* (College Station: Texas A.&M. Press, 1981).

51. Derek H. Aldcroft, "Urban Transport Problems in Historical Perspective," in *Business, Banking, and Urban History: Essays in Honour of S. G. Checkland*, ed. Anthony Slaven and Derek H. Aldcroft (Edinburgh: John Donald, 1982), 220-32.

52. Joel A. Tarr, "Urban Pollution: Many Long Years Ago," *American Heritage* 22 (1971). The eleven American cities were New York, St. Louis, Chicago, Cleveland, Cincinnati, Buffalo, San Francisco, New Orleans, Detroit, Milwaukee, and Washington, D.C.; Clay McShane, "Transforming the Use of Urban Space: A Look at the Revolution in Street Pavements, 1880-1924," *Journal of Urban History* 5 (1979), 280.

53. Walter Benjamin, *Charles Baudelaire: A Lyric Poet in the Era of High Capitalism*, trans. Harry Zohn (London: New Left Books, 1973).

54. Richard Sennett, *The Fall of Public Man* (New York: Random House, 1974; reprint 1978), 169.

55. Perry Duis, "Whose City? Public and Private Places in Nineteenth-Century Chicago," *Chicago History* 12 (1983).

56. McShane, "Transforming the Use of Urban Space," 284.

57. Schafer, *Tuning of the World*, 65-67. Charles Babbage estimated losing one-fourth of his intellectual effort from distractions by street musicians. He kept a partial list, recording 165 interruptions in 90 days. Michael T. Bass, *Street Music in the Metropolis* (London: John Murray, 1864).

58. M. J. Daunton, "Public Place and Private Space: The Victorian City and the Working-Class Household," in *The Pursuit of Urban History*, ed. Derek Fraser and Anthony Sutcliffe, 214. *See also* Leonore Davidoff and

Catherine Hall, "The Architecture of Public and Private Life: English Middle-Class Society in a Provincial Town 1780 to 1850," Ibid., 327–45; David R. Green, "Street Trading in London: A Case Study of Casual Labour, 1830–60," in *The Structure of Nineteenth-Century Cities*, ed. James H. Johnson and Colin G. Pooley, 129–52.

59. Raymond Williams, *The Country and the City* (New York: Oxford University Press, 1973), 222.

60. Ibid., 154–55. *See also* F. S. Schwarzbach, *Dickens and the City* (London: Athlone Press, 1979), an impressive, authoritative study which amplifies upon Williams's insights. Schwarzback points out that the characters in *Bleak House* "divide and isolate their public and private selves in an attempt to cope more easily with the unavoidable tensions of urban living" (125).

61. Hugh Duncan, *The Rise of Chicago as a Literary Center from 1885 to 1920* (Totowa, N.J.: Bedminster Press, 1964), and Sidney H. Bremer, "Lost Continuities: Alternative Urban Visions in Chicago Novels, 1890–1915," *Soundings* 64 (1981), provide alternative approaches to this kind of topic. On photography and the New York skyline, *see* Sam Bass Warner, Jr., "The Management of Multiple Urban Images," in *The Pursuit of Urban History*, ed. Derek Fraser and Anthony Sutcliffe, 383–94; and William Taylor, "New York et l'origine du 'Skyline': la cité moderne comme forme et symbole," *URBI*, no. 3 (1980); Peter Bacon Hales, *Silver Cities: The Photography of American Urbanization, 1839–1915* (Philadelphia: Temple University Press, 1983).

62. Chevalier, *Classes laborieuses et classes dangereuses à Paris*.

&❧ 5. The Regulatory Mode

1. *See*, for example, Bernard S. Katz, "Infrastructure," *Encyclopedia of Economics*, ed. Douglas Greenwald (New York: McGraw Hill, 1982), 522–23.

2. Thomas P. Hughes, *Networks of Power: Electrification in Western Society 1880–1930* (Baltimore: Johns Hopkins University Press, 1983).

3. Ibid., 197, 365.

4. Bonnie Maas Morrison, "Household Energy Consumption, 1900–1980," in *Energy and Transport: Historical Perspectives on Policy Issues*, ed. George H. Daniels and Mark H. Rose (Beverly Hills, Calif.: Sage, 1982), 202–33. Professor Morrison argues that, expressed in BTUs, household energy consumption of all sources has decreased in the twentieth century, and in 1969–70 was actually 31 percent below the historical peak of 1907. Total energy consumption per household in 1980 matched levels observed in 1936. *See also* Mark H. Rose and John G. Clark, "Light, Heat and Power:

Energy Choices in Kansas, Wichita, and Denver, 1900–1935," *Journal of Urban History* 5 (1979).

5. Reyner Banham, *The Architecture of the Well-Tempered Environment* (London: Architectural Press; Chicago: University of Chicago Press, 1979), 60–61.

6. Hughes, *Networks of Power*.

7. John P. McKay, *Tramways and Trolleys: The Rise of Urban Mass Transport in Europe* (Princeton: Princeton University Press, 1976).

8. Carl W. Condit, *The Port of New York*: vol. 1, *A History of the Rail and Terminal System from the Beginnings to Pennsylvania Station*; vol. 2, *A History of the Rail and Terminal System from the Grand Central Electrification to the Present* (Chicago: University of Chicago Press, 1980–81).

9. Barbara Miller Lane, "Changing Attitudes to Monumentality: An Interpretation of European Architecture and Urban Form, 1880–1914," in *Growth and Transformation of the Modern City*, ed. Thomas Hall and Ingrid Hammarström, 100–101.

10. *Fortune*, vol. 20, no. 1 (July, 1939); on skyscrapers, 117; on subsurface infrastructures, 126, 128, 194. In the United States, downtown office space increased by 3,000 percent between 1920 and 1930; there were 295 buildings twenty-one stories or taller in the five largest cities alone. Joseph Interrante, "The Road to Autopia: The Automobile and the Spatial Transformation of American Culture," *Michigan Quarterly Review* 19 (1980)–20 (1981), 506.

11. Quoted in *Cubism and American Photography*, ed. John Paltz and Catherine B. Scallen (Williamstown, Mass.: Sterling and Francine Clark Art Institute, 1981), 3. *See also* John R. Stilgoe, "Moulding the Industrial Zone Aesthetic: 1880–1929," *American Studies* 16 (1982).

12. Jules Romains, *The Sixth of October*, trans. Warre B. Wells, vol. 1, *Men of Good Will* (New York: Alfred A. Knopf, 1933), 143; quoted with permission of the publisher.

13. Ibid., 161–62.

14. Ibid., 157–58.

15. Idem, *The Seventh of October*, trans. Gerard Hopkins, vol. 14, *Men of Good Will* (New York: Alfred A. Knopf, 1946), 3, 4.

16. Mel Scott, *American City Planning Since 1890* (Berkeley and Los Angeles: University of California Press, 1969), 118.

17. Alan D. Anderson, *The Origins and Resolution of an Urban Crisis: Baltimore 1890–1930* (Baltimore: Johns Hopkins University Press, 1977), 107.

18. Mark Foster, "City Planning and Urban Transportation: The American Response, 1900–1940," *Journal of Urban History* 5 (1979), 367; *see also*

Blaine A. Brownell, "Urban Planning, the Planning Profession, and the Motor Vehicle in early Twentieth-Century America," in *Shaping an Urban World*, ed. Gordon Cherry (New York: St. Martin's Press, 1980), 59–77.

19. Lynch, *Theory of Good City Form*, 40. "[The] elements of the urban problem have been perceived as largely unrelated phenomena, leading to separate and frequently competing institutional bureaucracies." David Morely, Stuart Proudfoot, and Thomas Burns, eds. *Making Cities Work: The Dynamics of Urban Innovation* (London: Croom Helm; Boulder, Colo.: Westview Press, 1980), 17.

20. Jon Peterson, "The Impact of Sanitary Reform Upon American Urban Planning, 1840–1890," *Journal of Social History* 13 (1979), 95–96.

21. Erik Cohen, "Environmental Orientations: A Multidisciplinary Approach to Social Ecology," *Current Anthropology* 17 (1976), 54.

22. Federal Housing Authority, *A Handbook on Urban Redevelopment for Cities in the United States*, no. 2389 (Washington, D.C.: 1941), 62–66. Has the situation improved since the 1940s? Harvey Perloff observed recently: "A system of information is needed that cannot only report the condition of the city's physical plant at any given time, but which allows analysis of the relationship of physical condition to significant developments in the life of the people." *Planning the Post-Industrial City* (Washington, D.C., and Chicago: American Planning Association, Planners Press, 1980).

23. Reyner Banham, *Age of the Masters: A Personal View of Modern Architecture* (New York: Harper and Row, 1975), 110–11. For additional information on Marseille, *see* Rambert, *Marseille, cité moderne*; Jacques Gréber, *Plan d'aménagement et d'extension*, Bibliothèque de l'Institut d'urbanisme de l'Université de Paris (Paris: Vincent et Fréal, 1933); documents on the Quartier de la Bourse in Archives municipales, Marseille.

24. Banham, *Age of the Masters*, 14.

25. Lewis Mumford, "The City," originally published in 1922, reprinted in *City Development: Studies in Disintegration and Renewal* (New York: Harcourt Brace, 1945), 3–25; *see* especially 15–18.

26. Le Corbusier, *Towards a New Architecture*, trans. Frederick Etchells from *Vers une architecture*, 1923 (New York: 1927; reprint Praeger, 1960), 96–97.

27. Ibid., 88, 94.

28. Daniel J. Boorstin, *The Democratic Experience* vol. 3, *The Americans*, (New York: Vintage Random House, 1974), 535.

29. John Maxtone-Graham, *The Only Way to Cross* (New York: Macmillan, 1972), 113, 117.

30. Basil Greenhill and Ann Giffard, *Travelling by Sea in the Nineteenth*

Century: Interior Design in Victorian Passenger Ships (London: Adam and Charles Black, 1972); Frank O. Braynard, "Steamships of the Atlantic Seas," in *Decorative Arts of the Mariner*, ed. Gervis Frere-Cook (Boston: Little, Brown, 1966), 65–74.

31. David P. Billington, *The Tower and the Bridge: The New Art of Structural Engineering* (New York: Basic Books, 1983).

32. Banham, *Age of the Masters*, 58–62; idem, *Architecture of the Well-Tempered Environment*.

33. For some stimulating examples of environmental decisions on different scales, *see* John R. Stilgoe, *Metropolitan Corridor: Railroads and the American Scene* (New Haven: Yale University Press, 1983). Stilgoe mentions the problem of architects designing generators, which have to be built with expansion in mind and therefore have an incomplete form; yet ceaseless redesign violates aesthetic principles (123).

34. Roger Starr, "Making New York Smaller," *New York Times Magazine*, November 14, 1976, 105.

35. Peter W. Moore, "Public Services and Residential Development in a Toronto Neighborhood, 1880–1915," *Journal of Urban History*, 9 (1983).

36. Lewis, *Building Cycles and Britain's Growth*, 224.

37. Lampard, "Urbanization of the United States," 189–90.

38. Walter Isard, "A Neglected Cycle: The Transport-Building Cycle," *Review of Economic Statistics* 24 (1942), 149.

39. George F. Warren and Frank A. Pearson, *World Prices and the Building Industry* (New York: John Wiley and Sons, 1937).

40. Ibid., 113.

41. Ibid., 177.

42. Larry S. Bourne, "Private Redevelopment of the Central City: Spatial Process of Structural Change in the City of Toronto," research paper no. 112, Department of Geography (Chicago: University of Chicago, 1967), 2–3. There is no way to measure functional obsolescence, but regular procedures exist to monitor physical obsolescence. This perspective has been incorporated by Perloff in *Planning the Post-Industrial City*; for example, "A critically important, yet frequently overlooked, feature of urban planning should be the search for signs of system nonadaptability" (223). *See also* Peter Cowan, "Studies in the Growth, Change and Ageing of Buildings," *Transactions of the Bartlett Society* 1 (1962/63), 55–84.

43. Ibid., 4; italics in original.

44. Ibid., 133–34.

45. Ibid., 179.

46. Ibid., 176.

47. Peter Hall, *Great Planning Disasters* (London: Weidenfeld and Nicolson, 1980).

48. Stilgoe, "Moulding the Industrial Zone Aesthetic," 13.

49. "Tripping over the Office Wires," *The Economist*, April 16, 1983, 96.

50. André Vigarié, *Ports de commerce et vie littorale* (Paris: Hachette, 1979).

51. Konvitz, "Spatial Perspectives on Port City Development"; D. A. Pinder and B. S. Hoyle, "Cityports, Technologies and Development Strategies," in *Cityport Industrialization and Regional Development: Spatial Analysis and Planning Strategies*, ed. D. A. Pinder and B. S. Hoyle (Oxford: Pergamon, 1981), 328-38.

52. Ibid., 338. Marc J. Hershman, Stanley Euston, and Melissa M. Rohan, "The Future of U.S. Harbors," A Report to the Donner Foundation, Washington Sea Grant Program WSG AS 84-1 (Seattle: Institute for Marine Studies, University of Washington, 1983): "There is little understanding by policymakers and publics of the *harbor as a system* serving multiple and changing needs" (3). "The *harbor decision-making environment is complex*, fragmented, and often fails to recognize the interconnectedness of uses and the need for comprehensiveness in analysis and decision-making" (5).

53. Pierre Dansereau, *Inscape and Landscape: The Human Perception of Environment* (New York: Columbia University Press, 1975), 102-3.

54. Pat Choate, "Special Report on U.S. Economic Infrastructure," prepared for the House Wednesday Group, 1983; I am grateful to Steven Hofman and Matthew Cook of the Wednesday Group for letting me see a copy.

55. Lynch, *Theory of Good City Form*, 167.

56. Perloff, *Planning the Post-Industrial City*, 145.

57. Bjorn Linn, "Learning from Experience: The Use of Building and Planning History," in *Growth and Transformation of the Modern City*, ed. Ingrid Hammarström and Thomas Hall, 277-78.

ξ⋗ *6. Total War and Infrastructures*

HAROLD G. MARCUS read a draft of this chapter and provided useful advice for its revision.

1. Lynch, *Theory of Good City Form*, 184.

2. Gay Wilson Allen, *William James, A Biography* (New York: Viking Press, 1967), 445.

3. Michael Barkun, "Disaster in History," *Mass Emergencies* 2 (1977), 227.

4. Ibid., 223.

5. Ibid., 220, 230.

6. *See* the series *Histoire économique et sociale de la guerre mondiale*, série

française, published in the mid-1920s in Paris by Presses universitaires de France and in New Haven by Yale University Press. Volumes on Bourges were written by Claude Joseph Gignoux; on Paris by Henri Sellier and A. Bruggeman; on Bordeaux by Paul Courtenant; on Marseille by P. Masson; and on Rouen by J. Levainville. *See also* François Dutacq, *La ville de Lyon et la guerre: étude sur la politique économique d'une grande municipalité* (Paris: Presses universitaires de France, 1924).

7. Scott, *American City Planning*, 171–74.

8. Mark Swenarton, *Homes Fit for Heroes: The Politics and Architecture of Early State Housing in Britain* (London: Heinemann Educational Books, 1981).

9. Philip J. Funigiello, *The Challenge to Urban Liberalism: Federal-City Relations during World War II* (Knoxville: University of Tennessee Press, 1978).

10. Lowell Juilliard Carr and James Edson Stermer, *Willow Run: A Study of Industrialization and Cultural Inadequacy* (New York: Harper and Brothers, 1952), 313. *See also* Alan Clive, *State of War: Michigan in World War II* (Ann Arbor: University of Michigan Press, 1979); Frederick C. Lane, *Ships for Victory: A History of Shipbuilding under the United States Maritime Commission in World War II* (Baltimore: Johns Hopkins University Press, 1951), with excellent background on cities and shipyards; Richard H. Foster, Jr., "Wartime Trailer Housing in the San Francisco Bay Area," *Geographical Review* 70 (1980); Carl Abbott, "Portland in the Pacific War: Planning from 1940 to 1945," *Urbanism Past and Present* 6 (1980–81); Alonzo M. Smith, "Blacks and the Los Angeles Municipal Transit System, 1941–1945," Ibid.; Roger W. Lotchin, "The City and the Sword: San Francisco and the Rise of the Metropolitan Military Complex, 1919–1941," *Journal of American History*, 65 (1979).

11. Keith Mallory and Arvid Ottar, *Architecture of Aggression: A History of Military Architecture in North West Europe 1900–1945* (London: Architectural Press, 1975).

12. Department of the Navy, *Building the Navy's Bases in World War Two*, vol. 1, History of the Bureau of Yards and Docks and the Civil Engineer Corps, 1940–46 (Washington, D.C.: Government Printing Office, 1947); Lenore Fine and Jesse A. Remington, *The Corps of Engineers: Construction in the United States*, United States Army in World War Two, The Technical Services (Washington, D.C.: Government Printing Office, 1972).

13. Grant Hildebrand, *Designing for Industry: The Architecture of Albert Kahn* (Cambridge, Mass.: MIT Press, 1974).

14. Geoffrey Best, *Humanity in Warfare* (New York: Columbia University Press, 1980), 263.

15. David MacIsaac, *Strategic Bombing in World War Two: The Story of the United States Strategic Bombing Survey* (New York and London: Garland, 1976); Neville Jones, *The Origins of Strategic Thought and Practice up to 1918* (London: William Kimber, 1973); Sir Charles Webster and Noble Frankland, *The Strategic Air Offensive Against Germany, 1939–1945*, 4 vols., (London: Her Majesty's Stationery Office, 1961); W. W. Rostow, *Pre-Invasion Bombing Strategy: General Eisenhower's Decision of March 25, 1944* (Austin: University of Texas Press, 1981).

16. Richard Titmuss, *Problems of Social Policy*, History of the Second World War, United Kingdom Civil Series (London: His Majesty's Stationery Office, 1950), has excellent material on interwar estimates of potential casualties in another conflict. His book is also invaluable for an understanding of how civilians coped in England with evacuation and with life in cities under attack.

17. William Sansom, *Westminster in War* (London: Faber and Faber, n.d.); C. M. Kohan, *Works and Buildings*, History of the Second World War, Civil Series (London: His Majesty's Stationery Office, 1952); there is also much suggestive information about subterranean infrastructures for government functions in London in World War II in Peter Laurie's book, *Beneath the City Streets: A Private Enquiry into the Nuclear Perceptions of Government* (London: Allen Lane The Penguin Press, 1970).

18. Martin Middlebrook, *The Battle of Hamburg: Allied Bomber Forces Against a German City in 1943* (London: Allen Lane, 1980). To compare bombing against Germany with bombing against Japan, *see*: Thomas R. Havens, *Valley of Darkness: The Japanese People and World War II* (New York: W. W. Norton, 1976).

19. Fred Iklé, *The Social Impact of Bomb Destruction* (Norman: University of Oklahoma Press, 1950); *see also* Irving L. Janis, *Air War and Emotional Stress: Psychological Studies of Bombing and Civilian Defense*, Rand Corporation, (New York: McGraw Hill, 1951).

20. Evenson, *Paris*, 274–75.

21. Ibid., 41–49.

22. Marcel Smets, "The Reconstruction of Leuven after the Events of 1914," in *Villes en mutation XIXe–XXe siècles*, 499–533.

23. Stephen Spender, *Citizens in War and After* (London: George G. Harrap, 1945); for an American perspective on British cities at war which was very prescient for having been written so early in the conflict, *see* James L. Sundquist, *British Cities at War* (Chicago: Public Administration Service, 1940).

24. Funigiello, *The Challenge to Urban Liberalism*, 57 ff.

25. Ibid., 205–16, 248–49; *see also* John F. Bauman, "Visions of a Postwar City: A Perspective on Urban Planning in Philadelphia and the Nation, 1942–1945," *Urbanism Past and Present* 6 (1980–81).

26. Lutz Holzner, "The Role of History and Tradition in the Urban Geography of West Germany," *Annals of the Association of American Geographers*, 60 (1970); Percy Johnson-Marshall, *Rebuilding Cities* (Chicago: Aldine, 1966); Leo Grebler, *Europe's Reborn Cities*, Urban Land Institute, technical bulletin no. 28 (Washington, D.C., 1956); Anatole Kopp, Frédérique Boucher, and Danièle Pauly, *L'Architecture de la reconstruction en France* (Paris: Editions du Moniteur, 1982); Gerd Albers, "Town Planning in Germany: Change and Continuity under Conditions of Political Turbulence," in *Shaping an Urban World*, ed. Gordon E. Cherry (New York: St. Martin's Press, 1980), 145–60; Robert Fishman, "The Anti-Planners: The Contemporary Revolt against Planning and Its Significance for Planning History," Ibid., 243–52. The lessons of world war would indicate that the attitudes of antiplanners in favor of local control and individual initiative have some support in urban history. Very little has been done with the questions of cemeteries and monuments, but essential reading includes: "Silent Cities," exhibition catalog, Royal Institute of British Architects (London, 1978); Philip Longworth, *The Unending Vigil: A History of the Commonwealth War Graves Commission, 1917–1967* (London: Constable, 1967); George L. Mosse, "National Cemeteries and National Revival: The Cult of the Fallen Soldiers in Germany," *Journal of Contemporary History* 14 (1979).

ॐ 7. *Toward the Future*

1. Gerhard Mensch, *Stalemate in Technology: Innovations Overcome the Depression* (Cambridge, Mass.: Ballinger, 1979), especially 197.

2. Ibid., 219; Perloff, *Planning and Post-Industrial City*, 283. See also Pierre Laconte, ed., "Changing Cities: A Challenge to Planning," American Academy of Political and Social Science, *Annals* 451 (1980).

3. Lewis Mumford, *The Culture of Cities* (New York: Harcourt Brace, 1938), 443.

4. Kevin, Lynch, *What Time Is This Place?* (Cambridge, Mass.: MIT Press, 1972; reprint 1980), 108–9.

5. Ibid., 110. *See also* Peter Hall, *Great Planning Disasters*, 252, and Alice Coleman, "Is Planning Really Necessary?" *Geographical Journal*, 142 (1964).

6. Amos Rapoport, *Human Aspects of Urban Form: Towards a Man-Environment Approach to Urban Form and Design*, (Oxford: Pergamon, 1977), 356–57.

7. Richard G. Stein, *Architecture and Energy: Conserving Energy Through Rational Design* (New York: Anchor Press/Doubleday, 1977), 292–93.

8. Lynch, *Managing the Sense of a Region*, 7. "If the city is to maintain its adaptive quality, the public and private institutions that have created the city will be forced to make significant changes in their activities and management styles," wrote David Morely, Stuart Proudfoot, and Thomas Burns in the introduction to the essays they edited as *Making Cities Work: The Dynamics of Urban Innovation*, 19.

9. Lynch, *Managing the Sense of a Region*, 7; Anne Whiston Spirn, *The Granite Garden: Urban Nature and Human Design* (New York: Basic Books, 1983). A valuable survey of post-1945 writings on the cultural design process appears in "Camillo Sitte Reappraised," by George R. and Christiane C. Collins, 63–73.

10. Spirn, *The Granite Garden*, 231.

11. Ibid., 246.

12. Stephan A. Kliment, "Opening the Doors to Better Buildings: Choices for the Building Community," National Bureau of Standards, special publication no. 476 (Washington, D.C.: Government Printing Office, 1972): Marion Bowley, *The British Building Industry: Four Studies in Response and Resistance to Change* (Cambridge: Cambridge University Press, 1966). E. A. Johnson, *The Organization of Space in Developing Countries* Cambridge, Mass.: Harvard University Press, 1970), has many profound comments about the reasons for and consequences of inadequate attention to spatial and city-building concepts in education and politics, especially pp. 373–419.

13. National Commission on Urban Problems, "Building the American City," Report to the Congress and to the President of the United States (Washington, D.C.: Government Printing Office, 1968), 495–96.

14. Ibid., 497.

15. "Resilience is the capacity to use change to better cope with the unknown; it is learning to bounce back." Mary Douglas and Aaron Wildavsky, *Risk and Culture: An Essay on the Selection of Technical and Environmental Dangers* (Berkeley and Los Angeles: University of California Press, 1982).

16. Billington, *The Tower and the Bridge*, 213–32.

17. Jacob Bronowski, *The Visionary Eye: Essays in Art, Literature, and Science* (Cambridge, Mass.: MIT Press, 1978), 56.

18. Peter Szanton, *Not Well Advised* (New York: Russell Sage Foundation and Ford Foundation, 1981).

Bibliography

THE FOLLOWING LIST contains the books and articles cited in the Notes, plus a few additional items. A comprehensive listing of all secondary sources relevant to a history of city building would be impossible. Readers interested in further bibliographical guidance and in more specialized studies should consult the annual bibliographies in the *Urban History Yearbook* (Leicester: Leicester University Press), the bibliographies in *Urbanism Past and Present*, the review articles in the *Journal of Urban History*, Anthony Sutcliffe's bibliography of planning history, Eugene Moehring's bibliographic essay on American urban history and public works history, bibliographies published by the Council of Planning Librarians, and various national bibliographies of local and municipal history. Many of the other articles and books cited below contain extensive bibliographies as well.

Abbott, Carl. "Portland in the Pacific War: Planning from 1940 to 1945." *Urbanism Past and Present* 6 (1980–81): 12–24.

Agus, Irving A. *Urban Civilization in Pre-Crusade Europe.* 2 vols. New York: Yeshiva University Press, 1965.

Albers, Gerd. "Town Planning in Germany: Change and Continuity under Conditions of Political Turbulence." In *Shaping an Urban World*, edited by Gordon E. Cherry, 145–60.

Aldcroft, Derek H. "Urban Transport Problems in Historical Perspective." In *Business, Banking, and Urban History: Essays in Honour of S. G. Checkland*, edited by Anthony Slaven and Derek H. Aldcroft, 220–32. Edinburgh: John Donald, 1982.

Alford, B. W. E., and M. Q. Smith. "The Economic Effects of Cathedral and Church Building in Medieval England: A Reply." *Explorations in Entrepreneurial History* 6 (1969): 158–69.

Allen, Gay Wilson. *William James, A Biography.* New York: Viking Press, 1967.

Anderson, Alan D. *The Origins and Resolution of an Urban Crisis: Baltimore 1890–1930.* Baltimore: Johns Hopkins University Press, 1977.

Andreina, Griseri. "Urbanistica, cartografica e antico regime nel Piemonte Sabaudo." *Storia della Città,* nos. 12/13 (1979): 19–38.

Andrews, Richard Mowrey. "Paris of the Great Revolutions: 1789–1796." In *People and Communities in the Western World.* Vol. 2, edited by Gene Brucker, 56–112. Homewood, Ill.: Dorsey Press, 1979.

Argan, Giulio C. *The Renaissance City.* New York: George Braziller, 1969.

Artibise, Alan F. J., and Gilbert A. Stelter. *Canada's Urban Past: A Bibliography to 1980 and Guide to Canadian Urban Studies.* Vancouver: University of British Columbia Press, 1981.

Aspinall, Peter. "The Internal Structure of the Housebuilding Industry" in *Nineteenth-Century Cities,* edited by James H. Johnson and Colin G. Pooley, 75–106.

Åström, Sven-Erik. "Town Planning in Imperial Helsingfors, 1810–1910." In *Growth and Transformation of the Modern City,* edited by Ingrid Hammarström and Thomas Hall, 59–67.

Baker, John. *Enterprise versus Bureaucracy: The Development of Structural Air-Raid Precautions during the Second World War.* Oxford: Pergamon Press, 1978.

Banham, Reyner. *Age of the Masters: A Personal View of Modern Architecture.* New York: Harper and Row, 1975.

———. *The Architecture of the Well-Tempered Environment.* London: Architectural Press; Chicago: University of Chicago Press, 1979.

Barkun, Michael. "Disaster in History." *Mass Emergencies* 2 (1977): 219–31.

Barley, M. W., ed. *European Towns: Their Archaeology and Early History.* Council for British Archaeology. London and New York: Academic Press, 1977.

Bass, Michael T. *Street Music in the Metropolis.* London: John Murray, 1864.

Bauman, John F. "Visions of a Post-War City: A Perspective on Urban Planning in Philadelphia and the Nation, 1942–1945." *Urbanism Past and Present* 6 (1980–81): 1–11.

Bautier, Robert. *The Economic Development of Medieval Europe.* Translated by Heather Karolyi. London: Thames and Hudson, 1971.

Benjamin, Walter. *Charles Baudelaire: A Lyric Poet in the Era of High Capitalism,* translated by Harry Zohn. London: New Left Books, 1973.

Bercé, Y.-M. *Fête et révolte; des mentalités populaires du XVIe au XVIIIe siècle.* Paris: Hachette, 1976.

Beresford, Maurice. *New Towns of the Middle Ages: Town Plantation in England, Wales, and Gascony.* New York: Praeger, 1967.

Bernard, Leon. *The Emerging City.* Durham, N.C.: Duke University Press, 1970.

Best, Geoffrey. *Humanity in Warfare.* New York: Columbia University Press, 1980.

Bier, A. L. "Social Problems in Elizabethan London." *Journal of Interdisciplinary History* 9 (1978): 203–22.

Billington, David P. *The Tower and the Bridge: The New Art of Structural Engineering.* New York: Basic Books, 1983.

Billington, James. *Fire in the Minds of Men.* New York: Basic Books, 1980.

Blanchard, Anne. *Les Ingénieurs du 'Roy' de Louis XIV à Louis XV: étude des corps des fortifications.* Collection du Centre d'histoire militaire et d'études de défense nationale de Montpellier, no. 9. Montpellier: Université Paul-Valéry, 1980.

Blunt, Anthony. *Neapolitan Baroque and Rococo Architecture.* London: A. Zwemmer, 1975.

Bookchin, Murray. *The Limits of the City.* New York: Harper and Row, 1974.

Boorstin, Daniel J. *The Democratic Experience.* Vol. 3, *The Americans.* New York: Random House, 1974.

Bord, Gustave. *Les Inondations du bassin de la Seine, 1658–1910.* Paris: n.p., 1910.

Borsay, Peter. "Culture, Status, and the English Landscape." *History* 67 (1982): 1–12.

————. "The English Urban Renaissance and the Development of Provincial Urban Culture, c. 1680–1760." *Social History* 2 (1977): 581–603.

Bouchary, Jean. *L'Eau à Paris à la fin du XVIIIe siècle; la compagnie des eaux de Paris et l'entreprise de l'Yvette.* Paris: Rivière, 1946.

Boudon, Françoise. "La 'Haussmanisation' du centre de Paris: le nouveau parcellaire." *Storia della Città,* no. 5 (1977): 34–53.

————, André Chastel, Hélène Couzy, Françoise Hamon. *Système de l'architecture urbaine: le quartier des halles à Paris.* 2 vols. Paris: CNRS, 1977.

————, and Hélène Couzy. "Châteaux de cartes: l'histoire de l'architecture et la cartographie." *Storia della Città,* nos. 12/13 (1979): 63–78.

Bourne, Larry S. "Private Redevelopment of the Central City: Spatial Process of Structural Change in the City of Toronto," research paper no. 112, Department of Geography. Chicago: University of Chicago, 1967.

Bouwsma, William J. "Anxiety and the Formation of Early Modern Culture." In *After the Reformation: Essays in Honor of J. H. Hexter,* edited by

Barbara C. Malament, 215–46. Philadelphia: University of Pennsylvania Press, 1980.

Bowley, Marion. *The British Building Industry: Four Studies in Response and Resistance to Change.* Cambridge: Cambridge University Press, 1966.

Boyer, Marjorie Nice. *Medieval French Bridges: A History.* Publication no. 84. Cambridge, Mass.: Medieval Academy of America, 1976.

Braham, Allan. *The Architecture of the French Enlightenment.* London: Thames and Hudson, 1980.

Branner, Robert. *St. Louis and the Court Style in Gothic Architecture.* London: A. Zwemmer, 1965.

Braynard, Frank O. "Steamships of the Atlantic Seas." In *Decorative Arts of the Mariner,* edited by Gervis Frere-Cook, 65–74. Boston: Little, Brown, 1966.

Bremer, Sidney H. "Lost Continuities: Alternative Urban Visions in Chicago Novels, 1890–1915." *Soundings* 64 (1981): 29–51.

Brett-James, Norman. *The Growth of Stuart London.* London: Allen and Unwin, 1935.

Briggs, Asa. *Victorian Cities.* 1963; reprint, Harmondsworth: Pelican Books, 1968.

Brino, Giovanni, and Franco Rosso. *Colore e Città, il piano del colore di Torinio 1800–1850.* Milan: Idea Editions, 1980.

Bronowski, Jacob. *The Visionary Eye: Essays in Art, Literature, and Science.* Cambridge, Mass.: MIT Press, 1978.

Brownell, Blaine A. "Urban Planning, the Planning Profession, and the Motor Vehicle in early Twentieth-Century America." In *Shaping an Urban World,* edited by Gordon Cherry, 59–77.

Buisson, Sylvie. "Le Plan des Artistes, 1794–1797." *La Vie urbaine,* no. 55 (1950): 8–21; no. 57 (1950): 161–71.

Bull, G. B. G. "Thomas Milne's Land Utilization Map of the London Area in 1800." *Geographical Journal* 122 (1956): 25–30.

Burke, Gerald. *The Making of Dutch Towns.* London: Cleaver-Hume Press, 1956.

———. *Towns in the Making.* London: Edward Arnold, 1971.

Burke, Peter. *Popular Culture in Early Modern Europe.* New York: Harper and Row, 1978.

———. "Some Reflections on the Pre-Industrial City." *Urban History Yearbook* 1975, 13–21. Leicester: Leicester University Press, 1975.

Cain, Louis P. "An Economic History of Urban Location and Sanitation." *Research in Economic History* 2 (1977): 376–83.

Canetti, Elias. *Crowds and Power*, translated by Carol Stewart. New York: Seabury Press, 1978; reprint, New York: Continuum Press, 1981.

Cannadine, David. *Lords and Landlords: The Aristocracy and the Towns, 1774–1967*. Leicester: Leicester University Press, 1980.

———. "Urban Land Development in England and America in the Nineteenth Century: Some Comparisons and Contrasts." *Economic History Review*, 2d ser., 33 (1980): 309–25.

———, ed. *Patricians, Power, and Politics in Nineteenth-Century Towns*. Leicester: Leicester University Press, 1982.

———, and David Reeder, eds. *Exploring the Urban Past: Essays in Urban History by H. J. Dyos*. Cambridge: Cambridge University Press, 1982.

Carr, Lowell Juilliard, and James Edson Stermer. *Willow Run: A Study of Industrialization and Cultural Inadequacy*. New York: Harper and Brothers, 1952.

Carter, Howard. "The Map in Urban History." *Urban History Yearbook 1979*, 11–31. Leicester: Leicester University Press, 1979.

Cassirer, Thomas. "Awareness of the City in the 'Encyclopédie'." *Journal of the History of Ideas* 24 (1963): 387–96.

Castagnoli, Ferdinando. *Orthogonal Town Planning in Antiquity*. Cambridge, Mass.: MIT Press, 1971.

Chalklin, C. W. *The Provincial Towns of Georgian England: A Study of the Building Process 1740–1820*. London: Edward Arnold, 1974.

Chastel, André. "Problèmes d'urbanisme à Paris au XVIIIe siècle." In *Sensibilità e Razionalità del Settecento*, edited by Vittore Brana. Vol. 2, 617–28. Venice: Sansoni, 1967.

Cherry, Gordon, ed. *Shaping an Urban World*. New York: St. Martin's Press, 1981.

Chevalier, Bernard. *Les Bonnes villes de France du XIVe au XVIe siècle*. Paris: Aubier Montaigne, 1982.

Chevalier, Louis. *Classes laborieuses et classes dangereuses à Paris pendant la première moitié du XIXe siècle*. Paris: Plon, 1958.

Choate, Pat. "Special Report on U.S. Economic Infrastructure." House Wednesday Group, U.S. House of Representatives, 1983.

Choay, Françoise. *L'Urbanisme, utopies et réalités, une anthologie*. Paris: Editions du Seuil, 1965.

Cipolla, Carlo M. *Clocks and Culture, 1300–1700*. New York: W. W. Norton, 1977.

Clive, Alan. *State of War: Michigan in World War II*. Ann Arbor: University of Michigan Press, 1979.

Cobb, Richard. *Paris and its Provinces 1792–1802*. London: Oxford University Press, 1975.

———. *The Police and the People: French Popular Protest 1789–1820*. Oxford: Clarendon Press, 1970.

Cohen, Erik. "Environmental Orientations: A Multidisciplinary Approach to Social Ecology." *Current Anthropology* 17 (1976): 49–70.

Coleman, Alice. "Is Planning Really Necessary?" *Geographical Journal* 142 (1964): 411–37.

Collins, George R., and Christiane C. Collins. *Camillo Sitte and the Birth of Modern City Planning*. New York: Random House, 1965.

———. "Camillo Sitte Reappraised." In *Planning for Conservation*, edited by Roger Kain, 63–73. New York: St. Martin's Press, 1981.

Collins, Peter. *Changing Ideals in Modern Architecture, 1750–1950*. London: Faber and Faber, 1965.

Colquhoun, Patrick. *A Treatise on the Commerce and Police of the River Thames*. N.p., 1800.

Comer, John P. *New York City Building Control 1800–1941*. New York: Columbia University Press, 1942.

Condit, Carl W. *American Building: Materials and Techniques from the First Colonial Settlements to the Present*. Chicago: University of Chicago Press, 1967.

———. *The Port of New York*. Vol. 1, *A History of the Rail and Terminal System from the Beginnings to Pennsylvania Station*. Vol. 2, *A History of the Rail and Terminal System from the Grand Central Electrification to the Present*. Chicago: University of Chicago Press, 1980–81.

Les constructions civiles d'intérêt public dans les villes d'Europe au moyen-âge et sous l'ancien régime et leur financement. Colloque internationale, Spa 1968. Collection Histoire Pro-civitate, no. 26. Brussels: Crédit Communal de Belgique, 1971.

Contamine, Philippe. "Les Fortifications urbaines en France à la fin du Moyen-Age, aspects financiers et économiques." *Revue historique* 102 (1978): 23–47.

Cosgrove, Denis. "The Myth and Stones of Venice: An Historical Geography of a Symbolic Landscape." *Journal of Historical Geography* 8 (1982) 145–69.

Cowan, Peter. *The Office: A Facet of Urban Growth*. New York: American Elsevier, 1969.

———. "Studies in the Growth, Change and Ageing of Buildings." *Transactions of the Bartlett Society* 1 (1962/63): 55–84.

Cowan, Ruth Schwartz. "The 'Industrial Revolution' in the Home: Household Technology and Social Change in the 20th Century." *Technology and Culture* 17 (1976): 1–23.

Coyecque, E. "Les Plans cadastraux de la ville de Paris aux Archives nationales, d'après un rapport de la direction générale des contributions directes." *Bulletin de la société de l'histoire de Paris* 35 (1908).

Croix, Horst de la. "Military Architecture and the Radial City Plan in Sixteenth-Century Italy." *Art Bulletin* 42 (1960): 263–90.

————. *Military Considerations in City Planning: Fortifications.* New York: George Braziller, 1972.

Cruickshank, Dan, and Peter Wyld. *London: The Art of Georgian Building.* London: Architectural Press, 1975.

Daiches, David, and John Flower. *Literary Landscapes of the British Isles, A Narrative Atlas.* New York and London: Paddington Press, 1979.

Danville, François de. "Grandeur et population des villes au XVIIIe siècle." *Population* 13 (1958): 459–80.

Danbom, David. *The Resisted Revolution: Urban America and the Industrialization of Agriculture, 1900–1930.* Ames: Iowa State University Press, 1979.

Dansereau, Pierre. *Inscape and Landscape: The Human Perception of Environment.* New York: Columbia University Press, 1975.

Darlington, Ida. "Edwin Chadwick and the First Large-Scale Ordnance Survey of London." *Transactions of the London & Middlesex Archeological Society* 22 (1969): 58–62.

————, and James Howgego. *Printed Maps of London, circa 1553–1850.* London: G. Philip, 1964.

Daumard, Adeline. "L'Avenue de l'Opéra de ses origines à la guerre de 1914." *Bulletin de la société de l'historie de Paris,* (1967–68): 157–95.

————. "Quelques remarques sur le logement des Parisiens au XIXe siècle." *Annales de démographie historiques* (1975): 49–64.

Daumas, Maurice. "La Géographie industrielle de Paris au XIXe siècle." In *Villes en mutation XIXe–XXe siècles,* 91–145.

Daunton, M. J. "Public Place and Private Space: The Victorian City and the Working-Class Household." In *The Pursuit of Urban History,* edited by Derek Fraser and Anthony Sutcliffe, 212–33.

Davidoff, Leonore, and Catherine Hall. "The Architecture of Public and Private Life: English Middle-Class Society in a Provincial Town 1780–1850." In *The Pursuit of Urban History,* edited by Derek Fraser and Anthony Sutcliffe, 327–45.

Davis, Natalie Zemon. "The Sacred and the Body Social in Sixteenth-Century Lyon." *Past and Present,* no. 90 (1981): 40–170.

Delumeau, Jean. *Rome au 16e siècle.* Paris: Hachette, 1975.

Demangeon, Alain, and Bruno Fortier. "La Politique de l'espace urbain, la ville des années 1800." *Architectural Design* 48 (1978): 8–13.

————. *Les Vaisseaux et les villes, l'arsenal de Cherbourg.* Brussels: Pierre Mardaga, 1978.

Department of the Navy. *Building the Navy's Bases in World War Two.* Vol. 1, History of the Bureau of Yards and Docks and the Civil Engineer Corps, 1940–46. Washington, D.C.: Government Printing Office, 1947.

Dollinger, Philippe. *La Hanse.* Paris: Aubier, 1964.

Doucet, Michael J. "Urban Land Development in Nineteenth-Century North America: Themes in the Literature." *Journal of Urban History* 8 (1982): 299–342.

Douglas, Mary, and Aaron Wildavsky. *Risk and Culture: An Essay on the Selection of Technical and Environmental Dangers.* Berkeley and Los Angeles: University of California Press, 1982.

Doxiadis, Constantinos A. *Architecture in Transition.* New York: Oxford University Press, 1963.

Dresbeck, LeRoy. "Winter Climate and Society in the Northern Middle Ages: The Technological Impact." In *On Pre-Modern Technology and Science: A Volume of Studies in Honor of Lynn White, Jr.*, edited by Bert S. Hall and Delno C. West for the Center for Medieval and Renaissance Studies, University of California, Los Angeles. Malibu, Calif.: Undema, 1976.

Duby, Georges. *The Early Growth of the European Economy; Warriors and Peasants from the Seventh to the Twelfth Century*, translated by Howard B. Clarke. London: Weidenfeld and Nicolson, 1974.

————. "Les villes du Sud-Est de la Gaule du VIIIe au XIe siècle." In *Hommes et structures au moyen-âge: recueil d'articles*, by Georges Duby, 111–31. Paris and The Hague: Mouton, 1973.

Duis, Perry. "Whose City? Public and Private Places in Nineteenth-Century Chicago." *Chicago History* 12 (1983): 2–27.

Duncan, Hugh. *The Rise of Chicago as a Literary Center from 1885 to 1920.* Totowa, N.J.: Bedminster Press, 1964.

Dutacq, François. *La ville de Lyon et la guerre: étude sur la politique économique d'une grande municipalité.* Paris: Presses universitaires de France, 1924.

Dyos, H. J. "A Guide to the Streets of Victorian London." In *Exploring the Urban Past*, edited by David Cannadine and David Reeder, 190–201.

————. "The Speculative Buildings and Developers in Victorian London." In *Exploring the Urban Past*, edited by David Cannadine and David Reeder, 154–75.

————, and Michael Wolff, eds. *The Victorian City, Images and Realities.* 2 vols. London: Routledge and Kegan Paul, 1973.

Edgerton, Samuel Y., Jr. *The Renaissance Rediscovery of Linear Perspective.* New York: Harper and Row, 1975.

Eitlin, Richard. "L'Air dans l'urbanisme des lumières." *Dix-huitième siècle* 9 (1977): 123–34.

Elazar, Daniel J. "Urban Problems and the Federal Government: An Historical Inquiry." *Political Science Quarterly* 82 (1967): 505–25.

Epstein, Amy Kallman. "Multifamily Dwellings and the Search for Respectability: Origins of the New York Apartment House." *Urbanism Past and Present* 5 (1980): 29–39.

Erenberg, Ralph E. "Mapping the Nation's Capital: The Surveyor's Office, 1791–1818." *Quarterly Journal of the Library of Congress* 36 (1979): 279–319.

Ettlinger, Leopold D. "The Emergence of the Italian Architect during the Fifteenth Century." In *The Architect: Chapters in the History of the Profession,* edited by Spiro Kostof, 96–123. New York, Oxford University Press, 1977.

Evenson, Norma. *Paris: A Century of Change, 1878–1978.* New Haven: Yale University Press, 1979.

Everitt, Alan. "Country, County and Town: Patterns of Regional Evolution in England." *Transactions of the Royal Historical Society,* 5th ser., 29 (1979): 79–107.

————. "The English Urban Inn 1560–1760." In *Perspectives in English Urban History,* edited by Alan Everitt, 91–137. London: Macmillan, 1973.

Fales, Robert L., and Leon N. Moses. "Land Use Theory and the Spatial Structure of the Nineteenth-Century City." *Papers of the Regional Science Association* 28 (1972): 49–80.

Fanelli, Giovanni. *Firenze, archittetura e città.* 2 vols. Florence: Vallechi, 1973.

Federal Housing Authority. *A Handbook on Urban Redevelopment for Cities in the United States,* no. 2389. Washington, D.C.: 1941.

Ferguson, Eugene S. "Mr. Jefferson's Dry Docks." *The American Neptune* 11 (1951): 108–14.

Fine, Lenore, and Jesse A. Remington. *The Corps of Engineers: Construction in the United States.* United States Army in World War Two, The Technical Services. Washington, D.C.: Government Printing Office, 1972.

Fishman, Robert. "The Anti-Planners: The Contemporary Revolt against

Planning and Its Significance for Planning History." In *Shaping an Urban World*, edited by Gordon E. Cherry, 243–52.

Fitch, James M. *American Building*. 2 vols. New York: Schocken, 2d ed. 1966.

Fortier, Bruno. "La Maitrise de l'eau." *Dix-Huitième siècle* 9 (1977): 193–201.

————. "Public Space and Civil Society: From the Salines de Chaux to Milan's Foro Bonaparte." *Lotus* 24 (1970): 14–20.

————, and Bruno Vayssière. "L'Architecture des villes: espaces, cartes et territoires." *URBI*, no. 3 (1980): 53–62.

Foster, Mark. "The Automobile in the Urban Environment: Planning for an Energy-Short Future." *The Public Historian* 3 (1981): 23–31.

————. "City Planning and Urban Transportation: The American Response, 1900–1940." *Journal of Urban History* 5 (1979): 365–96.

Foster, Richard H., Jr. "Wartime Trailer Housing in the San Francisco Bay Area." *Geographical Review* 70 (1980): 276–90.

Fox, Edward Whiting. *History in Geographic Perspective*. New York: W. W. Norton, 1971.

França, José-Augusto. *Une Ville des lumières: la Lisbonne de Pombal*. Paris: SEVPEN, 1965.

Francastel, Pierre. "L'Esthétique des lumières." In *Utopie et institutions au 18e siècle, le pragmatisme des lumières*, edited by Pierre Francastel, 331–57. Ecole pratique des hautes études, 6e sec., Congrès et colloques, no. 4. Paris and The Hague: Mouton, 1973.

————. "Imagination et réalité dans l'architecture civile du Quattrocento." In *Hommage à Lucien Fevre: éventail de l'histoire vivante*. Vol. 2, 195–206. Paris: Armand Colin, 1953.

Fraser, Derek, and Anthony Sutcliffe, eds. *The Pursuit of Urban History*. London: Edward Arnold, 1983.

Frieden, Bernard. *The Environmental Protection Hustle*. Cambridge, Mass.: MIT Press, 1979.

Friedrichs, Christopher. "German Town Revolts and the Seventeenth-Century Crisis." *Renaissance and Modern Studies* 16 (1982): 27–51.

Frisch, Michael. "American Urban History as an Example of Recent Historiography." *History and Theory* 18 (1979): 350–77.

Funigiello, Philp J. *The Challenge to Urban Liberalism: Federal-City Relations during World War II*. Knoxville: University of Tennessee Press, 1978.

Gadol, Joan. *Leon Battista Alberti: Universal Man of the Early Renaissance*. Chicago: University of Chicago Press, 1969.

Gaillard, Jeanne. *Paris la ville, 1852–1870*. Paris: Plon, 1958.

Garin, Eugenio. "La cité idéale de la renaissance." In *Les Utopies à la Renaissance*, 11–37. Travaux de l'Institut pour l'étude de la renaissance et de l'humanisme, no. 1. Brussels: Presses universitaires de Bruxelles; Paris: Presses universitaires de France, 1963.

Garms, Jörg. "Le Plan d'urbanisme de Strasbourg dressé par Jacques-François Blondel en 1764–69." *Cahiers alsaciens d'archéologie, d'art et d'histoire* 21 (1978): 103–41.

Gauldie, Enid. *Cruel Habitations: A History of Working-Class Housing 1780–1918*. London: Allen and Unwin, 1974.

Geist, Johann Friedrich. *Passagen: ein Bautyp des 19 Jahrhunderts*. Munich: Prestel, 3d ed. 1979.

Gelfand, Mark I. *A Nation of Cities: The Federal Government and Urban America 1933–1965*. New York: Oxford University Press, 1975.

Gillispie, Charles C. *Science and Polity in France at the End of the Old Regime*. Princeton: Princeton University Press, 1980.

Glickman, Norman. *The Urban Impacts of Federal Policies*. Prepared for the U.S. Department of Housing and Urban Development. Baltimore: Johns Hopkins University Press, 1980.

Goldberger, Paul. "Organic Remedies: Building and the City." *Salmagundi* no. 49 (Summer 1980): 87–98.

Goldthwaite, Richard A. *The Building of Renaissance Florence: An Economic and Social History*. Baltimore: Johns Hopkins University Press, 1980.

———. "The Florentine Palace as Domestic Architecture." *American Historical Review* 77 (1972): 977–1012.

Gréber, Jacques. *Plan d'aménagement et d'extension*. Bibliothèque de l'Institut d'urbanisme de l'Université de Paris. Paris: Vincent et Fréal, 1933.

Grebler, Leo. *Europe's Reborn Cities*. Urban Land Institute, technical bulletin no. 28. Washington, D.C., 1956.

Green, David R. "Street Trading in London: A Case Study of Casual Labour, 1830–60." In *The Structure of Nineteenth-Century Cities*, edited by James H. Johnson and Colin G. Pooley, 129–52.

Greenhill, Basil, and Ann Giffard. *Travelling by Sea in the Nineteenth Century: Interior Design in Victorian Passenger Ships*. London: Adam and Charles Black, 1972.

Gruber, Karl. *Die Gestalt der deutschen Stadt*. Munich: Callwey, 1952; reprint, 1977.

Gutkind, E. A. *The Netherlands and Great Britain*. Vol. 6, *International History of City Development*. New York: Free Press, 1970.

———. *Urban Development in Southern Europe: Italy and Greece*. Vol. 4, *International History of City Development*. New York: Free Press, 1969.

Hales, Peter Bacon. *Silver Cities: The Photography of American Urbanization, 1839–1915*. Philadelphia: Temple University Press, 1983.

Hall, Peter. *Great Planning Disasters*. London: Weidenfeld and Nicolson, 1980.

Hall, Thomas. "The Central Business District: Planning in Stockholm, 1928–1978." In *Growth and Transformation of the Modern City*, edited by Ingrid Hammarström and Thomas Hall, 181–232.

Hammack, David. *Power and Society: Greater New York at the Turn of the Century*. New York: Russell Sage Foundation, 1982.

Hammarström, Ingrid. "Urban Growth and Building Fluctuations: Stockholm 1860–1920." In *Growth and Transformation of the Modern City*, edited by Hammarström and Hall, 29–47.

Hammarström, Ingrid, and Thomas Hall, eds. *The Growth and Transformation of the Modern City*. Stockholm: Swedish Council for Building Research, 1979.

Hammond, Mason, assisted by Lester J. Bartson. *The City in the Ancient World*. Cambridge, Mass.: Harvard University Press, 1972.

Harouel, Jean-Louis. "Les Fonctions de l'alignement dans l'organisme urbain." *Dix-huitième siècle* 9 (1977): 135–49.

Harvey, John. *The Master Builders: Architecture in the Middle Ages*. New York: McGraw-Hill, 1971.

———. *The Medieval Architect*. London: Wayland Publishers, 1972.

Harvey, P. D. A. *The History of Topographical Maps: Symbols, Pictures and Survey*. London: Thames and Hudson, 1980.

Havens, Thomas R. *Valley of Darkness: The Japanese People and World War II*. New York: W. W. Norton, 1976.

Hennock, E. P. "Central/Local Government Relations in England: An Outline 1800–1950." *Urban History Yearbook 1982*, 38–49. Leicester: Leicester University Press, 1982.

Herbert, Gilbert. *Pioneers of Prefabrication: The British Contribution in the Nineteenth Century*. Baltimore: Johns Hopkins University Press, 1978.

Hershman, Marc J., Stanley Euston, and Melissa M. Rohan. "The Future of U.S. Harbors." A Report to the Donner Foundation. Washington Sea Grant Program WSG AS 84–1. Seattle: Institute for Marine Studies, University of Washington, 1983.

Hibbert, A. B. "The Economic Policies of Towns." In *Economic Organization and Policies in the Middle Ages*, edited by M. M. Postan, E. E. Rich, and Edward Muller, 157–229. Vol. 3, *Cambridge Economic History of Europe*. Cambridge: Cambridge University Press, 1963.

————. "The Origins of the Medieval Town Patriciate." *Past and Present*, no. 3 (1954): 15–27.

Hildebrand, Grant. *Designing for Industry: The Architecture of Albert Kahn.* Cambridge, Mass.: MIT Press, 1974.

Holland, Laurence B. *Who Designs America?* Garden City, N.J.: Anchor Doubleday, 1966.

Hollestelle, Johanna. *De Steenbakkerij in de Nederlanden tot omstreeks 1560.* Assen: Van Gorkum, [1961].

Holzner, Lutz. "The Role of History and Tradition in the Urban Geography of West Germany." *Annals of the Association of American Geographers* 60 (1970): 315–39.

Horn, Walter, and Ernest Born. *The Plan of St. Gall.* 3 vols. Berkeley and Los Angeles: University of California Press, 1979.

Hughes, Diane Gwen. "Urban Growth and Family Structure in Medieval Genoa." *Past and Present*, no. 66 (1975): 3–28.

Hughes, Thomas P. *Networks of Power: Electrification in Western Society 1880–1930.* Baltimore: Johns Hopkins University Press, 1983.

Hugueney, Jeanne. "Les Halles Centrales de Paris au XIXe siècle." *La Vie urbaine* 66 (1968): 81–130.

Iklé, Fred. *The Social Impact of Bomb Destruction.* Norman: University of Oklahoma Press, 1950.

Interrante, Joseph. "The Road to Autopia: The Automobile and the Spatial Transformation of American Culture." *Michigan Quarterly Review* 19 (1980) –20 (1981): 502–17.

Isard, Walter. "A Neglected Cycle: The Transport-Building Cycle." *Review of Economic Statistics* 24 (1942): 149–58.

Jacquement, Gérard. "Belleville aux XIXe et XXe siècles: Une méthode d'analyse de la croissance urbaine à Paris." *Annales E.S.C.* 30 (1975): 819–43.

Janis, Irving L. *Air War and Emotional Stress: Psychological Studies of Bombing and Civilian Defense.* Rand Corporation. New York: McGraw-Hill, 1951.

Jarcho, Saul. "Yellow Fever, Cholera, and the Beginnings of Medical Cartography." *Journal of the History of Medicine and Allied Sciences* 25 (1970): 131–42.

Johnson, E. A. *The Organization of Space in Developing Countries.* Cambridge, Mass.: Harvard University Press, 1970.

Johnson, H. Thomas. "Cathedral Building and the Medieval Economy." *Explorations in Entrepreneurial History* 4 (1967): 191–210.

————. "The Economic Effects of Cathedral and Church Building in

Medieval England: A Rejoinder." *Explorations in Entrepreneurial History* 6 (1969): 170–74.

Johnson, James H., and Colin G. Pooley, eds. *The Structure of Nineteenth-Century Cities.* London and Canberra: Croom Helm; New York: St. Martin's Press, 1982.

Johnson-Marshall, Percy. *Rebuilding Cities.* Chicago: Aldine, 1966.

Jones, Eric L. *Environments, Economies and Geopolitics in the History of Europe and Asia.* Cambridge: Cambridge University Press, 1981.

————, and M. E. Falkus. "Urban Improvement and the English Economy in the Seventeenth and Eighteenth Centuries." *Research in Economic History* 4 (1979): 193–233.

————, S. Porter, and M. Turner, "A Gazeteer of English Urban Fire Disasters, 1500–1900." Historical Geography Research Series, forthcoming 1984.

Jones, Neville. *The Origins of Strategic Bombing: A Study of the Development of British Air Strategic Thought and Practice up to 1918.* London: William Kimber, 1973.

Jutikkala, E. "Town Planning in Sweden and Finland until the Middle of the Nineteenth Century." *Scandinavian Economic History Review* 16 (1968): 19–46.

Kain, Roger J. P. "The Rebuilding of Rennes." *The Connoisseur* 190 (1975): 248–57.

————, ed. *Planning for Conservation.* New York: St. Martin's Press, 1981.

Katz, Bernard S. "Infrastructure." *Encyclopedia of Economics*, edited by Douglas Greenwald, 522–23. New York: McGraw-Hill, 1982.

Kellett, John R. *The Impact of Railways on Victorian Cities.* London: Routledge and Kegan Paul, 1969.

King, Anthony, ed. *Buildings and Society: Essays on the Social Development of the Built Environment.* London: Routledge and Kegan Paul, 1980.

Kliment, Stephan A. "Opening the Doors to Better Buildings: Choices for the Building Community." National Bureau of Standards, special publication no. 476. Washington, D.C.: Government Printing Office, 1972.

Kohan, C. M. *Works and Buildings.* History of the Second World War, Civil Series. London: His Majesty's Stationery Office, 1952.

Konvitz, Josef W. *Cities and the Sea: Port City Planning in Early Modern Europe.* Baltimore: Johns Hopkins University Press, 1978.

————. "Grandeur in French City Planning under Louis XIV: Rochefort and Marseille." *Journal of Urban History* 2 (1975): 3–42.

————. "Spatial Perspectives on Port City Development, c. 1780–1980." *Urbanism Past and Present* 7 (1982): 23–33.

Kopp, Anatole, Frédérique Boucher, and Danièle Pauly. *L'Architecture de la reconstruction en France*. Paris: Editions du Moniteur, 1982.

Kostof, Spiro S. "The Architect in the Middle Ages, East and West." In *The Architect: Chapters in the History of the Profession*, edited by Spiro S. Kostof. New York: Oxford University Press, 1977.

Krautheimer, Richard. *Rome: Profile of a City, 312–1308*. Princeton: Princeton University Press, 1980.

Krings, Wilfried. "Perception et aménagement du centre historique des villes; contributions belges, 1870–1914." In *Villes en mutation XIXe–XXe siècles*, 395–425.

Lacave, Michel. "Stratégies d'expropriation et Haussmannisation: l'exemple de Montpellier." *Annales E.S.C.* 35 (1980): 1011–25.

Laconte, Pierre, ed. "Changing Cities: A Challenge to Planning." American Academy of Political and Social Science, *Annals* 451 (1980): 1–220.

Laithwaite, Michael. "The Buildings of Burford: A Cotswold Town in the Fourteenth to Nineteenth Centuries." In *Perspectives in English Urban History*, edited by Alan Everitt, 60–90. London: Macmillan, 1973.

Lampard, Eric E. "The Evolving System of Cities in the United States: Urbanization and Economic Development." In *Issues in Urban Economies*, edited by Harvey S. Perloff and Loudon Wingo, Jr., 31–139. Baltimore: Johns Hopkins University Press, 1968.

———. "The Nature of Urbanization." In *The Pursuit of Urban History*, edited by Derek Fraser and Anthony Sutcliffe, 3–53.

———. "The Urbanization of the United States: The Capitalization and Decapitalization of Place." In *Villes en mutation XIXe–XXe siècles*, 147–200.

Lane, Barbara Miller. "Changing Attitudes to Monumentality: An Interpretation of European Architecture and Urban Form, 1880–1914." In *Growth and Transformation of the Modern City*, edited by Ingrid Hammarström and Thomas Hall, 100–114.

Landes, David S. *Revolution in Time: Clocks and the Making of the Modern World*. Cambridge, Mass.: Harvard University Press, Belknap Press, 1983.

Lane, Frederick C. *Ships for Victory: A History of Shipbuilding under the United States Maritime Commission in World War II*. Baltimore: Johns Hopkins University Press, 1951.

Laurie, Peter. *Beneath the City Streets: A Private Enquiry into the Nuclear Perceptions of Government*. London: Allen Lane The Penguin Press, 1970.

Lavedan, Pierre, and Jeanne Hugueney. *La Représentation des villes dans l'art du moyen-âge*. Paris: Vanoest, 1954.

————. *L'Urbanisme au moyen âge*. Paris: Arts et métiers graphiques; Geneva: Droz, 1974.

Leblicq, Yvon. "L'Urbanisation de Bruxelles aux XIXe et XXe siècles (1830–1952)." In *Villes en mutation XIXe–XXe siècles*, 335–94.

Le Corbusier, *Towards a New Architecture*, translated by Frederick Etchells from *Vers une architecture*. New York: 1927; reprint Praeger, 1960.

Lees, Andrew. "Critics of Urban Society in Germany, 1854–1914." *Journal of the History of Ideas* 40 (1979): 61–83.

————. "Debates about the Big City in Germany, 1890–1914." *Societas* 5 (1975): 31–47.

————. "Perceptions of Cities in Britain and Germany, 1820–1914." In *The Pursuit of Urban History*, edited by Derek Fraser and Anthony Sutcliffe, 157–66.

LeGoff, Jacques. "Au moyen-âge: temps de l'église et temps du marchand." *Annales E.S.C.* 15 (1960): 417–33.

————. "Ordres mendiants et urbanisation dans la France médiévale: état de l'enquête." *Annales E.S.C.* 25 (1970): 924–46.

Leith, James A. "Desacralization, Resacralization, and Architecural Planning during the French Revolution." *Eighteenth-Century Life* 7 (1982): 74–84.

————. "Space and Revolution: Architecture and Urban Planning during the French Revolution." *Proceedings of the Consortium on Revolutionary Europe*, 2 vols. Vol. 2, 24–53. Durham, N.C.: Duke University Press, 1980.

Leonard, Charlene Marie. *Lyon Transformed: Public Works of the Second Empire, 1853–1864*. Vol. 67, University of California Publications in History. Berkeley and Los Angeles: University of California Press, 1961.

Lestocquoy, Jacques. *Aux origines de la bourgeoisie: les villes de Flandre et d'Italie sous le gouvernment des patriciens, XIe–XVe siècles*. Paris: Presses universitaires de France, 1952.

Lewis, Archibald R. "Northern European Sea Power and the Straits of Gibraltar, 1031–1350 A.D." In *Order and Innovation in the Middle Ages: Essays in Honor of Joseph R. Strayer*, edited by William C. Jordan, Bruce McNab, and Teofilo F. Ruiz, 139–64. Princeton: Princeton University Press, 1976.

Lewis, J. Parry. *Building Cycles and Britain's Growth*. London: Macmillan; New York: St. Martin's Press, 1965.

Linn, Bjorn. "Learning from Experience: The Use of Building and Planning History." In *Growth and Transformation of the Modern City*, edited by Ingrid Hammarström and Thomas Hall, 277–78.

Lis, C., and H. Soly. *Poverty and Capitalism in Pre-Industrial Europe.* Atlantic Highlands, N.J.: Humanities Press, 1979.

Lobel, M. D., and E. M. Carus-Wilson. "Bristol." In *The Atlas of Historic Towns.* Vol. 2, edited by M. D. Lobel. London: Scholar Press, 1975.

Logan, Thomas H. "The Americanization of German Zoning." *Journal of the American Institute of Planners* 42 (1976): 377–85.

Lombard-Jourdan, Anne. *Paris, genèse de la 'ville': la rive droite de la Seine des origines à 1223.* Paris: Editions du CNRS, 1976.

Longworth, Philip. *The Unending Vigil: A History of the Commonwealth War Graves Commission, 1917–1967.* London: Constable, 1967.

Lopez, Robert S. "Economie et architecture médiévales: celà aurait-il tué ceci?" *Annales E.S.C.* 7 (1952): 433–38.

———. *Naissance de l'Europe.* Paris: Armand Colin, 1962.

Lotchin, Roger W. "The City and the Sword: San Francisco and the Rise of the Metropolitan Military Complex, 1919–1941." *Journal of American History* 65 (1979): 996–1020.

Lotz, Wolfgang. *Studies in Italian Renaissance Architecture.* Cambridge, Mass.: MIT Press, 1977.

Loyer, François. "Rennes et ses deux places: unité ou hiérarchie?" *Monuments historiques,* no. 120 (1982): 49–56.

Lubove, Roy. "The Urbanization Process: An Approach to Historical Research." *Journal of the American Institute of Planners* 33 (1967): 33–39.

Lynch, Kevin. *The Image of the City.* Cambridge, Mass.: MIT Press, 1960.

———. *Managing the Sense of a Region.* Cambridge, Mass.: MIT Press, 1978.

———. *A Theory of Good City Form.* Cambridge, Mass.: MIT Press, 1981.

———. *What Time Is This Place?* Cambridge, Mass.: MIT Press, 1972; reprint 1980.

McGrath, Patrick, ed. *Bristol in the Eighteenth Century.* London: David and Charles, Newton Abbott, 1972.

Machin, R. "The Great Rebuilding: A Reassessment." *Past and Present,* no. 77 (1977): 33–56.

MacIsaac, David. *Strategic Bombing in World War Two: The Story of the United States Strategic Bombing Survey.* New York and London: Garland, 1976.

McKay, John P. *Tramways and Trolleys: The Rise of Urban Mass Transport in Europe.* Princeton: Princeton University Press, 1976.

McKendrick, Neil, John Brewer, and J. H. Plumb. *The Birth of a Consumer Society: The Commercialization of Eighteenth-Century England.* Bloomington: Indiana University Press, 1982.

McKitterick, Rosamond. "Town and Monastery in the Carolingian Period."

In *The Church in Town and Countryside*, edited by Derek Baker, 93–102. Vol. 16, Studies in Church History. Oxford: Basil Blackwell for the Ecclesiastical History Society, 1979.

McShane, Clay. "Transforming the Use of Urban Space: A Look at the Revolution in Street Pavements, 1880–1924." *Journal of Urban History* 5 (1979): 279–307.

Mallory, Keith, and Arvid Ottar. *Architecture of Aggression: A History of Military Architecture in North West Europe 1900–1945*. London: Architectural Press, 1975.

Marcus, Steven. *Engels, Manchester, and the Working Class*. New York: Random House, 1974.

Marcuse, Peter. "Housing Policy and City Planning: The Puzzling Split in the United States, 1893–1931." In *Shaping an Urban World*, edited by Gordon E. Cherry, 23–58.

Mark, Robert. *Experiments in Gothic Structure*. Cambridge, Mass.: MIT Press, 1982.

Markus, Thomas A. "Buildings for the Sad, the Bad and the Mad in Urban Scotland 1780–1830." In *Order and Space in Society: Architectural Form and its Context in the Scottish Enlightenment*, edited by Thomas A. Markus, 25–114. Edinburgh: Mainstream, 1982.

Marsan, Jean-Claude. *Montreal in Evolution*. Montreal: McGill-Queens University Press, 1981.

Maxtone-Graham, John. *The Only Way to Cross*. New York: Macmillan, 1972.

Meischke, Ir. R., *Het Nederlandse Woonhuis van 1300–1800; vijftig jaar vereniging 'Hendrik de Keyser'*. Haarlem: H. D. Tjeenk Willink & Zoon, 1969.

Melosi, Martin V. *Garbage in the Cities: Refuse, Reform, and the Environment, 1880–1980*. College Station: Texas A&M Press, 1981.

———, ed. *Pollution and Reform in American Cities: 1870–1930*. Austin: University of Texas Press, 1980.

Mensch, Gerhard. *Stalemate in Technology: Innovations Overcome the Depression*. Cambridge, Mass.: Ballinger, 1979.

Meyer, Jean. *Généralités—France*. Vol. 1, *Etudes sur les villes en Europe occidentale: milieu du XVIIIe siècle à la veille de la Révolution française*. Paris: Société d'édition d'enseignement supérieur, 1983.

Middlebrook, Martin. *The Battle of Hamburg: Allied Bomber Forces Against a German City in 1943*. London: Allen Lane, 1980.

Minchinton, W. E. "Bristol—Metropolis of the West in the Eighteenth

Century." *Transactions of the Royal Historical Society*, 5th ser., 4 (1954): 69–89.

Mioni, Alberto. "Industrialisation, urbanisation et changements du paysage urbain en Italie entre 1861 et 1921." In *Villes en mutation XIXe–XXe siècles*, 277–325.

Moehring, Eugene P. *Public Works and the Patterns of Real Estate Growth in Manhattan, 1835–1894.* New York: Arno Press, 1981.

———. *Public Works and Urban History: Recent Trends and New Directions.* Essay no. 13. Chicago: Public Works Historical Society, 1982.

Moeller, Bernd. "The Town in History: The Reformation in Germany." In *The Church in Town and Countryside*, edited by Derek Baker, 257–68. Studies in Church History. Vol. 16. Oxford: Basil Blackwell for the Ecclesiastical History Society, 1979.

Mollat, Michel, and Philippe Wolff. *Ongles bleus, Jacques et Ciompi: les révolutions populaires en Europe aux XIVe et XVe siècles.* Paris: Calmann-Levy, 1970.

Monin, H. "Les travaux d'Edme Verniquet, et, en particulier, le plan de Paris dit 'Plan des Artistes'." *Bulletin de la Bibliothèque des travaux historiques* 3 (1908): xv–xxxiii.

Monkkonnen, Eric H. "A Disorderly People? Urban Order in the Nineteenth and Twentieth Centuries." *Journal of American History* 68 (1981): 539–59.

Moore, Peter W. "Public Services and Residential Development in a Toronto Neighborhood, 1880–1915." *Journal of Urban History* 9 (1983): 445–71.

Morachiello, Giorgio, and Georges Geyssot. "State Town: Colonization of the Territory during the First Empire." *Lotus* 24 (1980): 24–39.

Morely, David, Stuart Proudfoot, and Thomas Burns, eds. *Making Cities Work: The Dynamics of Urban Innovation.* London: Croom Helm; Boulder, Colo.: Westview Press, 1980.

Morris, A. E. J. *History of Urban Form: Prehistory to the Renaissance.* London: George Godwin, 1972.

Morrison, Bonnie Maas. "Household Energy Consumption, 1900–1980." In *Energy and Transport: Historical Perspectives on Policy Issues*, edited by George H. Daniels and Mark H. Rose, 202–33. Beverly Hills, Calif.: Sage, 1982.

Mosse, George L. "National Cemeteries and National Revival: The Cult of the Fallen Soldiers in Germany." *Journal of Contemporary History* 14 (1979): 1–20.

Mullin, John R. "American Perceptions of German City Planning at the Turn of the Century." *Urbanism Past and Present* 1 (1977): 5–11.

————. "Planning Theory in Germany during the Years of the Weimar Republic." *Town Planning Review* 53 (1982): 115–30.

————. "Planning Theory in Germany under National Socialism." *Town Planning Review* 53 (1982): 259–72.

Mumford, Lewis. *City Development: Studies in Disintegration and Renewal.* New York: Harcourt Brace and World, 1961.

————. *The City in History: Its Origins, Its Transformations, and Its Prospects.* New York: Harcourt Brace and World, 1961.

————. "Concluding Address". In *City Invincible*, edited by Carl H. Kraeling and Robert M. Adams, 224–26. Symposium on Urbanization and Cultural Development in the Ancient Near East, The Oriental Institute, 1958. Chicago: University of Chicago Press, 1960.

————. *The Culture of Cities.* New York: Harcourt Brace, 1938.

National Commission on Urban Problems. "Building the American City." Report to the Congress and to the President of the United States. Washington, D.C.: Government Printing Office, 1968.

Nelson, Blake. *Water for the Cities: A History of the Urban Water Supply Problem in the United States.* Syracuse: Syracuse University Press, 1956.

Nichols, David M. "Medieval Urban Origins in Northern Continental Europe: State of Research and Some Tentative Conclusions." *Studies in Medieval and Renaissance History* 6 (1969): 53–114.

————. "Town and Countryside: Social and Economic Tensions in Fourteenth-Century Flanders." *Comparative Studies in Society and History* 10 (1968): 458–85.

Nières, Claude. *La Reconstruction d'une ville au XVIIIe siècle; Rennes, 1720–60.* Rennes: Université de Haute-Bretagne, Institut amoricain de recherches historiques de Rennes, 1972.

Offer, Avner. *Property and Politics 1870–1914: Landownership, Law, Ideology, and Urban Development in England.* Cambridge: Cambridge University Press, 1981.

Olsen, Donald J. *Town Planning in London: The Eighteenth and Nineteenth Centuries.* New Haven: Yale University Press, 1964.

Ozouf, Mona. "Le Cortège et la ville: les itinéraires parisiens des fêtes révolutionnaires." *Annales E.S.C.* 26 (1971): 889–916.

Paltz, John, and Catherine B. Scallen, eds. *Cubism and American Photography.* Williamstown, Mass.: Sterling and Francine Clark Art Institute, 1981.

Parent, P. *L'Architecture civile à Lille au 17e siècle.* Lille: Raost, 1925.

Le Parisien chez lui au XIXe siècle, 1814–1914. Paris: Archives nationales, 1976.

Parker, Geoffrey. "The Military Revolution: 1560–1660—A Myth?" *Journal of Modern History* 48 (1976): 195–214.

Patte, Pierre. *Mémoire sur les objets les plus importants de l'Architecture.* Paris, 1769.

————. *Monumens érigés en France à la gloire de Louis XV.* Paris, 1765.

Pearl, Valerie. "Change and Stability in Seventeenth-Century London." *London Journal* 5 (1979): 3–34.

Perloff, Harvey S. *Planning the Post-Industrial City.* Washington, D.C., and Chicago: American Planners Association, Planners Press, 1980.

Perrot, Jean-Claude. *Genèse d'une ville moderne, Caen au XVIIIe siècle.* 2 vols. Paris and The Hague: Mouton, 1975.

Peterson, Jon A. "The Impact of Sanitary Reform upon American Urban Planning, 1840–1890." *Journal of Social History* 13 (1979): 83–103.

Pevsner, Nikolaus. *A History of Building Types.* Bollingen ser. 35. Princeton: Princeton University Press, 1976.

————. *North Somerset and Bristol.* Harmondsworth: Penguin Books, 1958.

Pinckney, David. *Napoleon III and the Rebuilding of Paris.* Princeton: Princeton University Press, 1958.

Pinder, D. A., and B. S. Hoyle. "Cityports, Technologies and Development Strategies." In *Cityport Industrialization and Regional Development: Spatial Analysis and Planning Strategies,* edited by D. A. Pinder and B. S. Hoyle, 328–38. Oxford: Pergamon Press, 1981.

Pinto, John A. "Origins and Development of the Ichnographic City Plan." *Journal of the Society of Architectural Historians* 35 (1976): 35–50.

Porteous, John Douglas. *Canal Ports: The Urban Achievement of the Canal Age.* London: Academic Press, 1977.

Portoghesi, Paolo. *Rome of the Renaissance,* translated by Pearl Sanders. London: Phaidon, 1972.

Pounds, Norman J. G. *An Historical Geography of Europe, 450 B.C.–A.D. 1330.* Cambridge: Cambridge University Press, 1973.

Powell, C. G. *An Economic History of the British Building Industry, 1815–1979.* London: Architectural Press, 1980.

Power, M. J. "East London Housing in the Seventeenth Century." In *Crisis and Order in English Towns 1500–1700,* edited by Peter Clark and Paul Slack, 237–62. London: Routledge and Kegan Paul, 1972.

Price, Jacob. "Economic Function and the Growth of American Port Towns in the Eighteenth Century." *Perspectives in American History* 7 (1974): 123–86.

Pronteau, Jeanne. *Les Numérotages des maisons de Paris du XVe siècle à nos jours.*

Ville de Paris, Commission des travaux historiques, sous-commission de recherches d'histoire contemporaine, no. 8 (1966).

———. "L'Oeuvre architecturale d'Edme Verniquet." *Annuaire de l'Ecole pratique des hautes études*, 4th section, 108 (1975–76; pub. 1976): 641–49.

———. "Le Travail des limites de la ville et faubourgs de Paris, 1724–1729: législation et application des textes." *Annuaire de l'Ecole pratique des hautes études*, 4th section, 110 (1977–78; pub. 1979): 707–45.

Pudney, John. *London's Docks*. London: Thames and Hudson, 1975.

Pundt, Herman G. *Schinkel's Berlin: A Study in Environmental Planning*. Cambridge, Mass.: Harvard University Press, 1972.

Råberg, Marianne. "The Development of Stockholm since the Seventeenth Century." In *Growth and Transformation of the Modern City*, edited by Ingrid Hammarström and Thomas Hall, 13–26.

Rambert, Gaston. *Marseille, la formation d'une grande cité moderne*. Marseille: S. A. du Semaphore de Marseille, 1934.

Rapoport, Amos. *Human Aspects of Urban Form: Towards a Man-Environment Approach to Urban Form and Design*. Oxford: Pergamon, 1977.

———. *The Meaning of the Built Environment: A Nonverbal Communication Approach*. Beverly Hills, Calif.: Sage, 1982.

Reddaway, T. F. *The Rebuilding of London after the Great Fire*. London: Jonathan Cape, 1940.

Reynolds, Susan. *An Introduction to the History of English Medieval Towns*. Oxford: Clarendon Press, 1977.

Richter, Michael. "*Urbanitas-Rusticitas*: Linguistic Aspects of a Medieval Dichotomy." In *The Church in Town and Countryside*, edited by Derek Baker, 149–57. Studies in Church History. Vol. 16. Oxford: Basil Blackwell for the Ecclesiastical History Society, 1979.

Riddell, John F. *Clyde Navigation: A History of the Development and Deepening of the River Clyde*. Edinburgh: John Donald, 1979.

Rimbert, Sylvie. *Les Paysages urbains*. Paris: Armand Colin, 1973.

Ritchie, Thomas. *Canada Builds*. Toronto: University of Toronto Press, 1967.

Roberts, Michael. "The Military Revolution." In *Essays in Swedish History*, 195–225. London: Weidenfeld and Nicolson, 1967.

Rodger, Richard. "The Growth and Transformation of Scottish Towns: The Role of the Building Cycle, 1860–1914." In *Growth and Transformation of the Modern City*, edited by Ingrid Hammarström and Thomas Hall, 115–24.

———. "The Invisible Hand: Market Forces, Housing and the Urban

Form in Victorian Cities." In *Pursuit of Urban History*, edited by Derek Fraser and Anthony Sutcliffe, 190–211.

Romains, Jules. *The Seventh of October*, translated by Gerard Hopkins, vol. 14, *Men of Good Will*. New York: Alfred A. Knopf, 1946.

————. *The Sixth of October*, translated by Warre B. Wells, vol. 1, *Men of Good Will*, New York: Alfred A. Knopf, 1933.

Roncayolo, Marcel. "La Production de la ville." In *La Ville de l'âge industriel, le cycle haussmannien (1840–1950)*, edited by Maurice Agulhon, 71–155. Vol. 4, *Histoire de la France urbaine*, edited by Georges Duby. Paris: Editions du Seuil, 1983.

Rose, Mark H., and John G. Clark. "Light, Heat, and Power: Energy Choices in Kansas, Wichita, and Denver, 1900–1935." *Journal of Urban History* 5 (1979): 340–64.

Rosenau, Helen. *Social Purpose in Architecture*. London: Studio Vista, 1970.

Rostow, W. W. *Pre-Invasion Bombing Strategy: General Eisenhower's Decision of March 25, 1944*. Austin: University of Texas Press, 1981.

Rouleau, Bernard. *Le tracé des rues de Paris: formation, typologie, fonctions*. Paris: Editions du CNRS, 1967.

Royal Institute of British Architects. "Silent Cities," exhibition catalog. London: 1978.

Ruddock, Ted. *Arch Bridges and Their Builders, 1735–1835*. Cambridge: Cambridge University Press, 1979.

Rudé, George. "The Growth of Cities and Popular Revolt, 1750–1850, with Particular Reference to Paris." In *French Government and Society 1500–1871: Essays in Memory of Alfred Cobban*, edited by John Bosher, 166–90. London: Athlone Press, 1973.

Russell, Josiah Cox. *Medieval Regions and their Cities*. London: Newton Abbot, David and Charles, 1972.

Rykwert, Joseph. *The First Moderns: The Architects of the Eighteenth Century*. Cambridge, Mass.: MIT Press, 1980.

Saarinen, Eliel. *The City: Its Growth, Its Decay, Its Future*. Cambridge, Mass.: MIT Press, 1943.

Sansom, William. *Westminster in War*. London: Faber and Faber, n.d.

Schafer, R. Murray. *The Tuning of the World*. New York: Alfred A. Knopf, 1977.

Schulz, J. "Jacopo de Barbari's View of Venice: Map Making, City Views and Moralized Geography before the Year 1500." *Art Bulletin* 60 (1978): 425–74.

Schultz, Stanley K., and Clay McShane. "To Engineer the Metropolis: Sew-

ers, Sanitation and City Planning in Late Nineteenth-Century America."
Journal of American History 65 (1978): 389–411.

Schwarzbach, F. S. *Dickens and the City.* London: Athlone Press, 1979.

Scott, Mel. *American City Planning Since 1890.* Berkeley and Los Angeles:
University of California Press, 1969.

Sennett, Richard. *The Fall of Public Man: On the Social Psychology of Capitalism.* New York: Random House, 1974; reprint 1978.

Shapiro, Ann-Louise. "Housing Reform in Paris: Social Space and Social
Control." *French Historical Studies* 12 (1982): 486–507.

Shelby, Lon R. "The 'Secret' of the Medieval Mason." In *On Pre-Modern
Technology and Science: A Volume of Studies in Honor of Lynn White, Jr.*, edited
by Bert S. Hall and Delno C. West for the Center for Medieval and
Renaissance Studies, University of California, Los Angeles. Malibu,
Calif.: Undema, 1973.

Simon, Roger D. *The City-Building Process: Housing and Services in New Milwaukee Neighborhoods 1880–1910.* American Philosophical Society Transactions, 68, part 5 (1978).

Simpson, M. A. "Meliorists versus Insurgent Planners and the Problems of
New York, 1921–41." *American Studies* 16 (1982): 207–28.

Smets, Marcel. "The Reconstruction of Leuven after the Events of 1914." In
Villes en mutation XIXe–XXe siècles, 499–533.

Smith, Alonzo M. "Blacks and the Los Angeles Municipal Transit System,
1941–1945." *Urbanism Past and Present* 6 (1980–81): 25–31.

Smith, Peter F. *Architecture and the Human Dimension.* London: George Godwin, 1979.

Soly, Hugo. *Urbanisme en Kapitalisme te Antwerpen in de 16 de Eeuw.* Collection
Histoire Pro-Civitate, no. 47. Brussels: Crédit Communal de Belgique,
1977.

Sosson, Jean-Pierre. *Les travaux publics de la ville de Bruges, 14e–15e siècles: les
matériaux, les hommes.* Collection Histoire Pro-Civitate, no. 48. Brussels:
Crédit Communal de Belgique, 1977.

Spender, Stephen. *Citizens in War and After.* London: George G. Harrap,
1945.

Spirn, Anne Whiston. *The Granite Garden: Urban Nature and Human Design.*
New York: Basic Books, 1983.

Starr, Roger. "Making New York Smaller." *New York Times Magazine.* November 14, 1976, 105.

Steadman, Philip. *The Evolution of Designs: Biological Analogy in Architecture
and the Applied Arts.* Cambridge: Cambridge University Press, 1977.

Stein, Richard G. *Architecture and Energy: Conserving Energy Through Rational Design*. New York: Anchor Press/Doubleday, 1977.

Stelter, Gilbert A., and Alan F. J. Artibise, eds. *Shaping the Urban Landscape*. Ottawa: Carleton University Press, 1982.

Stilgoe, John R. *Common Landscape of America, 1580 to 1845*. New Haven: Yale University Press, 1982.

———. *Metropolitan Corridor: Railroads and the American Scene*. New Haven: Yale University Press, 1983.

———. "Moulding the Industrial Zone Aesthetic: 1800–1929." *American Studies* 16 (1982): 5–24.

Stone, Lawrence. "The Residential Development of the West End of London in the Seventeenth Century." In *After the Reformation: Essays in Honor of J. H. Hexter*, edited by Barbara C. Malament, 167–212. Philadelphia: University of Pennsylvania Press, 1980.

Summerson, Sir John. *Georgian London*. London: Barrie and Jenkins, 1962; rev. ed. 1970.

———. *The London Building World of the Eighteen-Sixties*. London: Thames and Hudson, 1973.

———. "The Victorian Rebuilding of the City of London." *London Journal* 3 (1977): 163–85.

Sundquist, James L. *British Cities at War*. American Municipal Association. Chicago: Public Administration Service, 1940.

Sutcliffe, Anthony. "Architecture and Civic Design in Nineteenth-Century Paris." In *Growth and Transformation of the Modern City*, edited by Ingrid Hammarström and Thomas Hall, 89–114.

———. *The Autumn of Central Paris: The Defeat of Town Planning 1850–1970*. London: Edward Arnold, 1970.

———. "Environmental Control and Planning in European Capitals, 1850–1914: London, Paris and Berlin." In *Growth and Transformation of the Modern City*, edited by Ingrid Hammarström and Thomas Hall, 71–88.

———. "The Growth of Public Intervention in the British Urban Environment during the Nineteenth Century: A Structural Approach." In *The Structure of Nineteenth-Century Cities* edited by James H. Johnson and Colin G. Pooley, 107–24.

———. *The History of Urban and Regional Planning, an Annotated Bibliography*. New York: Facts on File, 1981.

———. "In Search of the Urban Variable: Britain in the Later Nineteenth Century." In *Pursuit of Urban History*, edited by Derek Fraser and Anthony Sutcliffe, 234–63.

————. *Towards the Planned City: Germany, Britain, the United States and France, 1780–1914.* New York: St. Martin's Press, 1981.

————, ed. *Multi-Storey Living: The British Working-Class Experience.* London: Croom Helm, 1974.

————, ed. *The Rise of Modern Urban Planning, 1800–1914.* New York: St. Martin's Press, 1980.

Swann, D. "The Pace and Progress of Port Investment in England 1660–1830." *Yorkshire Bulletin of Economic and Social Research* 12 (1960): 32–44.

————. "The Engineers of English Port Improvements 1600–1830." *Transport History* 1 (1968): 153–68, 260–76.

Swenarton, Mark. *Homes Fit for Heroes: The Politics and Architecture of Early State Housing in Britain.* London: Heinemann Educational Books, 1981.

Szanton, Peter. *Not Well Advised.* New York: Russell Sage Foundation and Ford Foundation, 1981.

Tarn, John Nelson. *Five Per Cent Philanthropy: An Account of Housing in Urban Areas Between 1840 and 1914.* Cambridge: Cambridge University Press, 1973.

Tarr, Joel A. "The Separate vs. Combined Sewer Problem: A Case Study in Urban Technology Design Choice." *Journal of Urban History* 5 (1979): 308–39.

————. "Urban Pollution: Many Long Years Ago." *American Heritage* 22 (1971): 65–69, 106.

Taylor, William. "New York et l'origine du 'Skyline': la cité moderne comme forme et symbole." *URBI*, no. 3 (1980): 3–21.

Teaford, Jon S. *City and Suburb: The Political Fragmentation of Metropolitan America, 1850–1970.* Baltimore: Johns Hopkins University Press, 1979.

TeBrake, William H. "Air Pollution and Fuel Crisis in Preindustrial London, 1250–1650." *Technology and Culture* 16 (1975): 377–59.

Teisseyre-Sallmann, Line. "Urbanisme et société: l'exemple de Nimes aux XVIIe et XVIIIe siècles." *Annales E.S.C.* 35 (1980): 965–86.

Temple, Nora. "The Control and Exploitation of French Towns during the Ancien Regime." *History: The Journal of the Historical Association* 51 (1966): 16–34.

Thienel, Ingrid. "Verstädterung, Stadtische Infrastruktur und Stadtplannung: Berlin Zwischen 1850 und 1914." *Zeitschrift fur Stadtgeschichte, Stadtsociologie und Denkmalpflege* (now *Die Alte Stadt*), no. 4 (1977): 55–84.

Thompson, F. M. L. *Chartered Surveyors, The Growth of a Profession.* London: Routledge and Kegan Paul, 1968.

Tilly, Charles, and R. A. Schweitzer. "How London and its Conflicts Changed Shape." *Historical Methods* 15 (1982): 67–77.

Titmuss, Richard. *Problems of Social Policy*. History of the Second World War, United Kingdom Civil Series. London: His Majesty's Stationery Office, 1950.

Vance, James E., Jr. *This Scene of Man: The Role and Structure of the City in the Geography of Western Civilization*. New York: Harper and Row, 1977.

van Houtte, J. A. "The Rise and Decline of the Market of Bruges." *Economic History Review*, 2d ser., 19 (1966): 29–47.

van Werveke, H. "The Rise of the Towns." In *Economic Organization and Policies in the Middle Ages*, edited by M. M. Postan, E. E. Rich, and Edward Muller, 3–41. Vol. 3, *Cambridge Economic History of Europe*. Cambridge: Cambridge University Press, 1963.

Vidler, Anthony. "Paris under the Academy: City and Ideology." *Oppositions* 8 (1977): 95–115.

Vigarié, André. *Ports de commerce et vie littorale*. Paris: Hachette, 1979.

Vigier, François. *Change and Apathy, Liverpool and Manchester during the Industrial Revolution*. Cambridge, Mass.: MIT Press, 1970.

Villes en mutation XIXe–XXe siècles. Collection Histoire Pro-Civitate, no. 64. Brussels: Crédit Communal de Belgique, 1982.

Walker, Frank Arneil. "The Glasgow Grid." In *Order and Space in Society*, edited by Thomas A. Markus, 155–99.

Ward-Perkins, Bryan. *From Classical Antiquity to the Middle Ages: Public Building in Northern and Central Italy, 300–850*. New York: Oxford University Press, 1984.

Ward-Perkins, J. B. *Cities in Ancient Greece and Italy: Planning in Classical Antiquity*. New York: George Braziller, 1974.

———. "From Republic to Empire: Reflections on the Early Provincial Architecture of the Roman West." *Journal of Roman Studies* 60 (1970): 1–19.

Warner, Sam Bass, Jr. "The Management of Multiple Urban Images." In *The Pursuit of Urban History*, edited by Derek Fraser and Anthony Sutcliffe, 383–94.

———. *The Urban Wilderness*. New York: Harper and Row, 1972.

Warren, George F., and Frank A. Pearson. *World Prices and the Building Industry*. New York: John Wiley and Sons, 1937.

Weaver, John C., and Peter de Lottinville. "The Conflagration and the City: Disaster and Progress in British North America during the Nineteenth Century." *Histoire sociale/Social History* 13 (1980): 417–49.

Webster, Sir Charles, and Noble Frankland. *The Strategic Air Offensive Against Germany, 1939–1945*. 4 vols. London: Her Majesty's Stationery Office, 1961.

Westfall, Carroll William. *In This Most Perfect Paradise: Alberti, Nicholas V, and the Invention of Conscious Urban Planning in Rome, 1447–1555.* University Park, Pa.: Pennsylvania State University Press, 1974.

White, Lynn, Jr. *Medieval Technology and Social Change.* London: Oxford University Press, 1962.

Wilkinson, Catherine. "The New Professionalism in the Renaissance." In *The Architect: Chapters in the History of the Profession*, edited by Spiro S. Kostof, 124–60. New York: Oxford University Press, 1977.

Willan, T. S. *River Navigation in England 1600–1750.* London: Frank Cass, 1964.

Williams, Alan F. "Bristol Port Plans and Improvement Schemes of the 18th Century." *Transactions of the Bristol and Gloucestershire Archeological Society* 81 (1962): 138–88.

Williams, Raymond. *The Country and the City.* New York: Oxford University Press, 1973.

Wise, M. J. "Evolution of Jewellery and Gun Quarters in Birmingham." *Transactions of the Institute of British Geographers* 15 (1949): 59–72.

Wittkower, Rudolph. *Architectural Principles in an Age of Humanism.* London: A. Tiranti, 1952.

———. *Palladio and Palladianism.* New York: George Braziller, 1974.

———. *Studies in the Italian Baroque.* London: Thames and Hudson, 1975.

Wohl, Anthony S. *The Eternal Slum: Housing and Social Policy in Victorian London.* London: Edward Arnold, 1977.

Wolff, Philippe. "Pouvoir et investissements urbains en Europe occidentale et centrale du treizième au dix-septième siècle." *Revue historique*, no. 254 (1977): 277–310.

Wrigley, E. A. "A Simple Model of London's Importance in Changing English Society and Economy 1650–1750." *Past and Present*, no. 37 (1967): 44–70.

Yearley, C. K. "The 'Provincial Party' and the Megalopolises: London, Paris, and New York, 1850–1910." *Comparative Studies in Society and History* 15 (1973): 51–88.

Yelling, J. A. "The Selection of Sites for Slum Clearance in London, 1875–1888." *Journal of Historical Geography* 7 (1981): 155–65.

Young, Arthur. *Travels in France During the Years 1787, 1788, and 1789*, edited by Constantia Maxwell. Cambridge: Cambridge University Press, 1950.

Younger, A. J. *The Making of Classical Edinburgh 1750–1840.* Edinburgh: Edinburgh University Press, 1966.

Zunz, Olivier. "Etude d'un processus d'urbanisation: le quartier du Gros-Caillou à Paris." *Annales E.S.C.* 25 (1970): 1024–65.

Index